STAGE

COACH

WELLS FARGO AND THE AMERICAN WEST

PHILIP L. FRADKIN
FOREWORD BY J.S. HOLLIDAY

SIMON & SCHUSTER SOURCE
NEW YORK • LONDON • TORONTO • SYDNEY • SINGAPORE

SIMON & SCHUSTER
Rockefeller Center
1230 Avenue of the Americas
New York, New York 10020

For information about special documents for bulk purchases,
please contact Simon & Schuster Special Sales:
1-800-456-6798 or business@simonandschuster.com

DESIGNED BY LISA CHOVNICK

Manufactured in the United States of America

1   3   5   7   9   10   8   6   4   2

Library of Congress Cataloging-in-Publication Data

Fradkin, Philip L.
Stagecoach, Wells Fargo and the American West / Philip L. Fradkin.
p.   cm.
1. Wells, Fargo & Company—History.   2. Coaching—United States—History.   3. Express
service—United States—History.   4. West (U.S.)—History.   I. Title.
HE5903.W5 F73 2002
388.3'41'0978—dc21   2001054154
ISBN 0-7432-1360-2

FOR PATRICIA

CONTENTS

FOREWORD

by
J. S. Holliday

As you read Philip Fradkin's vivid history of Wells Fargo & Company, the question—more likely an exclamation—will surely come to mind: where else but in California and the West?! In other states and other nations, a bank brings to mind an institution managed by stern-faced functionaries in starched collars. The name Wells Fargo evokes the image of a horse-drawn, dust-covered stagecoach rumbling into town to deliver, on time, a strongbox heavy with customers' gold. A robust scene of Wells Fargo agents keeping their word, their schedule, and their customers' confidence in a time and place that often overlooked values like trust and dependability.

The origins of that now-classic image derive from the validity and longevity of the company's history, here colorfully recounted. How risk-takers—miners, merchants, speculators—expanded the mining frontier from California eastward to Virginia City, Nevada and finally to Deadwood, Dakota Territory. How they entrusted their mail and treasure to the expressmen and stagecoach drivers of Wells Fargo. How by 1865 the company had, in the words of a newspaper editor, "grown very much into the heart and habit of the people from the Rocky Mountains to the Pacific Coast. . . . It is the Ready Companion of civilization, the Universal Friend and Agent of the miner, his errand man, his banker, his post office. . . . Its offices are in every town, far and near." And how, as an earlier historian suggested, the express company known as Wells Fargo became "the nearest thing to a universal service company ever invented."

Central to the story of Wells Fargo and the American West was the curious demography of that masculine world, a society and economy shaped by the scarcity of women, the rarity of families. This gender imbalance offered a vast and profitable business for Wells Fargo and its competitors, delivering letters from scores of thousands of men "out west" to their families "back east"—from mining camps in California and Colorado, Montana and Arizona; from instant cities like San Francisco and Denver; from boomtowns like Helena and Tombstone. Equally important, these men also entrusted Wells Fargo to deliver money—bills of exchange—to their families in the eastern states, money gained from who-knew-what enterprise, maybe a mining claim, maybe a gambling table, maybe a business that would never be countenanced in Michigan or Maryland. These letters and remittances tied the West to the East long before the transcontinental railroad in 1869.

With broad perspective and intimate detail, Fradkin encompasses the 150-year history of this robust company, which prospered even in its early decades, in an era he describes as "an entrepreneurial free-for-all, a gouging, spitting, mud-wrestling match between unrestrained capitalists, whose only rule was to remain in the ring as long as possible." In such a society, dedicated to the self-interest of fortune hunting, and an economy energized by the exuberant acceptance of everything forbidden back in the States, one of the company's founders, "stern-visaged" Henry Wells, confessed: "I am called sanguine at home [New York City], but I am an old fogey here [in San Francisco] and considered entirely too slow for this market."

Yet slow proved wise. When other express companies and banks disappeared in the searing flames of speculation (Adams & Company in 1855, William C. Ralston's Bank of California in 1875), Wells Fargo met the demands of its depositors and gained new stature, while its hundreds of messengers carried mail, gold and silver on stagecoaches across the vastness of the West, more swiftly and more dependably than the United States Post Office. Nor were the company's agents in scores of offices laggardly in providing banking services to meet the needs of the region's in-a-hurry, risk-taking population. In all, Fradkin's scholarship and range of observation give substance to the judgment of an earlier historian that

Wells Fargo became "the single most widespread institution in the early West, being even more omnipresent than the U.S. government."

In describing this parallel growth of the company and the West, Fradkin includes (with contagious pleasure) a review of the richest source of western folklore which Hollywood has woven into our national mythology. In his chapter "Crime and Punishment," he clarifies and corrects oft-told tales of lawmen, robbers, lynchings, gun battles, bank heists, and stagecoach holdups. And throughout his narrative, he weaves in memorable descriptions by none less than Horace Greeley and Mark Twain, and delightful surprises, including the revelation at "his" death that one of the most competent of all stage drivers was—a woman!

Like the economy of California and the West, the company's prosperity in the twentieth century depended not on mining but on agriculture, not on gold and silver torn from the earth but on new treasures nurtured in orchards and fecund soil: peaches and oranges, melons and berries delivered unspoiled—fresh!—by Wells Fargo's specially designed refrigerated railcars coupled to fast passenger trains. This service carried thousands of tons of "delicate western fruits and vegetables to eastern consuming markets." Thus, whether by stagecoach or "Fargo Fast" freight cars, Wells Fargo secured its reputation for speed and reliability.

Through the many decades of boisterous prosperity and perilous crises, Wells Fargo adapted to change and challenge. By the first decades of the twentieth century, the company's ocean-to-ocean rapid freight delivery system utilized numerous regional railroads and several urban distribution centers, from which horse-drawn wagons (and soon trucks) delivered to city and countryside the nation's bounty—salmon from Seattle, grapefruit from Florida, flour from Minnesota, cheese from Wisconsin, and a myriad of consumer goods from the mail order catalogs of Sears, Roebuck and Montgomery Ward.

Then, in 1918, the wonderfully profitable express business felt the power of Washington, D.C. In that year the Wilson Administration forced Wells Fargo and its competitors to form the federally governed American Railway Express Company. After sixty-six years, from stagecoach to wagon to truck, Wells Fargo gave up its express business and concentrated on its future as a bank, enhanced by its remarkable past.

That history, that experience of having grown up with the trans-Mississippi West, remained an invaluable asset in the last decades of the twentieth century when, despite many mergers and acquisitions, the old monarch retained its proud name. Indeed, that identity proved indelible, even after the 1998 merger with the midwestern banking giant Norwest Corporation, headquartered in Minneapolis.

Now, on the eve of its 150th anniversary, that name is more closely than ever identified with its stagecoach, once a reality "out west" and now the ubiquitous brand of the nationwide Wells Fargo & Company. What a symbol, what a story.

ACKNOWLEDGMENTS

FIRST, FULL disclosure.

My wife and I financed our home with a construction loan from a local bank. On completion, that loan was turned into a home loan from the same bank and then purchased by another lending institution. It was refinanced twice. The loan wound up in the hands of a midwestern corporation named Norwest, which meant nothing to us. Then one day the monthly bill arrived with the bright red-and-straw-colored logo of Wells Fargo, which we did recognize. The payment has remained the same.

As with my previous eight books, I acted as my own fact checker, since book publishers do not supply that crucial service. I asked the people most familiar with the subject to read and comment on the manuscript. I also told them that I had the final responsibility for what went into the book that carried my name.

At Wells Fargo, Andy Anderson, Robert Chandler, Bev Smith, and Dick Kovacevich read the manuscript. The first three come from the old Wells Fargo side of the merger, while Kovacevich is familiar with Norwest history and the merger negotiations. They spotted errors and made a few suggestions.

Outside the bank, Jim Holliday, an author, and Doris Ober, a freelance editor, reviewed the manuscript and made recommendations, as did my wife, Dianne. All my contractual and editorial dealings were with Fred Hills, senior editor and vice president of Simon & Schuster. Fred asked me to write the book, had helpful editorial suggestions, and shepherded it to publication. Frances Tsay noted details.

Without the unstinting cooperation of Bev Smith, who heads the bank's Historical Services department, and her able staff (particularly Marianne Babal), and the completeness of the Wells Fargo archive and files to which I had unlimited access, I could never have produced this book. My many friends at the Bancroft Library at the University of California, Berkeley, were also a great help, as was the staff at the Huntington Library in southern California.

Our coach was a great swinging and swaying stage, of the most sumptuous description—an imposing cradle on wheels. It was drawn by six handsome horses, and by the side of the driver sat the "conductor," the legitimate captain of the craft; for it was his business to take charge and care of the mails, baggage, express matter, and passengers.
—Mark Twain's description of his 1861 journey westward in *Roughing It*

Photography: The stagecoach, our most recognizable symbol, should be used as the dominant image whenever possible. Photographs of the stagecoach racing across an open landscape are not only breathtaking to view, they evoke a sense of endless opportunity, optimism, and entrepreneurial spirit.
—Memorandum from Wells Fargo corporate marketing brand identity to all certified brand messengers, April 5, 2000

PREFACE

ANY ACCOUNT of Wells Fargo & Company involves a history of the more dramatic aspects of the Old West. There is, however, another story that is quite interesting in its own right and certainly more relevant to our times.

The company's operations bisected almost all social, cultural, and economic activities in the trans-Mississippi West and were conducted in such diverse physical landscapes as the Great Plains, the Rocky Mountains, the Great Basin Desert, the wet Northwest, the dry Southwest, the Sierra Nevada, and the Pacific coast.

Wells Fargo's early history meandered through and illuminated the booms and busts of gold and silver mining rushes, the collection and distribution of mail, the rise and failure of banks, the Pony Express, overland staging, the building of the transcontinental railroad, the Civil War and the Indian wars, the violence of robbers and gunfighters, the development of agriculture, the rise of capitalist entrepreneurs, and the regulation and disbanding of monopolies. In fact, more than any government agency or any other commercial enterprise, the history of Wells Fargo mirrored the history of the American West through the second decade of the last century.

Follow Wells Fargo and you follow the path of money and products through a vast network of western trails. Wells Fargo was a business dedicated to remaining in business and making a profit, which was sometimes considerable and a few times excessive. The company has managed to operate for one hundred and fifty years, an unusual length of time in a region renowned for its economic vicissitudes and the transience of its population. Along with the nostalgic appeal of its Old West identity, speed, security, service, and the ability to connect people, money, and goods have been constants in Wells Fargo's long history.

★　★　★

There is a set of historical bookends that illustrates Wells Fargo's long reach from the era of sailing ships to the age of the Internet.

On July 30, 1844, the twenty-two-gun sloop *Levant* anchored off Sausalito in San Francisco Bay. The passage of the American naval vessel from Hawaii had taken an unusually long three weeks. A few days later a party of seven rowed ashore. William A. Richardson, a middleman between the governing Mexicans and visiting foreigners, provided the group with horses and a guide for purposes of hunting. They rode north to the San Rafael Mission in what would become known as Marin County, just north of the Golden Gate.

A young acting lieutenant, Louis McLane Jr., kept a journal. He was amazed by the abundance of wildlife. "The whole country around is covered with quail & deer—the latter wild," he wrote.

They reached the mission in time for dinner, which was mutton: "a great rarity in this country, where a man kills a fat Beef for the quarters & a deer for the saddle [a prime cut of meat]," McLane commented.

Their host at the run-down mission, Timothy Murphy, managed the property for the Mexican government, California then being part of Mexico. Murphy was pleased to see them, since he only encountered one or two fellow Anglos a year. After dinner they mounted fresh horses and tracked down the large doe McLane had wounded earlier in the day. The dogs finished her off. Other members of the party shot two more does, and McLane bagged a fawn before they retired from the field.

The next day the group departed for the return ride to the ship before breakfast. They saw more than one hundred deer, but only managed to shoot three bucks, as the large party made too much noise. The three-hundred-pound Murphy regaled them with stories about grizzly bears, one of whom had pawed him in the back three weeks previously. "He showed us the wound, barely healed," said McLane.

It was a taxing day. The nine hours in the saddle were "the hardest riding I have ever seen or ever expect to see." The lieutenant had a fair amount to say about the durable California horses, finding them "swift, surefooted & of great bottom." They were much hardier than the eastern horses he was used to. McLane looked about and saw a bountiful land: "The pasturage is excellent—fine grass in the valleys & wild oats on the hills & mountains. In consequence, both horses & cattle are in fine order."

For a time, horses would power the stagecoaches that drove the commercial empire McLane oversaw on the West Coast. The offspring of a distinguished Maryland and Baltimore family—his grandfather served as a colonel in the Revolutionary War and his father was a congressman, U.S. senator, ambassador to the Court of St. James's, and secretary of treasury and secretary of state in the cabinet of President Andrew Jackson—McLane offered this assessment of his future domain: "From all I can learn Oregon has no good harbor, is unhealthy & has large tracts of poor Land. California has several fine harbors, (this bay of San Francisco, is one of the best in the World) has very little poor land & is remarkable for the purity of its atmosphere."

Louis McLane would return to San Francisco to head the Wells Fargo office in what had become a thriving city by the mid-1850s. He would eventually take over the West Coast operations and then ascend to the firm's presidency in New York City.

*   *   *

Some tens of millions of additional inhabitants later, Wells Fargo was firmly ensconced in California and the West in 1996, having gobbled up such lesser entities as Crocker and First Interstate banks, doubling in size each time. Wells Fargo was second only to Bank of America, which had been taken over by a North Carolina bank. It was the oldest bank in the West.

Wells Fargo had become so large and so successful that it made a tempting target for an aggressive "in-your-face" advertising campaign by Glendale Federal Bank, which was seeking to entice customers following Wells Fargo's takeover of First Interstate. If imitation is the sincerest form of flattery, then the southern California bank was guilty of gross adulation.

The bank's advertising agency, the aptly named Wise Guys of Pasadena, hired a tug to pull an eighty-foot barge around San Francisco Bay. Two sail-like square banners were rigged on the barge's deck. One had the international sign for no, a red circle and slash, superimposed over a stagecoach pulled by six horses—the Wells Fargo icon. The other banner sought to emulate the western theme that Wells Fargo has so successfully employed over the years: "Hit The Trail," it stated. "The *other* way to bank."

The campaign backfired. In an era when stadiums were being named after Internet companies, schools sold space for advertising in textbooks, and airships and biplanes circled lazily overhead with their forgettable messages, the commercialization of the ad-free waters of San Francisco Bay was too much. There was an outcry. One public agency banned nautical advertising in the wake of the ill-conceived campaign. Very soon thereafter Glendale Federal disappeared in a merger.

What the campaign demonstrated, however, was the drawing power and value of a recognizable corporate identity, or brand, as a company's *Geist* is now called. David A. Aaker, a former professor of marketing strategy at the University of California at Berkeley and vice chairman of Prophet Brand Strategy in San Francisco, wrote in his book *Managing Brand Equity:*

> A study of banks in California confirmed that their associations are very similar with respect to money, savings, checking account deposits, and tellers. Nothing distinctive—with the exception of Wells Fargo, which has had a host of associations going along with their ubiquitous stagecoach. In an industry in which similarity is the norm, the stagecoach is an enormous asset, in part because of the richness of the concept. In addition to providing associations with the Old West, horses, and the gold rush, it also effortlessly is linked to reliability in the face of adversity, adventurousness, independence, and even building a new society out of wilderness.

How true are these associations? Time—in this case one hundred and fifty years—would tell.

*   *   *

There are two layers to this story, as Henry Wells pointed out in an 1864 speech to the American Geographical and Statistical Society. Wells cited to that august body the need for "hard facts." But as one of the founders of the express business, and American Express and Wells Fargo in particular, he said the "Romance of the Express" also had its appeal. "I could tell of midnight adventures in the forest; of perils in the waters; of perils by robbers; of awful catastrophes . . . [and] of humorous, pathetic, and tragical occurrences."

The facts and romances of the express business and the American West are intertwined. The realities and myths need to be separated. A business that spans the history of the region provides the perfect tool for that exercise.

The emphasis of this book is on the period from 1852 to 1918 when Wells Fargo was an express company. During those sixty-six years, Wells Fargo made three major contributions to the well-being of the West and the nation as a whole. First, the company served as the principal communications conduit between East and West; second, it contributed to the Union victory in the Civil War; and last, it shipped fresh vegetables and fruits via fast refrigerated express, thus ensuring better health in the colder regions of the country. After 1918, Wells Fargo was just another bank until its reemergence as a major national financial institution in the 1990s.

HENRY WELLS (*1805–1878*), cofounder of Wells Fargo & Company, American Express Company, and Wells College for women in Aurora, New York.

WILLIAM FARGO (*1818–1881*), cofounder of Wells Fargo & Company; American Express Company; mayor of Buffalo, New York; and namesake of Fargo, North Dakota.

I

―――

1 8 5 2 – 1 8 6 9

BEGINNINGS

IMAGINE A business that combines the communications aspects of letter mail, e-mail, faxes, and the telephone; the transportation of heavier goods by parcel post and express mail, such private carriers as United Parcel Service and Federal Express, and an armored car service; and the plethora of financial arrangements supplied by modern intrastate, interstate, and international full-service banks. That was an express company in the nineteenth century; there simply is no equivalent today.

Wells Fargo came into the world as the younger sibling of the American Express Company, both having common parents. The two companies exist to this day as totally separate entities—one headquartered in San Francisco and the other in New York City. Wells Fargo's parents were distant overseers. Separation and a measure of maturity occurred at age seventeen.

Almost everything in the American West, meaning what lay beyond the Mississippi River, was strange and new to easterners in the mid-nineteenth century. The lack of rainfall, a vertical landscape of tremendous diversity, and the chimera of instant mineral riches lying just beneath the surface of the earth were the most startling differences. Imported institutions, including businesses, had to adjust to disparate natural conditions and human needs or they would wither and fail.

When Louis McLane, who resigned his naval commission in January 1850, stepped ashore in Gold Rush San Francisco four months later at the age of thirty-one, he commented in a letter to his wife of ten months: "Gold. Gold. Gold is the all absorbing idea here. It affects everything and everybody." Real estate, including underwater lots, was also a hot item. "Just now everyone who has money at command is speculating in lots. You hear of some new town or city (on paper) every week and the sales are real. . . . Money can be made out of it by any man who will set down, watch the current & not hold on too long." McLane sat down for a while.

While waiting to go into the steamboat business between San Francisco and Sacramento, he noted the poor level of mail service. "I know of no place where the post office wants more reform than here. Those who don't take boxes may wait a week & then not be served," he said. A box tax, "a very convenient piece of bribery," brought quicker service to box-holders. The lonesome McLane justified a bribe on the basis that "hope deferred maketh the heart sick."

A private express service, McLane said, was safer, surer, and speedier than the federal postal service. "You must know that no one in California mails an inland letter but sends by Express." He added, "The miners give their address & power of attorney to the Express agent who takes their letters out of the post office in San F. twice a month and delivers them to every town & camp in the placers. . . ."

There was opportunity here, to be sure. But no express service carried the name of Wells Fargo, yet. The major players were in place in New York City. Such a company would soon become a reality.

For an express business to succeed there were three functions that needed to be fulfilled: reliable communications, speedy transportation, and secure banking.

For most of the history of this country, the mail was the principal means of communication. It was central to our being as a nation. Daniel J. Boorstin, Pulitzer Prize–winning historian and former Librarian of the

Library of Congress, wrote of the mail: "No American institution has
been more intimately involved in daily hopes and fears. Nor has any institution been more effective in cementing community or more essential
to the function and growth of a democratic government."

Supposedly a monopoly established by law, the Post Office charged
high prices for poor service in 1840. It cost eighteen cents to send a letter
from New York City to Troy, New York, but only twelve cents to ship a
barrel of flour over the same route. (For longer distances, the letter rate
was twenty-five cents.) As a result, private express services who employed messengers proliferated. They carried the mails at up to one-fifth
the cost of the government service. The Post Office arrested messengers
and brought suit against some of the express services.

The harassment didn't bother the private concerns. Henry Wells, a
partner in an upstate New York express company, proposed that his firm
take over the entire postal business of the government and charge five
cents for a letter.

"Zounds, sir," reportedly replied an assistant postmaster general to
Wells's proposal, "it would throw 16,000 postmasters out of office!"

The appointment of postmasters was a major source of political patronage. Congress did not wish to do away with this "engine of patronage." So the solution would have to be an adjustment to marketplace
realities and tightening the monopoly.

The 1845 Postal Act reduced the cost of postage and made the government monopoly on letter mail virtually airtight. The law, however,
was honored more in the breach than observed in the West, where expediency and selective enforcement were the informal laws of the land.
This was a time of buccaneers, both in the gold fields and in the halls of
commerce. Wells Fargo and other express companies became, in effect,
opposition post offices.

The fast transportation function of the express service had a colorful
history that went back to runners on bare feet and riders on horses. "Life
and death often depended upon their speed, and not a few illustrious political offenders have had to thank the riders for their timely relief from

the edge of the axe, or the pressure of the rope," A. L. Stimson wrote in *History of the Express Business*. "Even whole cities, when about to yield to besieging armies, have been saved by these expresses."

Where railroads and steamboats had replaced horseback riders and stagecoaches on the major routes in the East by the 1840s, some of the romance involved in swift delivery had been lost. Looking back some years later, Henry Wells recalled:

> I was over the road between Albany and Buffalo for eighteen months, and for one year of that time I never lost a [weekly] trip. The railroad, where it was in existence, was a strap rail, very suggestive of snakeheads, and given to run-offs; and the common road, of which there was sixty-five miles, was to be endured in summer, and in the spring and fall was simply—horrible. I have been eighteen nights out of twenty-one upon the road, and "still live."

Besides the prosaic items of commerce and personal correspondence, Wells carried shucked oysters from Albany to Buffalo at the cost of three dollars per one hundred. The oysters caused a sensation when they arrived in Buffalo. The same enterprising caterer who ordered the oysters via Wells's express moved on to Chicago, where he cooked a lobster dinner delivered by express on the prairie. Wells defined his service as "the business of carrying parcels and packages as fast as possible, with special care to their safety in transportation and their sure delivery."

Wells credited banking, the third function of an express business, with helping him prosper. When the federal government closed the Bank of the United States in 1836, the only interbank messenger service ended with it. Paper financial instruments, hard cash, and bars of gold need to be moved. It was costly for the banks to undertake this specialized service, so the express companies performed it. A natural alliance was formed between the two business entities, one that Wells Fargo and other express companies would commingle in California.

California, however, was different. On the West Coast the means of monetary exchange was not symbolic paper money; it had to be a tangible entity. It was a cattle hide– and metal-based economy.

The dried hides of cows that could be turned into leather were known as "California bank notes" during the 1840s. With annexation, the coins of the realm were minted, at first privately by private concerns and then by the federal government. The coins were struck from the very minerals—namely, gold and silver—that were found within the territory. Gold and silver were called "our twin staples" by a California newspaper. Metallic money meant greater weights for express companies to carry.

Where the markup on goods imported from the East could be as high as 1,000 percent and instant wealth was a cultural totem, large sums of money were exchanged and smaller amounts were disdained. Following California statehood in 1850, the smallest denomination was a "bit," roughly 12.5 cents. Two bits equaled a quarter. In the 1860s, the dime was the smallest denomination, anything less being associated with poverty. The next decade saw the introduction of the detested nickel. The *Daily Alta California*, the state's leading newspaper, referred to the nickel as being "half-brother to arsenic." On the East Coast, greenbacks (called "this monster serpent, paper money" in California) and the lowly copper penny were in use. Such base metals as copper and nickel were shunned in the West.

Gold Rush Californians, mostly easterners who had had unfavorable experiences with banks, regarded those institutions and bankers "as something inherently evil." The legislature prohibited banks, but it failed to provide any means of enforcing the law. Banks, however, were a necessary evil, given the need to convert a mineral into a means of purchasing goods or something that could be easily transported and stored. Informal banking practices grew from merchants extending credit, dabbling in the buying and selling of gold, and operation of express services.

Government interference and regulations were unknown. Reputation, meaning the appearance or the reality of being solvent, substituted for regulation. Anyone could hang out a sign stating "Bank," as Wells Fargo and other express companies did. Expediency was the law, and it worked most of the time. On occasion, however, depositors were stung badly. There were scares, panics, and failures.

The need for adaptation in this new financial environment was described by Ira B. Cross, a professor of economics at the University of California who wrote a banking history of California seventy-five years after Wells Fargo arrived in the state. Cross said, "The conditions that existed at that time did not make for the establishment of banking institutions such as were commonly found in the eastern states. . . . Trafficking in gold dust dominated all channels of finance. . . . California was no place for financiers trained in the banking customs and practices of the more settled communities."

*   *   *

Henry Wells and William G. Fargo, who both began their express careers as messengers in upstate New York, joined forces in 1845 and commenced the process that would result in bringing the functions of communications, speedy transportation, and banking together in California. Both were stern-visaged, bearded men who exuded rectitude. Wells was the mediator and Fargo the aggressive entrepreneur.

Various express companies in which Wells and Fargo had an interest were formed and dissolved as the industry consolidated during the formative years of the late 1840s. Creation of the American Express Company in 1850 was the result of their joint endeavors. Wells was the first president and Fargo the secretary. The other faction on the board of directors was headed by John Butterfield. Fargo and Butterfield were both strong-willed and frequently clashed.

Wells and Fargo had consistently pushed their separate businesses westward from upstate New York, reaching as far as Chicago and St. Louis. With the surge of new business generated by the California Gold Rush, it made more sense to start from the other end of the continent and progress eastward. The American Express board of directors debated the proposal for a western express service in early 1852. Tempers flared. A successful western venture would add to Fargo's prestige and power. Butterfield opposed it, and he had the votes to defeat the proposal.

Ten days later Wells and Fargo invited a group of investors to the Astor House in New York. Wells Fargo & Company was formed on March 18, 1852, two years to the day after American Express had come into existence. Butterfield did not miss the significance of the date, nor would he forget. A former stagecoach driver, Butterfield was a legendary swearer. Years later the mild Wells recalled: "All of the profanity that one head could hold, or one tongue utter, was used to express his friendship toward me and Fargo."

Gold Rush California

Like American Express—the immediate business model—Wells Fargo was not incorporated; it was established in New York as a joint stock association. That meant the shareholders (the directors, for the most part) were personally liable for losses, but they could act autonomously and in total secrecy. There were no reporting requirements, neither to bothersome stockholders nor government overseers. The company was capitalized at $300,000, an amount equal to approximately $6 million in 2000, but it is unlikely there was anywhere near that amount of cash available at the time.

Edwin B. Morgan, an upstate New York merchant and banker, was named the first president; and Henry Wells and William Fargo faded into the background as powerful members of the board of directors. Although their names would be forever associated with the company that became a western institution, their main interests lay elsewhere.

Both men took a much more active role in the affairs of American Express. Wells soon retired to upstate New York and established Wells College for women in Aurora. His health and business acumen deteriorated in the 1860s. Fargo vigorously pursued other business interests and was mayor of Buffalo for two terms. He would serve briefly as president of the company that bore his name. Although Fargo remained a director of Wells Fargo until his death in 1881, he was president of American Express for a long time, vice president of the New York Central Railroad, and a director of other transportation concerns, including the Northern Pacific Railroad, whose express service competed with Wells Fargo. During their tenures as directors of Wells Fargo, each made only one short trip to the West Coast.

The principal agents in San Francisco ran the business on the ground and were subject to the vagaries of the mail as far as policy was concerned. If the ships did not sink, it took three to four months for a letter to be sent and an answer received. (The three letters Louis McLane wrote his wife in 1851 took an average of fifty-four days to travel one way from San Francisco to Baltimore via the Isthmus of Panama.) The president and directors in New York set policy. They struggled to keep up with fast-breaking developments and sought to understand what was happening in that strange, distant land.

A New York State mentality and American Express directors dominated the Wells Fargo board for its first seventeen years. Four of the seven directors of American Express were on the first nine-member Wells Fargo board. They were: Wells, Fargo, Johnston Livingston, and James McKay. Morgan—the first president, a longtime friend of Wells and Fargo's brother-in-law—was also a director. The banker Danford N. Barney became president of Wells Fargo in 1853 and served in that position until 1866. He also headed two other American Express offshoots.

Two Wells Fargo agents arrived in San Francisco in the early summer of 1852. Samuel P. Carter of American Express, who had been an express and telegraph agent for Wells in Albany, handled the express side of the business in California. Reuben W. Washburn, a Syracuse banker, took charge of the monetary transactions. Prices were 400 percent over what was charged in New York, and Carter apologized to Morgan for the cost of office space: "An awful price, I know, but it was that or nothing." The company opened its San Francisco office on July 13, 1852, at 424 Montgomery Street, on virtually the same site as the current corporate headquarters at 420 Montgomery Street. The brick building was located in what was called a fireproof block, fire being the scourge of early San Francisco.

Wells Fargo was not alone. In the *Register of First Class Business Houses in San Francisco*, fourteen banks, including Wells Fargo, were listed under "Banking and Exchange" in October. Other banks were found under such categories as "Banking and Commissions" and "Real Estate and Stocks." Besides Wells Fargo, there were four other aggressive advertisers for express services in the *Daily Alta California*, all using the printer's stock illustration of a sailing vessel as their identifying mark in ads.

Like a modern-day marketing rollout, Wells Fargo ads blossomed that summer in San Francisco, inland California, and Portland newspapers. A typical ad stated that Wells Fargo specialized in shipping "GOLD DUST, BULLION, SPECIE, PACKAGES, PARCELS & FREIGHT OF ALL KINDS, TO AND FROM NEW-YORK AND SAN FRANCISCO: Thence to Sacramento, Stockton, Nevada, Marysville, Sonora and all the principal towns of California and Oregon. They will also purchase and sell Gold Dust, Bullion and Bills of Exchange; pay and collect Notes, Bills and Accounts, &c. &c." As principal offices, the Montgomery Street address was listed along with the New York City address on Wall Street. The impressive figure of $300,000 and the names of the nine directors were given. At the bottom were the names of the two principal California agents.

By spending money on twelve branch offices, agents, and advertising, Wells Fargo quickly established a beachhead in 1852. During the last five months of that first year, the firm shipped $312,000 worth of gold to New York, compared to $5.5 million shipped by its main competitor, Adams & Company. Carter and Washburn acquired smaller express companies in the first of what would be many subsequent mergers and acquisitions, and they made mutually advantageous arrangements with existing ones. By such means the company expanded inland via Stockton and Sacramento and then moved further eastward into the central gold districts of the Sierra Nevada foothills.

Mail was accepted at its offices and picked up at post offices for delivery into areas not served by the government. One of Wells Fargo's future agents, Charles T. Blake, wrote home from the diggings at Sarahsville: "If you write me through the P.O., address Auburn. But the surest way of reaching me is through Wells-Fargo and Co's Express."

From the start, Wells Fargo paid close attention to the marketing and public relations aspects of establishing and expanding a business. "We were very particular in civilities to the newspapers," said Wells. Newspapers were carried free so that other newspapers in those pre–wire service days could copy the news and credit Wells Fargo for delivering it. Much like a town crier, election news was rushed westward and announced with fanfare. "The recent important intelligence of the [1852] presidential election gave opportunity for the display of great enterprise and daring on the part of the various [express] companies here," commented the San Francisco *Herald*, which singled Wells Fargo out for supplying the first news and being "a firm which has gained rapidly in public favor and is now fully and successfully established."

Within the state the *Daily Alta California* acknowledged receipt, via Wells Fargo messenger, of "carefully prepared special [election] returns" from the gold country. There were much-publicized pony express races between rival companies that were covered breathlessly by the press. Wells Fargo did not win all the races; but the name was repeated endlessly—a publicist's dream.

Image was important. Agents comported themselves like gentlemen, were seen with the right people, joined the appropriate civic organizations. At the top were the directors, who were prominently listed in the advertisements. "A glance at the list of directors will satisfy anyone of the unlimited confidence which may be reposed in the establishment," commented one California newspaper, whose editor, and certainly the vast majority of readers, had no way of knowing who all the nine men on the East Coast were.

*   *   *

Underneath the paper-thin surface of what little polite society existed, California was an entrepreneurial free-for-all—a gouging, spitting, mud-wrestling match between unrestrained capitalists whose only rule was to remain in the ring for as long as possible.

The principal Wells Fargo employees in California felt that the officers of the company back in New York did not understand what was happening in California. Capital, and lots of it, was needed to purchase gold dust from the miners. In return, miners received gold coins or drafts—bills of exchange—that were sent home in duplicate or triplicate copies via different mails in order to assure their safe arrival. The first copy to be delivered was paid. Money—quite a lot, actually—could be made on these exchanges.

Carter and Washburn were desperate for more capital; $50,000 was not nearly sufficient. They needed $100,000 to $150,000. The two agents borrowed from another bank to buy gold dust and practiced subterfuge: "It is understood here that our Capital is ample, and we do all we can to encourage the idea, but we dare not venture on a kind of business which would immediately show its fallacy, and expose our weakness." Washburn continued in a letter to the New York office: "Banking in San Francisco is a very different thing from Banking in the City or State of New York." Wells Fargo's credit in California was no better than that of other third-rate banks. The principal agent for banking added: "Our connection and supposed identity with the American Express Company is no doubt an advantage, but it aids us only to a very moderate extent—much less than some of our Directors seem to suppose."

Gold, not paper securities and notes, was the bedrock on which business was conducted in California. "This is the best Country that I know of to make money with money," wrote Washburn, "but the worst to do a Commercial or Banking business in without money, and plenty of it." The directors lacked the cash; it would take another year for them to raise the working capital for California to $150,000.

The personnel on the two coasts were at odds with each other. The directors wanted the California agents to concentrate on the more glamorous San Francisco–New York run. Carter thought he could eventually show a greater profit on the domestic express business, which was beginning to pick up letters, a practice that was "making and keeping friends."

The Wells Fargo California operation was a classic case of management by distant fiat. In letter after letter, Carter and Washburn pleaded that a director come out, spend three months, and see for himself what the realities were. They were glad to hear that Wells was on his way, but they also wanted Morgan and Fargo to visit. As an enticement, Washburn mentioned to Morgan the opportunity to make "perfectly safe" investments outside of Wells Fargo that would yield up to 50 percent in yearly interest.

The infighting on the American Express board, of which Wells was president, had reached its most intense level. Wells, the mediator who had a habit of disappearing at crucial times, decided to take a three-month leave of absence and travel to California in December of 1852. The board of directors insured his life.

Wells was exuberant upon reaching the Pacific Ocean. "Give me credit of being the first man across the Isthmus in a race of six hundred and all nearly men," he wrote his friend Morgan, "and very many are not in now and will not be for 24 hours. I passed everything on the road. I think for the dry season this is a tolerable moist climate. It has rained about six hours and part of the time poured." (Wells was on a mule, and undoubtedly his passage was expedited by the local express agent; most walked.)

By the time Wells reached San Francisco on February 5, 1853, fifteen fellow passengers had been buried along the way and a large number were ill when they disembarked. But Wells was fit. It was to be a whirlwind inspection tour of three weeks, rather than the desired three months, for the first director to visit California. He toured Sacramento for one day and then returned to San Francisco, where he stayed for the remainder of his time in California. Wells's goal, he said, was "to understand our true position, the wants of the business etc etc."

There were differences in attitudes between East and West. "I am called sanguine at home but I am an old Fogey here and considered entirely too slow for this market but I am content to remain as I am a conservative in all such matters," said Wells, who was approaching the age of fifty.

Carter and Washburn were doing a good job. There was a need for a "<u>competent</u>" bookkeeper. Living expenses were "enormous." Profits were increasing, however. Wells was told by fellow businessmen "that it is only a matter of time—that no concern ever started with better prospects [than Wells Fargo] or had been better managed during its 7 months existence & success was certain and positive." There was a need to increase capital, however, "as it is now but a one horse Bank compared with those around us."

California was not for Wells, but he could see that it fit the needs of others. He could hardly wait to return. "I am content to stay in NY if I ever get back." Then, for a moment, Wells got caught up in the contagion. At 11 P.M., as the firm rushed to get the shipment on the outbound steamer, Wells wrote: "This is a great country & a greater people."

In the Gold Country

THE SURVIVING portraits of the founders date the two men. The photograph of John Quincy Jackson, Wells Fargo's Auburn agent, is amazingly contemporary—perhaps a young man on the make in Silicon Valley in the late 1990s. The times were similar. Jackson and California fit each other.

Auburn was on the money trail. The mines in the nearby central district fed into Auburn, which was at the intersection of four main roads. From Auburn the gold went to Sacramento by stage and then San Francisco via river steamer.

Jackson arrived in California in 1849. After holding a series of jobs, he went to work for Wells Fargo at the age of twenty-one in 1852. He was one of Carter's hires and opened the Auburn office, of which he was quite proud: "The business I am engaged in requires my whole attention and is far beyond my years," Jackson wrote his family. "I might have staid in Virginia till I was as old as Mathusalem (or some such name) and never had $1000 entrusted to me or been worth anything myself, while here I have charge of a large Express Office and Banking house."

Jackson was ambivalent about California: "I have a great attachment for this country although I hate its ways." He loved the climate but found "the present appearance of society" a bit rough. He had had no luck mining with nine fellow Virginians and was "perfectly satisfied" working for Wells Fargo. He had gained instant status in the community: "My position throws me in contact with the heaviest business men of the state—Bankers, Lawyers, Judges, Merchants & all do business through us."

The young man wrote his brother a detailed description of what an agent's long work day consisted of in October of 1852:

> What I have to do is quite confining, staying in my office all day till 10 at night buying dust, forwarding & receiving packages of every kind from and to everywhere, filling out drafts for the Eastern Mails in all sorts of sums, from $50 to $1000, and drawing checks on the Offices below when men wish to take money to the cities, as it is a great convenience to them to have a check instead and it saves us the trouble of shipping coin up from below for purchasing dust. I have just come from the Post Office, from which I have got 100 letters to be forwarded to the different parts of the country to which they are ordered by Express. On these I make $25 as my charge on each is 25 cents. This comes around twice a month and I generally get out about a dozen 3 times a week besides letters from within the state. This alone pays quite a sum, nothing like my expenses however, as they are necessarily heavy, but not so heavy but that they leave me a handsome sum each month on all my income. Mother says rolling stones gather no moss, but whether they do or not I am always going to roll when the "ship is about to sink" and rolling will save me.

As the height of the Gold Rush receded, Jackson realized that he would "never make a great deal here." He purchased a small house that he rented at a modest profit, invested in a sawmill, and was too busy to help the visiting scout Kit Carson sell some sheep: "I could be of little service to him, as he knows everything about the market—likely a good deal more than I did."

Young Jackson had an eye for the married women, there not being many available single women. The crossroads location of the Auburn office aided business, which was increasing in 1854. Once a week Jackson rode to the river settlement of Murderers Bar to buy gold dust.

On the night of February 22, 1855, Jackson attended a ball, and he did not get to bed until 4 A.M. He wrote of his experiences the next morning when a financial panic struck San Francisco:

At 8 o'clock I was awoke up by a messenger handing me a telegraphic dispatch from our firm below, to the effect that Adams & Co had failed to prepare for a run. Here was a pleasant message and I instantly got up & at the moment I reached the door crowds were running towards the office. I knew that our funds would not meet all our outstanding draft certificates. . . . Very soon Adams Co here had paid out all their funds and still were short some $20,000. The crowd was now furious and banking hours drawing nigh. What was worse still was my being alone in the office, my assistant a short time since being transferred to the Iowa Hill office. I saw no other plan but to open and let it go as far as it would. Paying out commenced and the work got pretty warm when two or three of my personal friends came forward and offered their assistance to the extent of their means. One of them being very popular and a substantial man, his presence served to allay all excitement and to instill confidence, as to our means, to the crowd. As they dispersed and the matter became a little quieted I went outside and made arrangements for funds nearly to the amount of all the demands against us. The time ran smoothly till about 4 pm when it was telegraphed that Wells Fargo & Co had suspended in San Francisco. This fell like a death knell to me but as far as this office was concerned I could weather it. When the news was spread around the crowds commenced assembling and pretty soon the paying out was lively. But as there seemed to be no lack of funds and my giving personal assurance of their safety all was quieted for the day. This morning I recd a dispatch from San Francisco Office that their house would open on Monday next and through the day have rec'd several of the same purport. We have had but little trouble so far today & I am in hopes we will go through the storm safely.

For Jackson, the banking crisis "was the proudest time of my life." He was congratulated by his superiors in San Francisco and cheered by the grateful community. Four months later Auburn was destroyed by fire. Everything in the newly refurbished wooden office building was burned except the contents of the two-ton safe. Soon the town was alive with the sounds of rebuilding. The Wells Fargo office would be rebuilt of brick, the agent vowed.

Jackson left California in the early 1860s. Neither Jackson nor most of the '49ers had made their fortunes, but it had been a very lively time. His California friends wrote him about the hard, boring times they were having in their later years. There was a great deal of yearning in their letters. Jackson died in his hometown of Petersburg, Virginia, in 1899. The retired merchant left a small estate to his three daughters.

The Post–Gold
Rush Years

Two important events that related to Wells Fargo occurred in 1855. The boom went bust for the first time in American California (as it would periodically in later years), and Louis McLane took over the San Francisco office. McLane would emerge as the pivotal executive during the early years of the company's existence.

William Tecumseh Sherman had waded ashore in April 1853 when the S.S. *Lewis* grounded on a reef just north of San Francisco. He found a lumber schooner that would take him to San Francisco. The schooner capsized. "Satisfied that she could not sink, by reason of her cargo," Sherman wrote years later, "I was not in the least alarmed, but thought two shipwrecks in one day not a good beginning for a new, peaceful career."

The former army captain, who would become a San Francisco banker before assuming the rank of a Civil War general, was a reliable and forthright witness to events during the decade. Of the banking crisis, the new manager of the St. Louis branch of Lucas, Turner & Co. wrote:

Friday [February 23, 1855.] I was thunderstruck to see the crowd and tumult. Adams & Co. closed, Wells, Fargo & Co. afraid to open, Robinson & Wright's Savings Banks closed before a dollar could be called for and the assertion in every man's mouth that all must break, because Page Bacon & Co.'s circular said so. "There is no coin in the country" a base deliberate falsehood, conceived in folly, knavery or downright malice. . . .

Sherman had no faith in Wells Fargo, as he thought banking and the express business were different trades and should be separated. The banking side of Wells Fargo went briefly into the hands of receivers who verified its solvency, a fairly common technique used to restore the public's confidence in the years before government regulation.

Wells Fargo's banking business opened again on Tuesday. Except for three days at the height of the 1906 San Francisco earthquake and fire, this was the only time that Wells Fargo closed its doors. Adams & Co., the leading banking and express business, had failed, leaving Wells Fargo as the dominant express company in the state.

Although the firm now had fifty-five offices, mostly within California, the express business was operating at a net loss. The directors in New York took two actions: they decided not to assume the risk for any shipments over $20,000 and they authorized sending the company treasurer Thomas M. Janes to California "with full power to act for the Board" as the temporary head of the western operation.

Janes found Louis McLane in San Francisco, and he was hired as the general agent in November 1855. McLane and three of his brothers were involved in a number of interlocking California enterprises. They participated in mining ventures; an interstate railroad and a telegraph company; river and oceangoing steamship lines; a dry dock company; the Bank of California; insurance, gas, and water companies; and the profitable Pioneer Stage Company. McLane operated this staging company independent of Wells Fargo before the latter owned the wheeled vehicles that would become the company icon.

The early historian of the express business, A. L. Stimson, described the former naval lieutenant as "a fresh and unusually vigorous spirit of enterprise and improvement." The tart-tongued Sherman, who would one day march through Georgia to the sea, saw McLane and two others as "cautious, timid, prudent men." California banking historian Ira Cross described McLane as "strict in following rules of the greatest prudence." With his eight children, McLane was known as a disciplinarian. All hinted at a certain rigidity.

McLane was a community leader, as befit a Wells Fargo general agent. He was an Episcopalian; a contributor to charities and a member of their committees; foreman of the Grand Jury that was investigating vigilantes in 1856 and a member of the executive committee of a vigilante committee that same year; active in civic affairs, such as the Fourth of July committee and the welcoming committee for New York editor Horace Greeley; and vice president of the committee loyal to the Union cause.

Shortly after taking over, McLane wrote his wife back east on company stationery that defined the firm's pretensions. While really only a California operation, the letterhead announced:

New York, California and European Express and Banking Company
WELLS, FARGO & CO.
BANKERS, COMMISSION AGENTS AND EXPRESS FORWARDERS
Principal Offices,—New York, San Francisco, London, and Paris.

There was no trademark symbol on the stationery nor any mention of mail service, a profitable part of the business. Perhaps that was because the Post Office was attempting to crack down on the express companies' illegal mail business. In return, the San Francisco newspapers railed against the "useless" postal service.

One of McLane's two principal contributions while in California was figuring out how to get around the prohibition against Wells Fargo carrying the U.S. mail. The general agent hit upon the simple expedient of buying large quantities of government-stamped envelopes, adding the company's imprint, called the Wells Fargo frank, and selling the double-stamped envelope for two to three times what the Post Office would have charged for its service alone.

What did the customers receive in return? Security and speed and convenience, for which they were willing to pay more. Estimates of the percent of mail carried in California by the express companies varied from nearly 70 to 95 percent. The profits for Wells Fargo were commensurate with the popularity of the mail service—a net income of $15,000 a month by the end of the decade.

This service—what the historian Daniel Boorstin called "cementing community"—was Wells Fargo's first contribution on a national scale. From the late 1850s to 1880, when the Post Office challenged the express company, and then 1895, when Wells Fargo ended its letter service, the company was the primary means of sustained communications between the western portion of the country and the remainder of the nation. After Wells Fargo discontinued its letter service, the express company retained its dominance by shipping larger items until parcel post was introduced in 1913.

With so many alternative ways to communicate electronically today, and the relegation of regular mail to "snail" status, it is extremely difficult to imagine the sole dependence on the lowly letter that existed at the time. Other than by costly, brief telegrams that could not be sent across the country until 1861, there simply was no other efficient way to communicate.

From the beginning, the government could not keep up with demand or supply convenience, known as "service" in modern business parlance. Gold Rush historian J. S. Holliday wrote: "In a land where there had never been a postal delivery network, the postmaster general in Washington failed miserably to cope with the surge of mail sent to California in 1849 and for years thereafter."

The San Francisco Post Office was swamped by 2.6 million pieces of mail annually. Long lines formed. There were no post offices in the hinterland. Small, private express companies or individuals were the alternative. The postmaster threatened the enterprising expressmen with arrest for carrying the mail. McLane's solution placated the Post Office.

Wells Fargo added convenience to its basic mail service. Wells Fargo offices sprang up all over the West—126 by 1859, when the express service earned $46,000 and the company's capital stock was raised to $1 million. Letter carriers were employed in San Francisco, and bright green letter boxes were placed at accessible locations in urban areas, there being eighty-six such boxes in the city in 1877. There was a special mail route, called the China Route, serving San Francisco's Chinatown. Three Chinese employees sorted the mail, then stamped it by hand in red.

Directives to agents from the head office in San Francisco emphasized that the firm was in competition with the U.S. mail, and postal authorities were keeping a close watch on its activities. A 1858 notice sent "To Our Agents" stated: "We have to request a more strict observance to stamping letters. . . . We are called upon by the mail agent, who assures us that fines will be imposed for any infringement of postal laws."

Besides making money, the letter express won friends and influenced people. There were many testimonials.

William H. Brewer, a Yale University professor who was engaged in a survey of California, wrote home from San Juan Bautista, just south of San Jose, in 1861:

> Way mails in this state are so uncertain that all important letters are carried by private express in government envelopes. The company sends three-cent letters for ten cents, and to the states, ten-cent letters for twenty cents. Here in this state it is used very largely, the Wells & Fargo mail being often larger than the government mail. We avail ourselves of it, even on so short a distance as from here to San Francisco, if the letter has any special importance or needs to go with certainty of dispatch. I have had

letters two weeks in getting where they ought to go in two days with a daily mail.

To the north in Idaho, Wells Fargo agent Charles T. Blake (the same Blake who wrote home eleven years earlier asking that his family send him mail via Wells Fargo) approached his new post, the raw mining settlement of Placerville, in April of 1863. He carried a bag of letters in his pack train. The journey of nine days from Walla Walla, Washington Territory, was through deep snow. Blake didn't know what to expect, nor did the home office, except "it was reported rich last year, and that all the rush is that way this year." The agent previously appointed to the post had disappeared while attempting to make it to Placerville on snowshoes. Blake wrote to his fellow agents in balmy California:

One of the crowd that followed us in said to our guide "Can you tell us anything about Wells Fargo and Co? We understood that they were going to establish an agency here." "Yes" says the guide "they are, and that man in spectacles is the agent." The next instant I heard a shout taken up and repeated through the whole town "Wells Fargo have come." In less than three minutes I was surrounded by an excited crowd of two or three hundred men, who hardly allowed me time to get my saddle off from my mule before they almost dragged me into a large unfinished building on the Plaza, as they called the square. . . . I had brought in with me about 400 letters, and now proceeded to call them over. As news of my arrival spread, the crowd increased and for eight mortal hours my tongue had to wag without cessation. I disposed of a great many letters though at a dollar apiece and about eight o'clock at night broke up business in spite of the crowd, being very hungry and tired and started out to get something to eat. This was my introduction to Placerville.

The following year the San Francisco Chamber of Commerce committee that had been appointed to investigate the poor state of postal affairs cited the lack of cooperation of the San Francisco postmaster in its investigation. It estimated that the Post Office carried only one-third the amount of letters carried by the express companies. Postal service was poorer in rural areas. Politicians used the Post Office to serve "personal ambition and political traffic." Citing the higher price that Wells Fargo charged in hard currency, versus the paper money the Post Office accepted, the report went on to state:

> The general mismanagement of postal affairs on this coast, is sufficiently indicated by the fact that the letter business of a single enterprising Express Company, advertising about one hundred and fifty offices and agents in the Pacific States and Territories, and charging from 9 to 10 cents coin per single letter, far exceeds the entire letter business of the San Francisco postoffice, which is a distributing office for nearly the whole western coast of America, and is in direct communication with about six hundred and fifty other postoffices in the States and Territories above mentioned.

Looking back on this era in 1930, historian Carl I. Wheat wrote: "Wells, Fargo & Co's Express was at this period the most important agency for both express and mail service throughout California and particularly in the mining regions. . . . By 1858, Wells, Fargo went everywhere, did almost anything for anybody, and was the nearest thing to a universal service company ever invented. Next to the whiskey counter and gambling table, Wells, Fargo's office was the first thing established in every new camp or diggin's."

William Sherman, who had been east for a while, returned to San Francisco in early 1858 and found a number of changes, one of which was Wells Fargo's emergence as one of the leading banking houses. Success, however, had its drawbacks.

Near the end of the decade a phenomenon that hadn't bothered Wells Fargo before—armed robberies—began to hinder its operations. Sherman, that sharp-eyed observer, noted it: "There has been a good deal of talk about Wells, Fargo & Company who have agencies all over the country . . . and has been robbed several times. . . . Recently they have been very successful in recovering lost treasure but have had to pay liberal rewards."

Wells Fargo reacted aggressively. It hired armed guards and paid lawmen to pursue suspects. Expenses involved in the Angeles Road, Iowa Hill, Shasta, Trinity Center, and other robberies showed up for the first time in the company's profit and loss statement for the express department in 1860. Despite expenses of $48,415 that were mostly crime related, there was a profit of $127,418 generated by 108 offices, ten of which were outside California.

The Pony Express

THE PONY EXPRESS myth is well known, having been broadcast widely in words and images; daring young men on dashing steeds plunged through dark dangers to deliver the mail in record time.

The reality, particularly the role of Wells Fargo, is much murkier. As a profit maker, the Pony Express was a loser; as a necessity in order to acquire the lucrative transcontinental mail and express business carried by stagecoaches, it was a winner; as an indicator of how a new technology could replace an existing one and render the latter obsolete, it was a precursor to what would come later.

First, it needs to be made clear that there was "the Pony," as the newspapers of the time referred to the overland Pony Express, and more local pony expresses. The Pony Express ran for nineteen months and carried light mail from near St. Louis to Placerville, California, at an eventual cost of $1.00 for a half-ounce letter. At $23 in current dollars, it was not a service that was affordable for ordinary folks.

The one-way trip was supposed to be made in ten days in summer and twelve days in winter, no small feat at the time. "It took the people quite by surprise, for they had not yet fairly waked up to the idea that the continent could possibly be spanned in ten days time," wrote the St.

Louis correspondent of a San Francisco newspaper. First undertaken privately and then under government contract, the Pony Express lasted from April 3, 1860, to October 24, 1861.

Then there were bistate and intrastate pony expresses run by various individuals and express firms that employed slight men on fast horses for shorter distances. These feeder pony express routes were generally operated between 1852 and 1870. Wells Fargo was involved off and on in the shorter routes for most of those eighteen years and in the transwestern service for its last six months. At a time in the mid-1960s when the extent of Wells Fargo's role in the Pony Express was being challenged, W. Turrentine Jackson, professor of history at the University of California at Davis, wrote that the express company "was involved in the ownership, operation, and expense of running the trans-Missouri Pony Express in the last third of its brief and dramatic existence."

*   *   *

Since 1848 there had been scattered attempts to transport the mail overland to California. The vast bulk of mail went by steamship via the Isthmus of Panama until the Overland Mail Company, also known as the Butterfield Overland Mail after its president and major stockholder, John Butterfield of American Express, began to put a dent in the maritime delivery in 1858.

Congress had passed a bill in March 1857 sanctioning an overland stage service. Butterfield and William Fargo wrote a proposal letter to the postmaster general in June, and later that year Butterfield and his associates were awarded the contract. The Overland Mail Company was formed in October of 1857 specifically to fulfill the provisions of the $600,000 contract.

The Overland Mail Company was emblematic of the colonial nature of the West. It was an eastern or, to put it more precisely, a New York City–dominated consortium of the largest express companies in the country. Four of the first eleven directors of the Overland were also di-

rectors of Wells Fargo. A fifth Wells Fargo director was added to the Overland board in 1860. Five of the eleven largest stockholders were either
Wells Fargo directors or large stockholders in American Express.

The Overland company was mainly Butterfield's creation, five years
after Butterfield and Fargo had warred over establishing a West Coast
arm of American Express. The financial returns of Wells Fargo during the
intervening years had demonstrated to Butterfield the feasibility of investment in the West.

With sectionalism prevalent on the eve of the Civil War, the postmaster general, who was from Tennessee, chose a semicircular route. It
began in St. Louis and then dipped south to nearly touch the Mexican
border before heading toward the pueblo of Los Angeles and then northward to San Francisco. The route through large swaths of southern desert
was an all-year trail. The southern route also had political advantages.
The mail was viewed at the time as an instrument of settlement (as free-
ways and rapid transit are today), and thus a means to gain southern sympathizers.

The first relay of stages, drivers, mules, and horses westward made
the grueling, 2,700-mile journey in twenty-four days and nights in September and October of 1858. It carried the mail and one through passenger. This was the first true transcontinental mail and passenger service.

The Overland Mail Company lost money; and Wells Fargo, acting as
its banker, continued to advance it loans. The Wells Fargo directors on
Overland's board threatened foreclosure. It was Fargo, Butterfield's old
nemesis, who forced the issue in a March 1860 meeting of the Overland
board in Wells Fargo's New York office.

Fargo made a motion that the business be turned over to Wells Fargo.
A compromise was struck. Butterfield was ousted as president and Wells
Fargo directors and allied directors gained a majority on the board. They
now had control of the overland mail service.

Overland was the successful bidder in 1861 for a dual stagecoach and
Pony Express service via the central route, the outbreak of the Civil War
forcing transcontinental traffic north through Salt Lake City and over

the Sierra Nevada to Placerville. The $1 million government contract to carry the mail specified that the Pony Express obligation ended when the transcontinental telegraph line was completed.

The Pony Express had originally been the unsubsidized creation of Russell, Majors & Waddell, but the firm had experienced financial difficulties. The Overland Mail Company now conrolled the central route. The Wells Fargo–dominated Overland board subcontracted the service east of Salt Lake to the Russell firm and retained oversight of its operation. Overland ran the Salt Lake to Carson City, Nevada, segment. The Pioneer Stage Company, controlled by Louis McLane and managed by one of his brothers, operated the Carson City to Placerville run for Overland. Thus, while the Wells Fargo logo was not overtly emblazoned on Pony Express fixtures, it had de facto control for the last few months of its existence.

*   *   *

There was the romance and there was the reality of the Pony Express in action. Mark Twain spied a rider from the window of a stagecoach while crossing the plains in the summer of 1861. Eleven years later he penned this highly romanticized description in *Roughing It:*

> Presently the driver exclaims:
> "HERE HE COMES!"
> Every neck is stretched further, and every eye strained wider. Away across the endless dead level of the prairie a black speck appears against the sky, and it is plain that it moves. Well, I should think so! In a second or two it becomes a horse and rider, rising and falling, rising and falling—sweeping toward us nearer and nearer—growing more and more distinct, more and more sharply defined—nearer and still nearer, and the flutter of the hoofs comes faintly to the ear—another instant a whoop and a hurrah from our upper deck, a wave of the rider's hand, but no re-

ply, and man and horse burst past our excited faces, and go winging away like a belated fragment of a storm.

So sudden is it all, and so like a flash of unreal fancy, that but for the flake of white foam left quivering and perishing on a mail-sack after the vision had flashed by and disappeared, we might have doubted whether we had seen any actual horse and man at all, maybe.

Twain, who was primarily interested in telling a good story in *Roughing It*, and Robert H. Haslam, better known as Pony Bob, elevated the rider to the status of myth. Pony Bob Haslam achieved legendary status among riders when he set off in May of 1860 on a wild, 380-mile ride that set a record for endurance. He told the story with relish for the next half century, and it became embedded in the literature of the Pony Express.

Before the ride, the lean, twenty-year-old horseman had achieved a certain cachet among Pony Express riders. He had been wounded twice by Indians, once by an arrow that broke his jaw. In early April, Haslam had carried the first mail eastward for a distance of 120 miles "through a hostile Indian country," according to Alexander Majors, one of the founders of the Pony Express.

May was a time of even graver danger. The Paiute Indians had suffered terribly in the fierce winter of 1859–60. They blamed the whites for their starving condition. Miners from California were pouring into the Comstock Lode country of what would become known as western Nevada in four years. The isolated stagecoach and Pony Express stations dominated the few sources of water and the best grazing grounds in that arid region. The Indians were being pushed aside.

There was the usual back-and-forth of brutal incidents, capped by the kidnapping of two small Paiute girls. The Indians retaliated. The vulnerable Pony Express stations were the principal targets. Stations were razed, livestock driven off, and sixteen Pony Express employees killed.

Rumors spread as fast as four hooves could fly. Fear and frenzy contaminated the land.

Haslam's regular run was from Friday's Station at the south end of Lake Tahoe to Buckland's Station, seventy-five miles to the east. Armed with a Spencer rifle and a Colt revolver, Haslam slung the *mochilla*, a special saddlebag that fit over the saddle horn, on his horse and set off on May 11. He later told his story to Majors.

Pony Bob passed through the new mining community of Virginia City, where the inhabitants that remained feared an attack by the Paiutes. A stone hotel under construction on C Street had been converted into a temporary fort. A ragtag group of volunteers had taken off after the Indians. Charles Forman, newly hired in the local office of Wells Fargo, later wrote of the citizen militia: "We were very poorly armed . . . very poorly mounted, had but few rifles in the whole company, and had but little ammunition and a small amount of provisions."

The volunteers had requisitioned all the horses at Reed's Station on the Carson River. There was no fresh mount for Haslam when he arrived there. He fed his tired horse and rode fifteen miles further to Buckland's, where Fort Churchill would be constructed in a few months.

The next rider refused his assigned task. Haslam was astonished. The superintendent, W. C. Marley, offered Haslam a $50 bonus to continue the ride. Haslam accepted immediately.

The next leg was "a lonely and dangerous ride" to the Carson Sink station. He continued on to Sand's Springs, changed horses, changed again at Cold Springs, and finally ended his 185-mile run at Smith's Creek. Haslam had stopped only to eat and change horses. Now he slept for eight hours. Upon arising he ate and then returned with the westbound mail.

Unknowingly, Haslam had narrowly escaped death. "When I arrived at Cold Springs, to my horror I found that the station had been attacked by Indians, and the keeper killed and all the horses taken away."

What to do? There seemed to be no choice:

I watered my horse—having ridden him thirty miles on time, he was pretty tired—and started for Sand Springs, thirty-seven miles away. It was growing dark; and my road lay through heavy sagebrush, high enough in some places to conceal a horse. I kept a bright lookout, and closely watched every motion of my poor horse's ears, which is a signal for danger in an Indian country. I was prepared for a fight, but the stillness of the night and the howling of the wolves and coyotes made cold chills run through me at times, but I reached Sand Springs in safety and reported what had happened.

He advised the station keeper at Sand Springs to leave, and the frightened man joined Haslam on the ride to the Carson Sink station. A large party of Indians had been spotted in the vicinity. Haslam rested for one hour and then started out for Buckland's in the dark.

Upon reaching Buckland's, Marley paid Haslam $100 to continue. "I was rather tired," Haslam said, "but the excitement of the trip had braced me up to withstanding the fatigue of the journey." He rested for an hour and a half. Haslam reached Friday's Station on May 13, having covered 380 miles in some thirty-six hours of hard riding.

Meanwhile, the volunteer army of 105 men and boys had been lured northward to near Pyramid Lake. The Paiutes, derogatorily called Digger Indians by the whites, were led by Chief Numaga. The Indians killed seventy whites in a carefully executed trap. Forman, the Wells Fargo employee, was among the few to survive the battle, which has never been accorded the status it deserves in western lore. The news was delivered to Virginia City on May 13. The Pony Express shut down for one month.

That November, Abraham Lincoln was elected president. The news was telegraphed westward to Fort Kearny in what would become Nebraska. From there Pony Express riders sped westward. It is believed that Haslam was the rider who rode the last lap into Fort Churchill. A painting by the California artist Maynard Dixon showing a hatless Pony Express rider shouting "Lincoln Elected!" celebrates the event. From Fort Churchill the news was telegraphed to San Francisco.

Upon the demise of the Pony Express, Haslam put his considerable equestrian talents to work for Wells Fargo. He rode for the company in the spirited pony express races with the Pacific Union Express between Reno and Virginia City. Haslam won the first race, and Wells Fargo won most of the succeeding ones.

Pony Bob moved on to Idaho, where he delivered the mail on the Wells Fargo pony express routes. He passed the bleached remains of ninety Chinese immigrants who had been slain by Indians along a ten-mile stretch of road. Haslam's successor on the route was killed on his first trip.

After a brief stint as deputy U.S. marshal in Salt Lake City, Haslam went back to work for Wells Fargo as a messenger on the 720-mile Salt Lake City–Denver run. He eventually moved to Chicago, where he went to work for a large hotel. Haslam died peacefully in 1912 at the age of seventy-two. A photo of him in later life shows a distinguished gentleman with a black homburg in his left hand and a cigar and cane in his right.

The dash of realism that Sir Richard Burton applied to the Pony Express operation failed to dampen the myth set in motion by Mark Twain and Pony Bob. Burton was an English explorer, writer, and linguist who had made famous treks to Mecca and the source of the Nile. He was drawn to the exotic and set out in 1860 on a one-hundred-day stagecoach trip across the American West to appraise such unusual phenomena as the American Indian and the polygamous Mormons.

The experienced explorer prepared carefully for the new adventure. He took two revolvers, a Hawkin's rifle, "an air gun to astonish the natives," and a generous supply of opium and cigars. Burton had his hair cut short so "that my scalp is not worth having." He followed in Haslam's tracks five months after his long ride.

When Burton first spotted a Pony Express rider (like Twain, on the plains east of the Rocky Mountains) he wrote: "The riders are mostly youths, mounted upon active and lithe Indian nags." Crossing Nevada, Burton decried the slovenliness of the non-Mormon stations. The region, with a few exceptions, was "a howling wilderness." (Today's Highway 50, which follows the same general route, is advertised as "the Loneliest Road in America.") Of the Basin and Range Province, Burton wrote: "Nothing can be more monotonous than its regular succession of high grisly hills, cut perpendicularly by rough and rocky ravines, and separating bare and barren plains."

Burton saw the charred remains of the way stations in mid-October of 1860. A young express man he was riding with pointed to where another Pony Express rider had been wounded. The regular army was patrolling the trail. The Paiute Indians Burton encountered were peaceful. Pine nuts were exchanged for biscuits. Of a lazy Indian, Burton remarked, "Neither gospel nor gunpowder can reform this race."

The road was rough from Smith's Creek to Cold Creek Station, where Haslam had seen the stationkeeper's body that was later half-consumed by wolves before it could be properly buried. "The station was a wretched place," Burton wrote, "half built and wholly unroofed; the four boys, an exceedingly rough set, ate standing, and neither paper nor pencil was known amongst them." He slept that night under a haystack "and heard the loud howling of the wolves, which are said to be larger on these hills than elsewhere."

Sand Springs was deserving of its name. Burton observed:

The water near this vile hole was thick and stale with sulphury salts: it blistered even the hands. The station house was no unfit object in such a scene, roofless and chairless, filthy and squalid, with a smoky fire in one corner, and a table in the centre of an impure floor, the walls open to every wind, and the interior full of dust. Hibernia, herself, never produced aught more characteristic. Of the *employés*, all loitered and sauntered about *desœuvrés* as cretins, except one, who lay on the ground crippled and apparently dying by the fall of a horse upon his breast bone.

At Buckland's there was "the chance of being 'wiped out' in a 'differ-ence' between a soldier and a gambler, or a miner and a rider." At Carson City, Burton was told "that a dead man for breakfast was the rule" and "they reckoned per annum fifty murders."

Sir Richard hurried on to California and then sped home by boat via Panama, as did most distinguished visitors to the West at the time.

One year later the Pony Express was history beginning to fade into myth and nostalgia. Four shod hooves were replaced by the wire of the telegraph strung across the country, the stagecoach's four iron-rimmed wheels, and soon thereafter by the completely metallic wheels of the transcontinental train.

The Devil in Reality

BAD FOOD, delays in departures and arrivals, cramped seating, lost or damaged baggage, generally an unpleasant but necessary experience. Sound familiar?

Take the complaints of airplane passengers today, compare them with the experiences of the first travelers on regularly scheduled commercial journeys across the western half of the United States, add to the few hours of air travel some sixteen to twenty days or very likely more (including travel at night), mix in frequent accidents, incessant jolting, a thick coating of fine dust, lack of air-conditioning or heat, very little sleep, the lurking presence of trigger-happy robbers and vengeful Indians, and a ticket price that was up to eighteen times greater than what it now costs to fly from Missouri to California. The resulting stew was a stagecoach journey across the trans-Mississippi West in the 1860s.

When the eleven-year dominance of travel by overland stagecoach had passed, to be abruptly replaced by the transcontinental train, another western myth rose in its wake like dust trailing a Concord coach. The romance of staging had replaced its gritty reality.

In California, Louis McLane, who coaxed stagecoach travel to its peak, commented on a romanticized rendering of that means of transportation: "I thought staging looked very well to the lithographer, but was the devil in reality." At the other end of the line, the *Omaha Herald* described stage travel thus: "Don't imagine for a moment you are going on a picnic; expect annoyance; discomfort and some hardships. If you are disappointed, thank heaven."

The experiences of traveling overland by stagecoach from 1858 to 1869 are worth recalling in detail because Wells Fargo dominated that particular means of travel.

*   *   *

The 2,000-mile central route was the longest and costliest stagecoach line in the country, if not the world. Stagecoaches were an interim solution, and all recognized them as such, for the future was present at both ends of the trail. Steam in the form of steam-driven trains and boats bracketed the stagecoach line on either end in the early years. Steam up the Missouri River to Atchison, Kansas; steam-driven trains from Placerville or Folsom, California, to Sacramento, and then steamboats down the Sacramento River to San Francisco.

The terrain was varied. From the Missouri River the wagon road crossed the plains to Fort Kearny on the Platte River. There was a junction at Julesburg that led to Denver. The transcontinental route proceeded past Fort Laramie and Independence Rock to South Pass. It rose and fell across the undulating high plains landscape, then descended to the Green River, the northernmost tributary of the Colorado River. Past verdant Fort Bridger the tracks followed Echo Canyon to the Mormon enclave of Salt Lake City, where there was order and comfort in the midst of the wilderness.

On again it went across the barren Great Salt Lake Desert. It followed the Humboldt River southwest across the basin and range province of central Nevada. It swung south and passed through Austin to Carson City and Virginia City, outposts of California. The first real mountains to cross, the Sierra Nevada, were breached at Carson or Echo or Donner passes. The final leg was a long descent through verdant forests. The 1,913-mile journey was completed in approximately three weeks, if all went well.

From Kansas to California there were 153 stations, averaging about a dozen miles between each. At "swing" stations, horses or mules were changed; at "home" stations, drivers switched and meals were served, at an additional cost of between one and two dollars. The food was mostly poor to bad; fleas were rampant. Beds were for the drivers. The passengers wrapped themselves in blankets and napped on dirt floors. While under way, they attempted to sleep on the rocking stages. The stations had thick cedar-log walls and sod roofs, neither flammable nor easily breached by Indians. At home stations there usually was a family acting as caretakers; at swing stations there were two to four bachelor stock tenders.

The one-way throughfare varied from $225 to $500. It was more during the Civil War and less afterward. Very few passengers traveled the entire 2,000 miles; and, if they did, most returned on the more comfortable steamships via the Isthmus of Panama. The stagecoach was mostly for intermediate stops in the interior West.

The expenses of establishing and running an overland stagecoach company were enormous. On the payroll were headquarters personnel, division agents, harness makers, blacksmiths, carpenters, stock tenders, drivers, messengers, cooks, and agents. Stations had to be constructed. Then there were the costs of acquiring and feeding 2,750 horses and mules and buying harnesses and the stages.

The total annual operating cost was estimated at $2,425,000 in the early years when the mail contract was $1,000,000 per annum. The difference, it was hoped, would be made up by passengers and express traffic, which accounted for why the regular mail was delayed or dumped at times to make room for these additional revenue producers.

The costly overland line, versus the more profitable feeder lines, either broke its owners, forced them to sell, or seriously depleted their resources. An early historian of the overland stage, Frank A. Root, who had worked as a messenger in his youth, wrote: "It cost an enormous sum of money to equip and operate the 'Overland.' Prices for everything used in those days were way up on the high-pressure scale."

The experience of riding an overland stagecoach was documented by a number of journalists and writers. Horace Greeley of the *New York Tribune,* the preeminent editor of his time, was one of the early travelers, making the one-way trip in 1859 on the Russell line. He was primarily interested in promoting the idea of a transcontinental railroad.

The start was inauspicious. Atchison was described by one traveler as "certainly the last place a man would live for pleasure." The windswept, gullied ground was "desolate and uninviting," not a place to tarry in long. It rained hard in May of 1859. Streams rose and Greeley, the author of the phrase "Go West, young man!" was treated to an extended display of "celestial pyrotechny," meaning thunder and lightning. Tornadoes occasionally swept the trail.

The stage departed at 8 A.M. every morning, which coincided with the mail coming from the east via train and ferry. Depending on the weather, terrain, or what was available, the stage was pulled by either mules (for endurance) or horses (for speed). When Greeley eventually boarded the overland, after first traveling about Kansas on various local contrivances, it was a Concord stage propelled by four Kentucky mules. The editor wrote, "Adieu to bedrooms and washbowls!"

Had it been available at the time, Greeley could have availed himself of the hints for stage travelers published a few years later by the *Omaha Herald.* They remain a classic description of what to expect and how to prepare for it:

> The best seat inside a stage coach is the one next the driver. You will have to ride with back to the horses, which with some people, produces an illness not unlike sea-sickness, but in a long journey this will wear off, and you will get more rest, with less than half the bumps and jars than on any other seat. When

Henry Wells pioneered the express business in the Northeast in the 1840s. His philosophy for success: "There was one very powerful business rule, it was concentrated in the word—courtesy."

Telegraph Hill, 1849: California gold transformed San Francisco from a tent city into the West's leading metropolis.

Wells and Fargo opened their first banking and express office on Montgomery Street in San Francisco on July 13, 1852.

The company advertised its extensive banking services in *Parker's San Francisco Business Directory for 1852.*

Wells Fargo opened offices in hundreds of Gold Rush mining towns like Iowa Hill, California. *Courtesy California Historical Society.*

John Quincy Jackson, banker, assayer, gold buyer, and express agent at Auburn, California, 1852–1861.

In California mining camps women were scarcer than gold, which makes this photo of prospectors working near Auburn, California, in 1852 quite unusual. *Courtesy California Section, California State Library, Sacramento.*

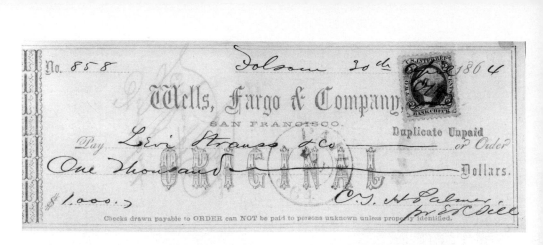

Businesses like Levi Strauss & Company used Wells Fargo checks.

Louis McLane, Wells Fargo president from 1866 to 1868, built the largest stagecoach operation in the West.

Stagecoach and express service helped connect residents of remote towns like Bear River, California, with the rest of the country.

"Lincoln Elected!" Artist Maynard Dixon captures the excitement generated by the arrival of a Pony Express rider with the latest news.

This envelope addressed to Wisconsin went east as far as St. Joseph, Missouri, by Pony Express.

GREAT OVERLAND
MAIL ROUTE.

PACIFIC AND ATLANTIC STATES.

WELLS, FARGO & CO.

SOLE PROPRIETORS.

FARE REDUCED !   TIME SHORTENED !

On and after the 1st day of April, 1867, passengers will be
forwarded through at the following reduced rates, viz:

Sacramento to Omaha	*$300.*
Virginia City to Omaha	*275.*
Austin to Omaha	*225.*
Sacramento to Cheyenne	*250.*
Virginia City to Cheyenne	*225.*
Austin to Denver	*175.*
Salt Lake to Bannock, Montana	*120.*
" *Virginia*	*120.*
" *Helena*	*145.*
" *Fort Benton*	*175.*

ALL LEGAL TENDERS OR THEIR EQUIVALENT.

12

An 1867 advertisement for Wells Fargo's Great Overland Mail Route.

A Wells Fargo stage in Salt Lake City, Utah, in 1869. *Courtesy Historical Department, Church of Jesus Christ of Latter Day Saints, Salt Lake City.*

Stages could carry as many as eighteen passengers inside and on top, along with luggage, mail bags, and the treasure box.

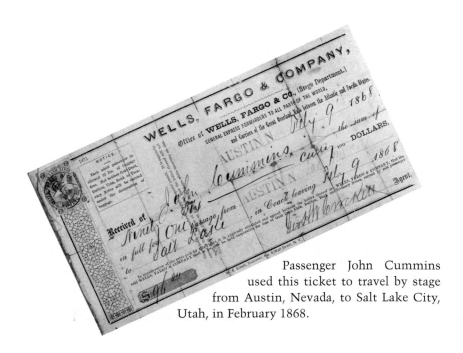

Passenger John Cummins used this ticket to travel by stage from Austin, Nevada, to Salt Lake City, Utah, in February 1868.

Artist Charles M. Russell depicted the peril of stagecoach travel.

Stage driver William H. "Shotgun" Taylor dressed for a Montana winter.

President Ulysses S. Grant described George Monroe as the finest stage driver he had ever seen. *Courtesy California Historical Society.*

Chief detective James B. Hume's methods earned him a two-thirds conviction rate for stage and train bandits from 1870 to 1885.

From 1875 to 1883, Black Bart the "Po8" held up stages, leaving a poem at the scene of the crime to taunt detectives. A dropped handkerchief provided the clue that led to his arrest.

REWARD

WELLS, FARGO & CO.'S EXPRESS BOX

on SONORA AND MILTON STAGE ROUTE, was ROBBED this morning, near Reynolds' Ferry, by one man, masked and armed with sixteen shooter and double-barreled shot gun. We will pay

$250

for ARREST and CONVICTION of the Robber.

JNO. J. VALENTINE, Gen. Supt.

San Francisco, July 26, 1875.

The "one man" described in this reward poster was Black Bart, and the robbery his first.

Hired gun Wyatt Earp rode shotgun for Wells Fargo in Tombstone, Arizona. *Courtesy Arizona Historical Society, Tucson.*

Lawman Bob Paul, Wells Fargo special officer and shotgun guard, sheriff, and U.S. marshal, brought law and order to some of the West's toughest towns.

Shotgun guards like these in Reno, Nevada, protected treasure boxes.

Jack the Dog: an alert guard dog atop the treasure box became a symbol of security in the express business.

Steamers carried gold, mail, and passengers between Pacific ports.

Steamer messenger Pillsbury "Chips" Hodgkins.

Lucy Miller and her sister Julia Jones ran the Wells Fargo office in Mariposa, California, from 1885–1909.

Before becoming an express agent in Pantano, Arizona, in 1880, Esteban Ochoa was mayor of Tucson.

Express wagons carried this dramatic advertising banner in 1915.

Lloyd Tevis, railroad, mining, and business entepreneur, and Wells Fargo president from 1872 to 1892.

Railroad mogul Edward H. Harriman gained control of Wells Fargo & Company in 1902 and split the company's express and banking businesses.

After 1869, Wells Fargo messengers increasingly rode the rails into thousands of American communities, such as Napa, California.

Denver, Colorado, 1892.

Ashland, Oregon, circa 1895. Agent Emma F. Howard, center.

Railroad depot, Albuquerque, New Mexico, 1913.

Houston, Texas, circa 1904.

Since Gold Rush days, Chinese miners and merchants were among Wells Fargo's most loyal customers. In 1882 the company issued a bilingual directory of Chinese merchants.

Pharmacy in San Francisco's Chinatown.

any old "sly Eph," who traveled thousands of miles on coaches offers, through sympathy to exchange his back or middle seat with you, don't do it. Never ride in cold weather with tight boots or shoes, nor close-fitting gloves. Bathe your feet before starting in cold water, and wear loose overshoes and gloves two or three sizes too large. When the driver asks you to get off and walk, do it without grumbling. He will not request it unless absolutely necessary. If a team runs away, sit still and take your chances; if you jump, nine times out of ten you will be hurt. In very cold weather abstain entirely from liquor while on the road; a man will freeze twice as quick while under its influence. Don't growl at food at stations; stage companies generally provide the best they can get. Don't keep the stage waiting; many a virtuous man has lost his character by so doing. Don't smoke a strong pipe inside especially early in the morning, spit on the leeward side of the coach. If you have anything to take in a bottle, pass it around, a man who drinks by himself in such a case is lost to all human feeling. Provide stimulants before starting; ranch whiskey is not always nectar. Be sure and take two heavy blankets with you; you will need them. Don't swear, nor lop over on your neighbor when sleeping. Don't ask how far it is to the next station until you get there. Take small change to pay expenses. Never attempt to fire a gun or pistol while on the road; it may frighten the team and the careless handling and cocking of the weapon makes nervous people nervous. Don't discuss politics or religion, nor point out places on the road where horrible murders have been committed, if delicate women are among the passengers. Don't linger too long at the pewter wash basin at the station. Don't grease your hair before starting or dust will stick there in sufficient quantities to make a respectable "tater" patch. Tie a silk handkerchief around your neck to keep out dust and prevent sunburns. A little glycerine is good in case of chapped hands.

When twenty-five-year-old Mark Twain and his brother, Orion Clemens, arrived in Atchison in July of 1861, they found that their luggage was over the twenty-five-pound weight limit, so they shipped their nonessential items home. The brothers took with them only necessities. They included revolvers, blankets, pipes and tobacco, two large canteens filled with water, and small change. "We jumped into the stage, the driver cracked his whip, and we bowled away and left 'the States' behind us," wrote Twain in *Roughing It.*

*   *   *

The Concord coaches that Greeley and the Clemens brothers stepped into were marvels of their time and are the present-day symbol for Wells Fargo Bank.

The Rolls-Royces of stagecoaches were built with a care, precision, and level of craftsmanship unknown and economically unfeasible today. At a time when brands were rare, the Concord coach was as recognizable as the Colt revolver, the McCormick reaper, and the Singer sewing machine. The name Concord was inserted in advertisements for stage lines, much as airlines might use the designation of a particular aircraft, if it was well made and provided a comfortable and safe ride.

The Concord mail coach was manufactured by the Abbot-Downing Company of Concord, New Hampshire. From 1830 to 1900 some 3,700 coaches were sold to customers in the United States, Canada, Europe, South Africa, South America, and Australia. The company's catalogue copy emphasized its universal acceptance in the English-speaking world: "The use of our Coaches and Wagons on all the Mail routes in America and the English Colonies for many years is a guarantee of their superiority."

What distinguished the Concord stages was their design, suspension, workmanship, and price, which was at the top end of the scale. The cost varied between $1,000 and $1,200, depending on accessories and model, meaning the six-, nine-, or twelve-passenger versions. Up to a dozen additional passengers could sit on the flat top of the coach in "relative comfort."

The design of the boxy, steel-springed English mail coach was modified for rougher American roads. Before aerodynamics was a known science, those Yankee craftsmen—many of whom were raised on farms—took the box form and modified it into a horizontal, egg-shaped body. Besides cutting down on drag, not an overriding consideration at stagecoach speeds, the modified oval shape allowed a lower center of gravity, thus lessening the chance of upsets. Also, a hen's egg, if stood on end, could support more than one hundred times its weight. A thin veneer covering the body of the coach could thus be strong and light.

When steel springs compressed and the body hit the axle as a conventional coach passed over a rock or pothole, there was a bone-jarring jolt. The lateral rigidity of boxy, top-heavy coaches caused them to capsize, much like some modern sports utility vehicles. The suspension had to be improved, especially for frontier road conditions.

The answer was to suspend the coach on two 6- to 8-ply bullhide belts that cradled the coach like a body in a hammock. The result was a floating, swaying, or rocking motion that made some passengers seasick but did not jar teeth loose. "Our coach was a great swinging and swaying stage," Mark Twain wrote, "of the most sumptuous description—an imposing cradle on wheels."

The wheels were an example of the extremely high level of craftsmanship employed throughout the coaches. Hand-tooled joinery work had been perfected by the middle of the nineteenth century and, in fact, had begun to decline as the Industrial Age, with its emphasis on mass production, continued to advance. The Abbot-Downing works were an exception. Great care was taken with a minimum of machinery. The use of iron, because of the weight factor, was limited. Choice straight-grained ash and white oak were the woods of choice. Abbott-Downing wheels, unlike modern tires, were never recalled.

Beyond practicality, there was aesthetics. Multiple coats of pomegranate red paint were rubbed down with pumice. Then two coats of spar varnish were applied to the finish. The mirror-like, blood-red surface gleamed. A beckoning landscape—usually an idealized New England scene—was painted on the door panels for an additional $20, if the customer desired it. Elaborate wooden scrollwork set off the oil painting. The metal trim was painted black, the undercarriage was straw colored, and the lettering was sometimes gold leaf or gold colored. The names of the stage line and whose mail and packages it carried, whether the government or a private express company, were painted above the doors and on the driver's box. The result was circus-like when contrasted with the predominant sage grays and khaki tans of the western landscape.

When Wells Fargo ordered Concord coaches in 1867, the specifications emphasized sturdiness. There was a touch of luxury, however. Damask-lined leather curtains were specified for the interiors. The company favored the one-ton, nine-passenger model, meaning that there were three seats inside: one facing backward, one in the middle with no backrest, and one facing forward. There were fifteen inches of room for each passenger, versus the seventeen to eighteen inches in the coach section of today's commercial jets.

The stage companies used lesser vehicles for unusual terrain or specialized tasks—mud wagons for real tough going and lighter celerity wagons for speed. They cost approximately half as much as a full-sized mail coach. What Abbot-Downing called mail coaches in its catalogues were both the flagships and workhorses of the overland fleets.

Looking back, the Concord coaches seem too elegant for the dusty, muddy, snow-clogged trails of the West, where they received a constant battering from the elements, both human and natural. So much was makeshift in the Old West that those fragile-looking craft seem like anomalies. The coaches, however, belied their looks; some lasted beyond their times. Two coaches from the 1867 order are currently on display in Wells Fargo offices.

Perhaps the most famous coach was the stage driven pell-mell with the driver's guns ablazing through various arenas in the United States and Europe by William F. ("Buffalo Bill") Cody, a former Pony Express rider and stagecoach driver. Its origins are uncertain. The coach, smaller than regular models, was reportedly ordered by McLane for his Pioneer Stage Company in 1864. From California it seemingly made its way eastward to Deadwood, Wyoming, where Cody acquired it and used it in his Wild West show.

In London, the story goes, Buffalo Bill took four European kings for a ride. They sat inside. The place of honor beside Cody on the box was given to the Prince of Wales. The prince, perhaps wanting to appear western, remarked, "This coach now holds a big poker hand." "Yes," said Bill, "four kings inside and the 'joker' on the box." Wells Fargo acquired the coach in the late 1930s.

When the Abbot-Downing Company finally went out of business in 1927 because it was unable to compete successfully in building trucks, the name was bought by Wells Fargo, "which sought to perpetuate a great corporate identity in the history of America's West," according to a history of the stagecoach company published in the journal of the New Hampshire Historical Society.

*   *   *

Greeley, Twain, and others were confronted by an alien landscape as they proceeded westward over the High Plains, which the editor referred to as "the American Desert." Easterners making the trip for the first time—almost all in the more pleasant summer months—were intoxicated by the mountain scenery but depressed by the lack of vegetation and the aridity of the flat country, be it high plains or desert.

The travelers were overwhelmed by the vast spaces and lack of humans or trees: something, anything, that might provide a recognizable scale. "The Plains are nearly destitute of human inhabitants," lamented Greeley. He added, "Take away the buffalo, and the Plains will be destitute far beyond their present desolation." The editor bemoaned the lack of trees: "Yet not a tree nor shrub relieves the sameness, the bareness, the desolation, of thousands after thousands of acres." Of the Great Basin

Desert west of Salt Lake City, Greeley wrote, "If Uncle Sam should ever sell that tract for one cent per acre, he will swindle the purchaser outrageously."

This land was becoming Wells Fargo territory in the 1860s. Earlier, in order of appearance on the scene, it had encompassed Native American, Spanish, Mexican, U.S. government, and private holdings. Some cited the "austere beauty" of the plains landscape; Greeley saw "desolation."

As the passengers proceeded westward, they could find little to entertain them (other than taking random shots at buffalo and antelope) or take their minds off the unpleasantness of the journey. Demas Barnes, a New York businessman, traveled overland between 1862 and 1865 to assess western properties. He wrote of the road to Denver:

> It is not a <u>pleasant</u>, but it is an <u>interesting</u> trip. . . . Coaches will be overloaded, it will rain, the dust will drive, baggage will be left to the storm, passengers will get sick, a gentleman of gallantry will hold the baby, children will cry, nature demands sleep, passengers will get angry, the driver will swear, the sensitive will shrink, rations will give out, potatoes become worth a gold dollar each, and not to be had at that, the water brackish, the whiskey abominable, and the dirt almost unendurable.

Barnes's stage was accompanied by two to four cavalry soldiers on his 1865 trip. "We did not encounter any Indians, but saw many remains of their barbarity." Other travelers wrote in the same vein of the conflicts east of Salt Lake City between 1864 and 1867. They were called the Indian wars but could just as well been named the stagecoach wars. The lumbering stages, the many stations, and the demands of thousands of horses and mules for pasturage were the first wheeled incursions into territory the Indians regarded as their own.

The result was chaos. Stage lines ground to a halt, passengers were isolated at remote stations, mail accumulated, and the travelers demanded more protection from troops, commanded in the West after the Civil War by none other than that former San Francisco banker, Lt. Gen. William Tecumseh Sherman. Fear pervaded the overland route from Kansas to the California border.

Young Frank Root took a job as a mail agent at a station near present-day Greeley, Colorado. In the summer of 1864 traffic on the overland trail came to a halt and one hundred and fifty passengers and inhabitants from nearby homesteads took refuge in the station. There were rumors of nine hundred Indians poised to attack.

The women fashioned a flag that flew bravely above the impromptu fort. The men drilled. More than one hundred sacks of mail were used to form a breastworks. "I felt little uneasiness," wrote Root some forty years later, "in regard to the safety of the mail and was satisfied that, if an attack was made on the premises, I could, with my fortifications, two shot-guns, an improved breech-loading rifle, a brace of navy revolvers, and a keg of powder 'hold the fort.'"

Rumors intensified, and the excitement and fear mounted accordingly. A freighter, who had been standing guard duty, woke Root with a trembling hand. The Indians were coming and could be heard fording the nearby South Platte River, he said.

"The night was clear but quite dark and the splashing of the water in the river could be distinctly heard," said Root. "Every person in the house was soon up and dressed. Extra skirmishers were promptly deployed. The 'enemy' was soon discovered and proved to be nothing else than a drove of cattle crossing the river." Soon thereafter, the road to Denver and Salt Lake was reopened after being closed for six weeks.

The first sight of the Rocky Mountains was balm to the vegetation-starved travelers. Greeley wrote with relief and insight: "And the Rocky Mountains, with their grand, aromatic forests, their grassy glades, their frequent springs, and dancing streams of the brightest, sweetest water, their pure elastic atmosphere, and their unequaled game and fish, are destined to be a favorite resort and home of civilized man."

Although Greeley barely acknowledged his presence in dispatches, another eastern newspaperman was traveling on the same stage. Albert D. Richardson of the *Boston Journal*, who went to work for Greeley at the *Tribune* during the Civil War, would return to Denver in 1860 and again in 1865, when he made the trip all the way to San Francisco.

Denver was in 1860, according to Richardson, "a city of the dead" with many fresh graves, log cabins, clapboard shacks, three daily newspapers for four thousand inhabitants, a brick Catholic church under construction, dens of vice and iniquity, a proper drug store, a combination bank–assay office–private mint for the dominant business of mining, and a "huge frame two-story express office" with a long line "of anxious inquirers" waiting to collect their mail. The eastbound Concord stage was about to depart: "A motley crowd waits to witness the departure."

Five years later great changes had been wrought in Denver. Change, more rapid than elsewhere, was the one constant in the West. There were, said Richardson, "many imposing buildings. The hotel bills-of-fare did not differ materially from those in New York or Chicago." The newsman was surprised to find libraries, paintings, rich carpets, pianos, silver, and wine. Such was the measure of progress.

Across Colorado and southern Wyoming there were complaints about the mail service. A. K. McClure, whose letters also appeared in Greeley's *Tribune*, took Wells Fargo to task in 1867, the last year of the Indian troubles. "Congress has practically given up to Wells, Fargo & Co. a monopoly of the mails, exclusive of letters, at enormous rates, as the responsibility of a company of common carriers gives them a positive preference over the Post-Office Department."

While in Montana, McClure found that letters and newspapers shipped by Wells Fargo express, as opposed to the regular mail, arrived "promptly." There was a reason for that, he said. Greater profits were to be made carrying the double-stamped Wells Fargo mail. "At different stations on the way tons of [regular] mail piled up; and sometimes mail-bags are scattered along the road, apparently dropped off and carelessly abandoned."

He also found the stock in bad shape, either stolen by the Indians or in poor condition "because of the want of grain and hay." McClure met James J. Tracy, Wells Fargo's general superintendent of stage lines, on his way east. Tracy told him they had acquired the entire overland operation too late in the fall of 1866 "to supply it properly with forage."

Others, like Barnes, the businessman whose letters appeared in the *Brooklyn Eagle,* cited the same problems with the overland mail experienced by previous contractors, such as Ben Holladay, who sold his business to Wells Fargo in 1866. Barnes had found bags of mail stashed at stations west of Denver in 1865. "I have seen the stages pass through here loaded with passengers," Barnes wrote, "and not carrying a pound of mail, while perhaps two week's mail, or more, lay heaped up in the office."

He thought the public was being swindled by the owner of the stage line. Some western editors agreed, others didn't, citing conditions, such as Indian attacks and the weather, that were beyond the control of Wells Fargo and other express companies.

The stage journey bumped onward through what would become known as Wyoming. There was a patch of badlands to pass east of the Green River and then a well-watered oasis along the route in northern Utah. The noted New York editor, clad in his white duster, perched alone for more than four days and nights on top of seventeen mailbags, sixteen of which contained knobby patent office records being sent by a Utah congressman to his constituents. The rolling terrain, he noted, was "very scantily grassed and often thickly covered for miles by the everlasting sagebrush of the region." The alkali-laden dust along this section of the trail "parched the lips and irritated the nose with a keenness almost equal to quicklime," said another traveler.

At Fort Bridger on the north slope of the Uinta Mountains there were "gurgling rills threading its green parade grounds," Richardson noted, and good food, the cultured daughters of the post sutler playing the piano (hauled from the East Coast), and an old trapper telling tales. Richardson recounted the following conversation with the grizzled trapper:

"But the most singular thing I ever did was to make a hundred and fifty Blackfeet Indians run."

"How was that?" we asked.

"It was one year when the red devils were very hostile, and lifted the hair of every white man they could catch. Riding a swift horse, I suddenly came upon a party of them. I turned and ran and they all ran after me; but they didn't catch old Jack."

Fort Bridger was an exception, the food elsewhere along the line not being anywhere near as good. Referring to the meals he had consumed, a traveler noted: "Some were evidently filthy, but they were made to look passable on the table, and, with a little forgetfulness, enough could be worried down to satisfy the demands of hunger." Twain was served condemned army bacon, week-old bread, and a beverage called slumgullion. When he refused to eat the meal, the stationmaster told him to eat the mustard.

*   *   *

It all changed when the tired travelers arrived in Salt Lake City, a permanent settlement that was everything the surrounding territories were not. There was order, calm, safety, shade, fresh food, thrift, and a theocracy. Greeley, who spoke for a generation of overland travelers, said: "Salt Lake City wears a pleasant aspect to the emigrant or traveler, weary, dusty, and browned with a thousand miles of jolting, fording, camping, through the scorched and naked American desert."

For the writers, the Mormons and their inland empire were the biggest draw on the overland trail. The travelers who were charged with writing newspaper accounts approached the Mormons as if they were an alien race, centering their inquiries on the issue of polygamy. Sir Richard

Burton, Greeley, and Twain met the Mormon leader, Brigham Young. Twain, playing the fool, said he asked Young impertinent questions. Young remained calm. On leaving, the bearded patriarch placed his hand on the young man's head and asked Twain's older brother, "Ah—your child, I presume? Boy, or girl?"

Four years later Richardson visited Salt Lake City, and his description of the Mormon settlement differed markedly from his impressions of Denver in that same year of 1865: "Before us was the city, with its flashing streams, its low, adobe houses with trellised verandahs; its green gardens, and shade-trees of locust, aspen, popular, maple, walnut, elder and cottonwood; its bustling marts of trade, and cloistered retreats for the offices of a strange religion." All of this had been achieved just eighteen years after Brigham Young had supposedly said, "This is the place." This was the only place for tired travelers who wanted to be refreshed before hitting the trail again.

Salt Lake City was the well-organized hub for the carefully crafted spokes of the transportation wheel that radiated throughout most parts of the interior West. Much as Chicago is to United Airlines, so was Salt Lake to express companies. The jurisdictions of the various companies tended to begin and end there. The overland route passed through Salt Lake, and the feeder lines formed a semicircle from west to east, the Colorado River being an impenetrable barrier to large-scale commercial traffic directly to the south.

An 1868 table of distances, contained in instructions to Wells Fargo express agents at the height of the company's involvement in staging, illustrated the city's crossroads role: Salt Lake City to Cheyenne, Wyoming, 557 miles; Salt Lake City to Omaha, Nebraska, 1,073; Salt Lake City to Denver, Colorado, 606; Salt Lake City to Virginia City, Nevada, 572; Salt Lake City to Sacramento, California, 740; Salt Lake City to Boise City, Idaho, 393; Salt Lake City to Helena, Montana, 546. The transportation historian W. Turrentine Jackson wrote that "Salt Lake City was the most important and widely publicized transportation center between the Missouri frontier and California" at that time.

Two years after the famous New York editor had passed through Salt
Lake, one of the *Tribune*'s most loyal readers arrived to take charge of
the Overland Mail Company office. Hiram S. Rumsford engaged in a
lengthy correspondence with his wife back in Tiffin, Ohio. His main
concern was that she pay the subscription to the *Tribune* on time so
that he could keep his set of back issues unbroken. Keeping the subscription current rated higher than "the matter of house renting for
the ensuing year" for his family. He also received a copy of the paper in
Salt Lake.

Cordial relations with the Mormons was the first priority of his job.
That was the policy of his company, controlled in large part by Wells
Fargo directors. From time to time he met with Young, Heber C. Kim-
ball, and other Mormon leaders. One way to win "their undivided confidence, friendship, and affection," he noted, was to purchase supplies
from the Mormons—"several hundred thousand dollars . . . in glittering
gold" were spent in the first eleven months.

The public relations gesture was costly. The inflated prices for feed
"were enough to cripple any company," according to an overland historian. Rumsford cited a price of fifty to sixty cents for a bushel of oats.
One year the company raised its own feed, but still had to depend partially on the Mormons in later years.

Rumsford attended services in the Tabernacle, but was less than flat-
tering in his private comments about the Mormon religion and its ad-
herents. He praised the weather and the abundance of fresh vegetables,
fish, and game. The agent was particularly proud of his Indian policy, another company priority.

Shortly after Rumsford arrived in Salt Lake the Indians to the west
showed "some hostile signs," like attacking a station. No one was killed.
The problem, Rumsford told his wife, was: "The Government treated
with them last summer and promised them ample supplies of food and
clothing for the winter. This promise, unfortunately, has not been com-
plied with, and the poor savages are now preparing to remind the officials

of their faithlessness by commencing hostilities on the Overland Mail Co." Rumsford spoke to the regional superintendent of Indian Affairs, who promised "to quiet the Indians by providing for their wants."

The trouble centered around the Deep Creek Station, some 170 miles west of Salt Lake. Rumsford set off on an inspection tour in 1862. He found the station to be a veritable oasis amidst the desolation of the Great Basin Desert, which he described as "a succession of brazen looking, barren mountains, and alkali flats." The valley, in which the station was located, "is a beautiful one. It is traversed by a never-failing stream of water," the deep creek. A settlement of about a half dozen Mormon families was nearby. The late June day had been "hot and the dust along the road almost suffocating." It was beginning to cool in the early evening when the stage pulled into the station.

A painting by Francis L. Horspool depicts the Wells Fargo station in 1868, and a description accompanies it:

> Looking at the painting, you will see at the left corner of the barn a little child with a wagon. Below the child, at the pond is a post with an animal skull on it. Near the front part of the barn is a sleigh, at the right of the sleigh is a log dog house with two dogs on it. In front of the barn is the old pony express stable, then a freighter's wagon and Aaron Y. Ross, the guard. The freighter is seen over the back of the black horse. In front of the black horse is a gray horse with an artificial left hind leg, and below it is a dog in the rushes. William F. Horspool, the painter's father, is on the stage. Below the stage, near the wagon tongue is a dog, or is it a colt? In front of the horses hooked to the stage is a woman on a horse. It may be the wife of the station agent, James Ferguson, who is holding a mail sack in front of the horse. At the corner of the house are travelers. In the pond, among the rushes, are crosses which are fallen down fence posts, with ducks here and there in the pond.

A young couple by the name of Egan ran the station in 1862. Rumsford found Mrs. Egan beautiful and accomplished. He was much taken with her singing: "How home-like the associations and how chastening to the soul of the weary way-faring stranger, are the gentle tones of the female voice," he wrote his wife.

A large Indian encampment was one mile distant. "As game of all kinds," Rumsford noted, "has left the valley since the Overland Mail Company established its route along here, the poor savages have had no means of subsistence, except that furnished by the Company. We have fed them liberally acting upon the principal that it is cheaper to feed them than to fight them." The company paid Egan $1,800 to furnish beef to the Indians for the first three months of 1862. "Twenty thousand dollars will not pay their 'board bill' for the winter," lamented the cost-conscious agent.

Rumsford thought his company's Indian policy vastly superior to that of Russell's firm, which operated the overland route east of Salt Lake. There had been interruptions of service on that line. "We have 10 indians on our line to one of their's and yet we have no trouble with the savages. We give them plenty to eat and that is all they want. . . . If the Eastern Company had pursued the same line of policy everything would have gone along smoothly."

In March of 1863, after again fussing about the *Tribune* subscription, Rumsford said an "unexpected announcement" had arrived by telegraph from the Deep Creek Station. A party of hostile Indians had suddenly appeared in the valley and attacked the stage ten miles west of Deep Creek. He thought they were Snake or Shoshone Indians from the north. Rumsford was mistaken. This incident was the start of the Goshute War, the Goshutes being a local tribe.

The driver was killed and a passenger gravely wounded. Another passenger, Gordon N. Mott, a Nevada judge who became the state's territorial representative to Congress, climbed atop the driver's box, seized the reins, and guided the horses to Deep Creek. The wounded passenger was found inside the stagecoach, his two small sons huddled beside him. The father recovered from his head wound.

The Shoshone and Ute Indians had just agreed to peace. The commanding general in Salt Lake reported to his superiors:

Thus at last I have the pleasure to report peace with the Indian on all hands, save only a few hostile Goshutes west and north of Deep Creek. These cannot number more than 100 braves, and I have dispatched two companies of the Second Cavalry under Capt. S. P. Smith, who will scour the entire surrounding country and kill or drive off the last remaining hostile band. . . . I may therefore confidently report the end of Indian difficulties on the Overland Stage Line and within this district, from the Snake River, on the north, to Arizona, on the south, and from Green River to Carson Valley.

At 8 Mile Station, the first station eight miles to the west of Deep Creek, the soldiers found the structures in ashes, the horses gone, and the two stockmen "lying dead, naked and scalped upon the ground." Armed guards were posted at the more vulnerable stations. "This is the first Indian difficulty we have had upon our road since the line was started," Rumsford explained, "and such has been the sense of security, against attack, that passengers and employees were seldom armed when upon the road."

That spring Rumsford was busy preparing for the visit of three Wells Fargo directors. The president, Danford H. Barney, and William G. Fargo and Benjamin P. Cheney were on an inspection tour of the West. The agent was like any employee who has to entertain the company brass: "I shall be glad to see them—and, perhaps, will be equally glad to see them off again." (The three directors were in California a little over one month and returned to New York via steamship. Other than Wells's 1853 visit, it was the only time New York–based Wells Fargo directors visited California. After he resigned his directorship, Wells visited the state for health reasons.)

The taking of scalps was not confined to the Indians. Rumsford also found time that spring to send a scalp to his wife. It had been lifted from an Indian's head at Spring Valley Station, thirty-nine miles west of Deep Creek. He wished that he could have sent "many dozens" such scalps and apologized to his wife that he had been unable to find anyone in Salt Lake to tan the scalp, which had turned green from rot.

Nearing the end of his Salt Lake tour, Rumsford visited San Francisco for the fourth time in 1865. The agent purchased a silk dress for his wife and lamented the high prices. He noted the cool summer weather but said he preferred living in the East. Rumsford, too, was no fan of staging: "How glad I would be could I take the Steamer for New York instead of having to trudge over these horrible mountains again."

*　*　*

At Deep Creek the driver said "Git!", and the westward-trending stagecoach soon passed out of what would become known as Utah.

The stage driver, like an airline pilot, was the king of all he surveyed from his perch atop the box. The whip was his scepter, a personalized tool, and the symbol of his trade. Some were decorated with silver, others were simply deadly efficient. The drivers sat on the box "and cut a fly off the back of either of the lead horses or mules with the lash, while going at a lively trot," said Root, who, as a messenger, had sat beside many drivers. A stage traveler referred to the driver as "the hero of the whip and lines."

The drivers represented a cross-section of society. A college-educated driver from Massachusetts wrote his parents that he had gone "on the stage." Older drivers had driven stages from the Alleghenies to the Sierra Nevada, for they were a transient lot. They sang or were silent. One announced his stage's arrival with a bugle call. They were well armed and handy with repairs. Speed, when the road was relatively flat, was addictive, along with being necessary to keep to the schedule and ahead of harm's way.

The exposed drivers were perfect targets for arrows, bullets, and the lash of extreme weather, whether the blazing sun or blinding snow. In cold weather a driver wrapped himself in buckskin, wool, and buffalo robes, except for his hands, which were needed to communicate with the horses or mules. The driver's hands were clad in silk liners covered by thin buckskin gloves, which gave him minimal protection while still providing sensitivity to the tug of the reins. The two or three pairs of reins were held between the fingers of both gloved hands, as was the whip. The brake was applied by foot. There was a lot to do at one time.

In minus-zero-degree weather a stage pulled up to a one-room station in 1867. McClure wrote:

> A tolerable dinner was prepared and enjoyed by the company; but the badly-frozen hands of the driver who should have taken us on, was not a pleasant reminder of the cold snaps of the mountains. His fingers were swollen to thrice their natural proportions, and just before we started, he was coolly debating with the landlord whether the fingers must be amputated.

Accidents and being thrown from the stage, sometimes with fatal results, were occupational hazards for the drivers and nonlitigious risks for the passengers. The coach in which Greeley was traveling capsized when the mules were frightened by Indians while descending a steep hill. The editor was thrown about inside the coach and emerged badly cut. He shook off his injuries and continued the journey.

A few drivers stood out from the crowd. One such was Charley Parkhurst. J. Ross Browne, who wrote in the same exaggerated style as Twain, recounted his trip over the Sierra Nevada with a stage driver named Charlie, who was thought to be Parkhurst. The express agent for the Pioneer stage line had given Browne the honored seat beside the driver:

> The driver was Charlie. Of course every body knows Charlie—
> that same Old Charlie who has driven all over the roads in Cali-

fornia, and never capsized any body but himself. On that occasion he broke several of his ribs, or as he expressed it to me, "Bust his sides in." I was proud and happy to sit by the side of Charlie—especially as the road was supposed to be a little undulating even by its best friends.

The night passed in amiable conversation between the grizzled driver—depicted by Browne, also an illustrator, with a cigar clenched in his jaw—and the traveler, attired in a frock coat and top hat. Delivered safely to his destination, Browne praised Charley in the pages of *Harper's New Monthly Magazine:* "Sweet and gentle ladies shall pay the tribute of admiration to your manly features; and honest men shall award you honor, to whom honor is due. For in the vicissitudes of my career have I not found brave and sterling qualities in all classes of men. . . ."

Some fifteen years later Charley died. While preparing his body for burial, his friends were surprised to discover that Charley was a woman. The *San Francisco Call*'s obituary referred to Charley as "one of the most dexterous and celebrated of the famous California drivers" and called the discovery "literally astounding."

Charley, perhaps born Charlotte, originally came from Providence, Rhode Island, where she drove carriages for the gentry. The *Providence Journal* commented on the discovery: "The only people who have any occasion to be disturbed by the career of Charley Parkhurst are the gentlemen who have so much to say about 'women's sphere' and 'the weaker vessel.'" But the newspaper judiciously balanced its views by stating at the end of the article that perhaps "the opponents" of women's equality issues were right after all. The *San Francisco Chronicle* said Charley was the first woman to vote in California, although such a view neglects other women who may have posed as men. (Greeley came across such a woman on the trail to Denver.)

Charley worked as a messenger as well as a driver. It was the messenger's job to sit beside the driver; accompany important documents, valuable minerals called treasure, and the express mail; function as a conductor; and be the overall guard. The messengers were armed with a sawed-off double-barreled shotgun, a breech-loading rifle, a Colt navy revolver called a "hip howitzer," or some combination of the above.

The messengers and agents served as the public presence of Wells Fargo's express operation. Except for some scattered rural lines and its urban service, Wells Fargo only operated stages under its own name on major routes from 1866 to 1868. Wells Fargo may have owned outright a stage company and preferred to operate it under a more locally recognizable name, as was the case with the Pioneer Stage Company; it may have had an interest in a firm, the Overland Mail Company being an example; or it may have had an arrangement, perhaps pegged at some percent of the value carried, of sending its messengers and freight on an associated stage line. Generally, except for those two years, Wells Fargo preferred contractual arrangements with other stage companies to a large capital investment in the generally unprofitable business of staging over long distances.

In the public's mind, however, stagecoaches became synonymous with Wells Fargo, regardless of who owned them. The newspapers, ever grateful for the free news that Wells Fargo messengers carried, were responsible for this mistaken identity when they reported that a stage had been robbed. More commonly, it was the green, iron-bound Wells Fargo treasure box guarded by the company messenger that had been the target, the stagecoach having belonged to someone else.

The twenty- by twelve- by ten-inch boxes weighed twenty-four pounds empty and bore the white lettering, "Wells, Fargo & Co." They were made of ponderosa pine and had an oak trim. A San Francisco father-and-son carpenter team made the chests between the years 1862 and 1906. They are much sought after now by collectors.

Within the hierarchy of staging, the vaunted drivers were at the top; but it was the agents and the messengers who, along with the company image, represented the company. Generally messengers were young and inexperienced and came and went with greater frequency than drivers. Certainly that was the case with the young Bret Harte, before he

achieved literary fame. Frank Root was a messenger before becoming a
mail agent. He left one of the few accounts of the job:

> I never realized fully the dangers connected with the position of
> messenger on this stage line until I had resigned, after making
> thirty-two trips between the Missouri river and the Rockies, and
> riding, in the aggregate, a distance of 22,500 miles. The messen-
> gers simply took their lives in their hands. Those employed on
> the main line were obliged to ride six days and nights without
> taking off their clothes, catching what sleep they could from
> time to time while the stage was moving across the plains and
> over the mountain passes. Their place on the stage was supposed
> to be on the box, with the driver, and the safe containing the trea-
> sure was placed in the front boot, under the driver's feet.

Although Root never worked for Wells Fargo, he was familiar with
the company. "They were, in a measure, considered public benefactors,"
he said. As a former stage messenger he was particularly impressed with
the fact that they were "extremely liberal" with their pay.

*   *   *

Across what is now the State of Nevada the stagecoach flew at record
speeds. Was it being chased by Indians or robbers? No. Wells Fargo
wanted to impress an important congressman and his party of journalists
who were on a summer junket to the West in 1865. The journey was
characterized by speed, comfort, speeches, brass bands, and the careful
handling of the dignitaries.

The party consisted of Schuyler Colfax, speaker of the House of Representatives; William Bross of the *Chicago Tribune*; Samuel Bowles, editor of the *Springfield* (Massachusetts) *Republican*; and Richardson of the
Tribune. They were well armed and accompanied partway by a cavalry

escort and the commanding general for the military district to the east of Salt Lake in that year of Indian troubles. In addition, according to Bowles, they carried "every possible mitigation of the fatigues and discomforts of the long ride."

George K. Otis of the Overland Mail Company and secretary to the Wells Fargo board of directors rode along with the party to Salt Lake. Now they were in the hands of a division superintendent of the Overland "whose stockholders are New Yorkers, and mainly the same as those of the great express company of Wells, Fargo & Co., which monopolizes the express business in all these western States and Territories," Bowles reported to his New England readers.

The company established a speed record: from Salt Lake to Austin, Nevada, nearly four hundred miles in fifty hours, two-thirds the regular time; from Austin to Virginia City, Nevada, two hundred miles in twenty-two hours, fourteen hours less than the scheduled time. The swift ride would be their most memorable experience that summer, but not one they wished to repeat. The jolting, dust, and lack of sleep were constant. "The passengers are content that it should be a single experience for them," said Bowles. They were relieved to leave "these unpromising valleys, gray and brown with unnatural sunshine" behind. "Mountains are always beautiful," he observed.

Across the Sierra Nevada there was "the first real staging," said Barnes, the New Yorker, on a graded road with dashing horses at great speed. Six years earlier Greeley had written of the precipitous road over the summit:

> Yet along this mere shelf, with hardly a place to each mile where two meeting wagons can pass, the mail stage was driven at the rate of ten miles an hour (in one instance eleven), or just as fast as four wild California horses, whom two men could scarcely harness, could draw it. Our driver was of course skillful; but had he met a wagon suddenly on rounding one of the sharp points or

projections we were constantly passing, a fearful crash was un-avoidable.

In California, said Greeley, he found himself "once more among friends, surrounded by the comforts of civilization, and with a prospect of occasional rest." The West, to which Greeley exhorted his young read-ers to emigrate, was a coastal West, or at least that was where he and oth-ers like him felt most comfortable. The influential editor ended his dispatches with a ringing endorsement for a railroad to the Pacific Ocean, which would become a reality in ten years. Citing the large num-bers of emigrants to the West Coast, Greeley asked: "Can there be any doubt that nine-tenths of these would have traveled by railroad?"

When Bowles, who probably traveled for free as Greeley had done, ar-rived in California in 1865, he found a company that "has grown very much into the heart and habit of the people." The editor wrote of the un-usual commercial enterprise:

> There is no institution of the Coast that has interested me more than Wells & Fargo's Express. It is the omnipresent, universal business agent of all the region from the Rocky Mountains to the Pacific Ocean. Its offices are in every town, far and near; a billiard saloon, a restaurant, and a Wells & Fargo office are the first three elements of a Pacific or Coast mining town; its messengers are on every steamboat, the rail-car and stage, in all these States. It is the Ready Companion of civilization, the Universal Friend and Agent of the miner, his errand man, his banker, his post-office. It is much more than an ordinary express company; it does a gen-eral and universal banking business, and a great one in amount; it brings to market all the bullion and gold from the mining re-gions—its statistics are the only reliable knowledge of the pro-duction; and it divides with the government the carrying of letters to and fro.

The reception at the official end of the stage line in Placerville for Speaker Colfax and his party "seemed to come straight from the heart," according to Richardson. James B. Hume, the town marshal who would later go to work for Wells Fargo, led a parade featuring the honored guests through the pleasant Sierra Nevada foothill town of four thousand inhabitants that had formerly supplied the mines in the region. "The procession was large and enthusiastic, and the reception of the party cordial in the extreme," stated the *Mountain Democrat*.

There were, however, nine more miles to ride in the morning to Shingle Springs, where they boarded the train for Sacramento. "After two thousand miles of stage-coaching, here was the locomotive again!" Richardson wrote, "From the bottom of my heart I felt like embracing or, at the very least, apostrophizing it."

Wells Fargo
Goes to War

T HE EXPRESS companies prospered greatly during the Civil War, each in their different ways. For eastern companies there was the gruesome task of shipping bodies home and serving the needs of soldiers on the battlefields. Wells Fargo's contribution to the Civil War effort centered around the activities of the rich Comstock Lode in Virginia City, just over the line from California in what became the State of Nevada in 1864. The Civil War years were the second time the company had a major impact on the national scene.

The Comstock Lode, which went through extreme cycles of boom and bust during its twenty years of significant production beginning in 1860, was to Nevada what the Gold Rush had been to California. It attracted large hordes of people and was chaotic. Out of chaos came statehood. That scenario, played out first in California, would be repeated elsewhere in the West. The possession of valuable minerals was the path toward statehood. In the case of Nevada, the promise of an antislavery state and three electoral votes was an added inducement.

Put simply, Nevada provided most of the gold and silver; Wells Fargo transported the valuable minerals; and the Union used the bullion to fund the Civil War. The war was financed on vast amounts of credit secured by the gold and silver. In his book on banks and politics during the Civil War, *Sovereignty and an Empty Purse*, Bray Hammond made numerous references to the "unprecedented shipments" of gold from San Francisco that sustained eastern banks and the federal government. Along with the sword, the purse, he said "is one of the two basic supports of sovereignty."

When William M. Stewart, a Lincoln Republican and one of Nevada's first two senators, went to Washington, D.C., in February of 1865 (via steamboat), he met with President Abraham Lincoln the morning after he was sworn into office. The president told the new senator: "We need as many loyal States as we can get, and, in addition to that, the gold and silver in the region you represent has made it possible for the Government to maintain sufficient credit to continue this terrible war for the Union." President Lincoln later showed his gratitude by seating Senator Stewart next to General Ulysses S. Grant on the reviewing stand during the parade of the Union Army at its Virginia headquarters shortly before the surrender at Appomattox.

The Comstock, as if conjured into existence by a Union genie, appeared on the scene just in time; and Wells Fargo arrived in Virginia City shortly after the discovery. The express company's first agent set up office in a tent in 1860. The company erected a two-story brick structure and shared it with two other firms: the Pioneer Stage Company, owned by its general manager and run by his brother, and the Overland Mail Company, which Wells Fargo controlled. The Express Bar, a popular watering hole, was located in the basement of the building.

Concord coaches and heavy-duty, canvas-topped, fast freight wagons were soon plying the one-hundred-mile road from Virginia City to Placerville, the most popular route from the busy mines and mills to San Francisco. Constantly graded and watered to keep the dust down, the road was comparable to a modern freeway.

There was no doubt which side those staunch Yankee directors from upstate New York would take during the Civil War. When questioned about their loyalty, Henry Wells, speaking for the American Express

Company, of which he was the president, said that goods shipped by the express companies would not find their way to the South. "The officers of the federal, State, and city governments," he said, "are fully aware of the course we have pursued from the beginning, and approve of the same, and are constantly employing us in transporting for them."

Wells Fargo and American Express made sizable donations to the Union cause, but they also profited greatly from the increased business. The arithmetic tells the story in terms of Wells Fargo stockholders, who were mostly the directors. During the war years, cash dividends were 12 percent annually, except for the banner year of 1863, when the directors voted themselves 22 percent in regular cash dividends and a special stock dividend of 100 percent. The Wells Fargo directors who sat on the boards of other express companies were further enriched by the excessive profits of those firms.

A national interest was served at the same time, at least from the viewpoint of the North. Taxes paid for only a small portion of the Union's Civil War expenses. The vast bulk of the expenditures—$2.3 billion in military costs alone—came from borrowed and printed money, both of which were backed by gold and silver reserves. The federal government borrowed huge amounts of money to fight the first major war of the Industrial Age. In 1859 the national debt was $58 million. By 1866 it had risen to $2,756 million. For years afterward, the government was saddled with debt retirement.

One year serves as an example of the size of the company's contribution. The yield of the Comstock Lode in 1864 was $16 million, of which Wells Fargo transported $12.4 million. The Comstock was the first big silver strike in the West, but it also yielded gold in a ratio of 60 percent silver to 40 percent gold. The value of gold was sixteen times greater than silver, but most European nations, frightened by the huge production of California gold in the 1850s, maintained a silver standard. Silver was at a premium in the 1860s.

The Union was quite fortunate on a number of levels. Beginning in 1863 and reaching panic stages in 1865, the production of the Comstock mines declined. They held up just long enough to help the war effort. During the years of the Civil War, the Comstock Lode produced more than $50 million in gold and silver.

The Comstock, however, was only part of the story. Other mines in Nevada and California were producing gold and silver. Wells Fargo's San Francisco office handled more than $50 million in bullion in 1864 alone. More than a ton was shipped downriver each day from Sacramento. The weight was so great that a stateroom on board the steamboat *Antelope* had to be specially reinforced so that the heavy bars of bullion would not crash through the deck and hole the vessel.

It was a highly organized, efficient operation that ran on a tight schedule. Wagons and trains converged on Sacramento, where a side-wheel steamboat departed every day for San Francisco at 2 P.M. The heavy bullion was trundled on board in specially designed iron carts. Armed Wells Fargo messengers guarded the treasure. Mail and newspapers were sorted as the vessels steamed through the flat Sacramento Valley so that they could be delivered on arrival. If all connections were made, it was a thirty-hour trip from Virginia City to San Francisco.

* * *

The year 1864 also marked a departure by the New York–based Wells Fargo directors from their usual modus operandi when they purchased the Pioneer Stage Company, which had a monopoly on the lucrative Virginia City–Placerville run. The decision to expand had been made in the previous year when the three Wells Fargo directors visited California and witnessed firsthand the peak of the stage traffic from Virginia City. The price for the stage line paid to their employee, Louis McLane, was $175,000 in gold, deliverable in San Francisco.

The Pioneer company was the well-run, profitable commuter airline of its era. It handled more than ten thousand passengers in the first half of 1863 at $30 a head and grossed some $4.2 million annually. Of course, there were huge operating costs.

For the first time, Wells Fargo owned outright a major stage company. It was now responsible not only for carrying the cargo but also for the means of transportation. The Pioneer name was retained because the company had an excellent reputation.

The various components of the transportation system that served the entire needs of the Comstock—meaning in and about the many mines and mills, the town, and intrastate and interstate traffic—employed some two thousand men and used from twelve to fifteen thousand mules and horses. Wells Fargo dispatched its heaviest daily shipment from Virginia City in 1864, with three tons of bullion valued at $150,000.

All of this activity did not escape the notice of Confederate sympathizers in California.

*   *   *

The bloodiest episode of Civil War–related violence in California followed the 1864 robbery of a stage carrying bullion from Virginia City. The robbery was carried out in the name of the Confederacy.

It was evident to southerners, wrote Benjamin Franklin Gilbert nearly one hundred years later in the *California Historical Society Quarterly*, that stopping the flow of bullion "would weaken the credit and purchasing power of the Union. The large annual shipments of gold and silver from San Francisco to Northern and European ports appeared as rich prizes to Confederate adventurers."

They first outfitted the ninety-ton schooner, the *J. M. Chapman*, in 1863 as a privateer, intending to intercept the bullion shipments on the high seas, but the ship never cleared San Francisco Bay. It was halted on the morning of departure by the navy and boarded by the police.

The "Secesh" men, or Copperheads, as they were called, were charged with treason. Some were jailed, a few skipped bail, and others were recruited for further exploits. They centered their attention on stagecoaches carrying treasure.

The summer of 1864 was a time of heightened tension in California. The war seemingly hung in the balance, and the presidential election was looming. There were countless rumors of plots. The ranks of the volunteer police and the state militia swelled. They drilled and practiced "street fighting."

A Confederate captain, named Rufus Henry Ingram or Ralph Henry, and nicknamed the "Red Fox," surfaced in San Jose, a hotbed of secessionist activity. He organized a guerrilla band and named it Captain Ingram's Partisan Rangers. It was modeled on the notorious Quantrill's Raiders, with whom Ingram had supposedly served.

The raiders, in classic guerrilla style, had cut a bloody swath across Kansas and Missouri early in the war. Ingram, who was educated and well mannered, chose Tom Poole as his lieutenant. Poole, a former undersheriff of Monterey County, had refused to delay the death sentence of one José Anastacio, as ordered by the governor, because the temporary reprieve was mistakenly issued in the name of Anastasio Jesús. Poole hanged the Indian. He would pay dearly for his hasty work.

The band lingered in Placerville for a few days in early May of 1864, scouting the Wells Fargo silver shipments. One of their members got drunk and tried to recruit a local man. Fearing discovery, they fled back to San Jose. Six returned in late June, and on the last day of the month rode eleven miles east of Placerville to a sharp bend in the road, hereafter known as Bullion Bend.

The six masked men, armed with fourteen six-shooters and a shotgun, hid in the brush and waited for night. John Boessenecker wrote in his study of lawlessness in early California: "The six-horse Concord coaches of the Pioneer Stage Company carried much of the silver bullion across from the Comstock, treasure which helped greatly to finance the Union's war effort. Few but the Pioneer stages traveled the road after nightfall."

Two Pioneer stages had departed from Virginia City that morning. Each carried fourteen passengers and four bags of bullion weighing a total of 250 pounds and valued at $26,000. The second coach had a green, iron-bound Wells Fargo chest containing an additional $700 in coin.

At ten o'clock that night the first stage rattled around the bend. The Confederate captain, armed with the shotgun, stepped onto the road. "Hold on, or I'll fire," he commanded. The slow-moving stage ground to a halt. Poole ran out to steady the lead horses.

Ingram ordered the driver to throw down the bullion. "Come and get it," the driver replied insolently. Two of the masked men jumped up and threw the bags to the ground.

At this moment the second coach rounded the bend. The first stage was ordered to move on. As it did so, a Virginia City policeman leaned out the window and foolishly got off one wild shot that frightened the horses. The bandits held their fire.

Ingram addressed the occupants of the second stage: "Gentlemen, I will tell you who we are. We are not robbers, but a company of Confederate soldiers. All we want is Wells, Fargo and Company's treasure to assist us to recruit for the Confederate Army."

One of the passengers later described Ingram as "a tall, rawboned and slim man, who spoke with confidence, as if he understood the business he was engaged in." The newspapers called him "the gentlemanly robber" and his gang was referred to as "Jeff Davis men."

As the guerrillas proceeded to remove the bullion, a young girl asked Ingram a number of questions: Where was their flag, how would they carry the heavy treasure, what would they do with it? When Ingram asked if any of the passengers would like to contribute to the Confederate cause, the plucky youngster said she had a five-cent stamp "but I won't give it up without a fight."

Asked later why she had been so inquisitive, the seventeen-year-old replied that she wanted to hear their voices so she could identify them when they were captured. "She was smarter than we men," a passenger commented, "and, I might add, considerably more self possessed."

Ingram gave the driver a receipt he had prepared earlier for the treasure that would be used "for the purpose of outfitting recruits in California for the Confederate States Army." In the haste of the moment, or the lack of a writing instrument, he forgot to fill in the blank where the amount was to go. The receipt may have been an attempt to qualify the robbery as an act of war, and thus enable the "soldiers" to be treated as prisoners of war if they were caught. A treasonable act could get them hung.

The robbers were pursued vigorously. The rangers were surprised while resting at a boardinghouse not far from the scene of the crime. Scores of shots were exchanged. A deputy sheriff was killed and another was wounded. Poole was wounded and captured during the melee.

The other five guerrillas escaped and were pursued by a posse led by Jim Hume, the undersheriff who worked out of Placerville. Hume gave up too soon, and the gang made its getaway.

A short time later, Hume heard that the gang was at a ranch near San Jose. Another posse was organized, and for the second time the guerrillas were surprised. The two sides exchanged a fusillade of small arms fire, accuracy not being the forte of either group. A deputy and the sheriff were wounded. One robber was wounded and two were killed. Ingram and another guerrilla escaped and fled to Missouri. They were never captured.

Trials of the captured rangers, which attracted a lot of public attention, were held in Placerville. Wells Fargo, in at least in one instance, paid for a Sacramento firm of lawyers to prosecute the case while the El Dorado County district attorney sat in the courtroom.

In the minds of the guerrillas, Grant's army and Wells Fargo were one and the same. "They were robbing our people back home," said a participant in the robbery on the witness stand, "and it was nothing but right to rob the Federal Government, or rob Wells, Fargo & Co's Express. We had a right to retaliate."

A different governor, perhaps mindful of the earlier hanging incident, refused to commute the former lawman's death sentence for his role in the shooting of the deputy sheriff. Poole was hung in Placerville five months after Appomattox. Thus ended what Boessenecker called "without question the most daring and desperate undertaking by any members of California's Secessionist movement."

Wells Fargo listed as charges against the express operation that year $12,726.46 in expenses for the robbery. Of this total, $5,470.05 in reward money was allocated, $1,500 being earmarked for the two "robbers killed at San Jose." Although the listed firms were not identified as lawyers, it seems like a fair amount was paid in attorney fees to prosecute the "Secesh" men. Wells Fargo had sent a costly message to robbers and also those lawmen who needed an extra incentive to be more active on behalf of the company's interests.

End of an Era

IRONY ABOUNDS in history. Louis McLane was responsible for Wells Fargo's greatest glory and its near demise. Wells Fargo prospered in the 1860s and then very nearly failed. That decade defined Wells Fargo in terms of the resiliency that allowed the name and the business, if not exactly the same personnel, to survive drastic changes.

Wells Fargo, as an express, banking, and post office conglomerate, had come late to the Gold Rush, the Pony Express, and overland staging. But in each era it became the dominant business entity in its field. The large amounts of capital its eastern directors could command, along with its management skills and its attractive public persona, enabled Wells Fargo to last while others failed. Wells Fargo was not an innovator; it was a consolidator and, in the long run, added value to what had preceded it.

In the late 1860s, however, Wells Fargo almost put itself out of business, with the help of a push from more robust western buccaneers. The company's leadership—in place for nearly a generation and out of touch with the West—was tired and preoccupied with other ventures. As with any enterprise that survives for a measurable length of time, fortunes rise and fall. Cycles are an historical constant. For Wells Fargo the boom nearly went bust in the following manner.

Fed by the profits made during the Civil War, new mineral discoveries in the interior West, and new staging routes to serve the newfound sources of wealth, the 1860s were a time of great expansion for Wells Fargo. It was during this decade that the wave of population that had engulfed California in the 1850s rebounded eastward and flooded, albeit in lesser numbers, such future states as Nevada, Idaho, Montana, and Colorado. And Wells Fargo followed the population, which, for the most part, was intent on mining.

Between 1860 and 1869 the number of Wells Fargo offices doubled from 147 to 293. The company expanded into Oregon, Washington, Nevada, and Idaho. Branch banks were added to express functions in Denver and Salt Lake City, and in 1866 Wells Fargo entered Montana Territory after big strikes in Alder and Last Chance gulches. When gold appeared in the hot, bare hills above La Paz on the lower Colorado River, so did Wells Fargo, establishing the first express office in the brand-new Territory of Arizona before the arrival of the U.S. Post Office.

Ben Holladay, a flamboyant New York entrepreneur, controlled the stagecoach routes east of Salt Lake to the Missouri River. That changed dramatically in late 1866. Indian troubles, high operating expenses, and the coming of the railroad were factors in Holladay's selling his interest to Wells Fargo in what became known as the Grand Consolidation. Wells Fargo obtained the monopoly in the West that it had been seeking for fourteen years. On November 1, Louis McLane was elected president of the company, which was now capitalized at $10 million. Wells Fargo incorporated in the Territory of Colorado in 1866, a move that limited the liability of the directors of the expanding business, but the company's corporate headquarters remained in New York City.

Of the company's dominant position, one historian referred to Wells Fargo after the consolidation as "the greatest staging empire in history."

Another wrote: "Taken as a whole, it was the most powerful institution of any kind in the West—looming even larger than the U.S. government, whose departments had then only tenuously penetrated the trans-Mississippi frontier." Greeley's *New York Tribune* was more guarded in its assessment:

> Whether the consolidation will work good or ill for the heavy interests of the vast territory it covers, remains to be seen. If the business be transacted as well as it has been done in California, the improvement for Utah, Montana and Colorado will be very great. But it is the tendency of all our leading express and telegraph companies to combine into vast monopolies; and the instances are very rare in which monopolies do not become oppressive. We trust this may prove one of the exceptions.

It had been a memorable year for McLane. The events he had set in motion when the three directors visited California in the summer of 1863 had come to fruition in 1866. McLane had escaped serious injury earlier in the year when a shipment of nitroglycerine had exploded and shattered part of the San Francisco office, killing nine employees and seriously injuring fourteen. The son of an illustrious father, who became president of the Baltimore & Ohio Railroad after his career in government; an early visitor to California as a naval lieutenant; and a successful San Francisco businessman and community leader, McLane had risen to the top of the company in a mere eleven years.

There was just one slight blot on McLane's record. The business of the Pioneer Stage Line, which he had sold to Wells Fargo, had proved to be "discouraging, to say the least," according to the minutes of the Wells Fargo board. Mineral production had fallen off at the Comstock Lode, depleting the stage line's profits.

★ ★ ★

Wells Fargo's brand—the stagecoach—emerged at this time. It was never in constant use over the following years, but it was the symbol that has survived to become ubiquitous today.

Standard printing cuts of a rudimentary stage with anywhere from one to three pairs of horses appeared in advertisements in smaller California and Nevada newspapers and publications. A more finely designed illustration, with four prancing horses, was used widely in advertisements by the company. An 1867 stock certificate signed by Louis McLane bore a stylish rendition of a stagecoach drawn by six horses in a spectacular mountain scene. The stage in the upper-left-hand corner was counterbalanced in the upper-right-hand corner by a steam engine with thick, dark smoke trailing from its stack.

The stock certificates illustrate the quandary McLane and the Wells Fargo directors should have faced more realistically. There was no doubt the transcontinental railroad was coming and that it would impact the express business in some drastic way. The question was when and how.

*   *   *

Why did Wells Fargo miss the significance of the railroad and almost sink itself just as it was clearing the harbor and setting off on a long journey through history? The study of one company's response, or lack of it, to the technological revolution of going from horse-drawn to steam-driven transportation is worthy of study at the MBA level today.

There are two prevailing theories: Wells Fargo was aware of what would happen but thought it had at least ten years remaining in its stagecoach monopoly before adjustments would have to be made. The second theory maintains that Wells Fargo, and Louis McLane in particular, were so blinkered by the horse and carriage that they failed to foresee its obsolescence on the transcontinental route within three years of obtaining the monopoly on stagecoach travel.

No major decision—whether of a business, political, or personal nature—is made on the basis of a single reason. Undoubtedly, elements of the two theories were operative. What has been overlooked, however, is the human equation. Wells Fargo backed the wrong railroad, and in the process antagonized the eventual winners. Personal gain, dislike, and vengeance dominated subsequent business decisions.

McLane and his associates wanted to build a railroad over the Sierra Nevada from Placerville to tap the mineral wealth and population growth envisioned in Nevada. They tried to block the Big Four of the Central Pacific Railroad (Charles Crocker, Leland Stanford, Collis P. Huntington, and Mark Hopkins), whose more ambitious plans were to build a transcontinental railroad via Donner Pass that only incidentally would serve Nevada. The Big Four won, then retaliated. McLane was at the center of the dispute.

McLane's first year as president started badly. The company had acquired the Holladay lines too late in 1866 to stock the stations with adequate feed for the horses and mules. Indians burned a large amount of company property east of Salt Lake, ran off horses, and killed three employees. Mail piled up at stations and was abandoned along the trail. Monetary losses amounted to several hundred thousand dollars. Shares in Wells Fargo fell 60 percent and no dividend was paid for the year.

The company fought back in 1867 by spending money. In April, McLane ordered ten nine-passenger stages from the Abbot-Downing concern in New Hampshire. In October, he followed up that order with a request for thirty more of the ornate coaches—the largest single order ever fulfilled by the factory. The coaches were to transport Union Pacific crews who were building the railroad westward.

The thirty gleaming stages, each with two original landscape scenes ("gems of beauty," said a New Hampshire newspaper) hand-painted on the door panels, were shipped on fifteen railroad flatcars from Concord to Omaha in April 1868. Four additional boxcars carried sixty sets of custom-made harnesses and spare parts.

It was a widely celebrated event captured on film and canvas. The

---

---

82   PHILIP L. FRADKIN

Concord Daily Monitor called it "a novel sight" and the *New Hampshire Statesman* referred to "the beautiful train." No one, however, has noted the irony of shipping horse-drawn stagecoaches via railroad to help crews build the very transportation facility that would force Wells Fargo to sell the coaches at a huge loss within one year.

One month later the carefully constructed edifice that was the solid-seeming corporate structure known as Wells Fargo throughout the West began to crumble from within. A flurry of directors' meetings were held in New York. The normally terse board minutes were more lengthy than usual and reflected the tension in the late spring and summer of 1868.

There was a lot of activity behind the scenes at the headquarters office of Wells Fargo at 84 Broadway shortly before the May 14 board of directors meeting when McLane dropped his bombshell. The president outlined the poor financial shape of the company and then said he was resigning because "his private interests in California required his personal attention." The resignation, if it was that, was immediately accepted. A committee of three was appointed to look into the finances.

To raise money quickly, the board decided to sell the headquarters building to Danford N. Barney, its former president and a director, for $130,000. It then took the most drastic step in the company's long history on May 16. Another committee was formed to negotiate "the sale of the Stage lines owned and operated by this company, reserving the Express privileges over the same for the benefit of the Company if practicable." The action was later amended to those routes that were losing money, leaving Wells Fargo open to retain certain feeder lines.

The committee went looking for buyers. The board was told that the Union Pacific Railroad, for whose crews the new stages had been purchased, was not interested. Other prospective buyers of routes, stages, equipment, and buildings were desperately sought.

While on his way to San Francisco in early August, McLane had a chance to see firsthand the forces at work that had deposed him. He wrote his wife from Salt Lake City:

We arrived here yesterday P.M. by 6—tired dirty and sore from the heat dust and jolting of the ride from "Benton" present termini of Rail Road—the Road from Benton to Green River [Wyoming] is execrable—cut up by the heavy wagons teaming supplies for the Rail Road and our wagon though built & fitted up in the best style is very rough, owing to faulty construction of the rocker.

In mid-August twenty of the new stagecoaches McLane had ordered arrived in Salt Lake, driven from the end of the railroad line. The next month Wells Fargo closed down staging operations at its hub location. Some coaches, equipment, and structures in Salt Lake were sold to A. Harras, who then resold them. The company's repair shops and offices that had originally cost $50,000 were sold to Brigham Young, the Mormon leader, for $30,000. Other stages were sold for one-third their original cost.

A Salt Lake newspaper bemoaned the departure of Wells Fargo, noting that the company had "paid over five million of dollars for grain, etc. to our citizens. During all that time and with all that business, we never heard of but one man who ever complained of them. . . . We will miss the stage company."

Meanwhile, the sharks had begun circling the wounded leviathan. In his history of American Express, Peter Z. Grossman noted: "While no competitors disrupted the smooth flow of profits in the 1850s, one other group could and did pose problems for the expresses—the railroads. When railroad men finally realized just how much money the express business produced, they began to regret that they had not absorbed the express for themselves." One railroad set out to do just that.

Dating back to 1855, Louis McLane and his associates had been backers of the Sacramento Valley Railroad, California's first line that ran from Sacramento to Folsom. Later the same group financed the Placerville & Sacramento Valley Railroad that ran from Sacramento to Shingle Springs, near Placerville. They were also behind the proposed extension of that line over the mountains to Nevada.

When the Big Four went looking for financial backing in San Francisco for the Central Pacific Railroad, the Sacramento merchants were rebuffed. Crocker later recalled: "We came to San Francisco and tried our very best to get the capitalists to come in with us, but they laughed at the idea and would not touch it." McLane was one of the businessmen who ridiculed the Sacramentans. That rankled.

The San Franciscans opposed the Big Four at the local, state, and national levels. There was "outright hostility," according to John Hoyt Williams, author of a book on the transcontinental railroad. He wrote, "Shipping companies—Wells, Fargo and other stage and freight companies, and rival railroaders—all fought the Central Pacific from its inception." Angus D. McDonald, president of the Southern Pacific Railroad, wrote in the *Wells Fargo Messenger*, the company's internal publication, some seventy years later:

> The Central Pacific was the first unit of what is now Southern Pacific Company.
>
> As long as the transcontinental railroad was in the Congressional debate stage, everybody in the West was for it. When it became evident that the men who started the Central Pacific really intended to build a railroad, the transportation interests already in the field organized to throw obstacles in the way of the intruder. Wells Fargo & Co., I am compelled as a good historian to relate, was one of the railroad's opponents.

The fight got nasty when both sides sought a subsidy from the newly formed Nevada Legislature in 1865. There were charges and countercharges.

Charles McLane, brother of Louis and president of the Placerville railroad, and Lester L. Robinson, a civil engineer and stockholder in the Sacramento Valley company, "began a slander campaign . . . which soon degenerated into accusations of personal corruption" aimed at the Big Four, according to Williams. He was referring to an anonymous pamphlet published in San Francisco, titled "The Great Dutch Flat Swindle," which maintained that the Big Four were not interested in building a railroad over Donner Summit but rather just wanted to maintain control of the existing wagon road. Robinson, who was closely associated with the interests of the McLane brothers, repeated those same charges in a letter to the Nevada Legislature.

Stanford replied in a blistering attack. Robinson, he said, represented "the bitter and vindictive opposition" of other railroads and stagecoach lines that would be harmed by the new railroad. Stanford accused Robinson of "falsifying the facts," "vilifying the dead as well as the living," and distributing "the most slanderous articles."

As a result of the contentious debate, neither side received a subsidy from Nevada.

A quarter century later Charles Crocker, a self-described "mad bull," dictated his memoir. He vehemently and repeatedly recalled the opposition the Central Pacific faced, singling out San Francisco capitalists, owners of the Sacramento railroads, and Robinson for special mention. The McLane brothers, Wells Fargo director Barney, and at least one other high-ranking Wells Fargo employee, Theodore F. Tracy, were a visible part of that opposition.

Payback time came with a vengeance two months after completion of the transcontinental railroad. The Big Four, with the help of their front man, Lloyd Tevis, created a dummy company in July 1869. It was not an unknown tactic. Barney and Fargo had invented straw companies at least twice at American Express in order to fool the public into thinking there was competition.

The name Pacific Express Company bore a very close resemblance to Pacific Union Express Company. The names were so similar that journalists, the public, and many historians—including Edward Hungerford, a former advertising manager for Wells Fargo—have confused the two entities by using the names interchangeably or thinking they were one and the same company. Most probably that was the intent of the Big Four.

There was a vast difference, however. The Pacific Express Company was the creation of the Big Four. Although announcing it was ready to do business on a large scale, Pacific Express possessed only stationery and a bare office. The Pacific Union Express Company was an ambitious and energetic rival of Wells Fargo. It had participated in a number of highly publicized pony express, buggy, and stagecoach races with Wells Fargo in California and Nevada from the summer of 1868 to the early fall of 1869. The competition had forced Wells Fargo to lower its rates.

Most important, the dummy company held an exclusive contract with its sibling, the Central Pacific, for express privileges on the transcontinental railroad. The Central Pacific notified Wells Fargo that it would no longer carry its mail and express matter. Crocker and Tevis had also been quietly buying depressed Wells Fargo stock, which had fallen from $100 to $13.

The squeeze was on; the revenge was complete. "What happened next has to rank as one of the all-time corporate raids," wrote Robert D. Livingston, an historian of the express business, in the journal of early western mails *Western Express.*

Wells Fargo was brought to its knees and assumed the position of a supplicant. The company needed that contract in order to survive—the monopoly provision being "the great consideration," according to later testimony by Tevis. The contract cost Wells Fargo one-third of its stock, a minimum of three new directors from the West, and a headquarters in San Francisco that would make it difficult for eastern directors to attend board meetings. The only money Pacific Express had to put up was an infusion of $166,000 in cash into the lagging bank business.

The agreement, termed the Treaty of Omaha, was signed on October 4, 1869. William Fargo and President Barney told stockholders shortly afterward that there was no choice. "The terms were severe," wrote Livingston, "but the alternative for Wells Fargo, without access to the transcontinental railroad, was oblivion." The stockholders ratified the agreement.

At a hearing of the United States Pacific Railway Commission some years later, Tevis was asked if Wells Fargo was in a "dilapidated" condition in 1869. Tevis, who by then had been president of Wells Fargo for fifteen years, replied:

"Well, hardly dilapidated. That is too strong a word."

"It was not a prosperous concern?"

"It was not a prosperous concern before we went into it," Tevis replied.

THE IRON HORSE overtakes the stagecoach on this wagon banner advertisement.

II

———

1 8 7 0 – 1 9 0 6

THE NEW REGIME

UNDER LLOYD TEVIS and the westerners, Wells Fargo prospered once again. Kentuckians, who had come west at an early date, replaced upstate New Yorkers in the Wells Fargo hierarchy.

After graduating from college in Kentucky, Tevis read law with his father and then helped a relative run a dry goods store in Louisville. In May 1849, he moved westward to St. Louis and then paid $200 to join a wagon train that was headed for California in that Gold Rush year.

It was an arduous journey, and there were no riches for young Tevis in the El Dorado County diggings. He did not linger long in pursuit of the financial chimera that disappointed so many. Aided by his legal background, Tevis obtained a job in the Sacramento recorder's office. There he discovered a surer source of riches in California—the acquisition of real estate. Ten years later he was able to build a mansion in San Francisco.

"When I came to California young, poor, ambitious," Tevis later told some friends, "I had to decide whether I would strike for political fame or for money. I concluded to go for money."

Tevis formed a lasting friendship and partnership with another Kentuckian, James Ben Ali Haggin, who would join him on the Wells Fargo board. They married sisters from Kentucky. Their real estate and mining holdings were vast. Haggin and Tevis added existing San Francisco companies that dealt in steamships, dry docks, the telegraph, gaslights, water, food, and ice to their holdings. The firm of Haggin & Tevis became "the foremost private business association of the Pacific coast," according to the *Contemporary Biography of California's Representative Men*, a laudatory work published in 1881. The biography of Tevis was the opening sketch.

Tevis was the first president of the Southern Pacific Railroad, a small line attempting to make its way south from San Francisco to San Jose and thence on to Los Angeles. He was rich, a potential source of funds, and the Big Four repeatedly tried to interest Tevis in purchasing Central Pacific stock.

He declined, thinking the venture too speculative and knowing the stockholders would be held liable for debts. "They applied to me, I might say hundreds of times," Tevis recalled years later. "I occasionally loaned them money, and assisted them in procuring money from others."

A bond was formed. Tevis acted for the Big Four in their takeover of Wells Fargo. The 1881 biographical sketch stated: "He was foremost in starting the Pacific Express Company on this coast, which finally caused Wells, Fargo & Company to absorb it, on conditions which gave to himself and his associates the control of the latter, of which he is now president."

A cautious investor who foresaw the failures of the Bank of California and the Pacific Insurance Company, Tevis's forte was conducting large-scale negotiations, such as the Treaty of Omaha. Of his tenure, Robert Livingston wrote: "The takeover was a shock to the expressmen founders of Wells, Fargo & Co. but the company benefited from Tevis. His presidency from 1872 to 1892, still the longest in company history, brought stability. Furthermore, as a financier, Tevis took a special interest in the banking aspects of the business."

Tevis was a neatly bearded man with piercing eyes. A young Wells

Fargo employee took him some papers to sign. "He had a great way of barking at people," this employee recalled years later. " 'Talk quickly and to the point. I can think five times as fast as any man in San Francisco.' And so he could. He was a mental wonder and one of the smartest men in this town at the time."

In 1872 he succeeded Fargo, who had served two years as president. Ten years into his long reign, Tevis traced the origins and development of Wells Fargo, which by then had more than seven hundred agencies stretching from the Mexican border into Canada and from the Pacific Coast to the Mississippi River. In a major address to the American Banker's Association, Tevis portrayed Wells Fargo as being synonymous with San Francisco, California, and the West.

"San Francisco is not merely the metropolis of the State of California," he told the bankers assembled in Niagara Falls, New York, "it is also the metropolis of the greater part of this vast region. How far extends the commercial and financial system which centers in San Francisco, the operations of the express and banking company with which I am connected give an idea. Wells, Fargo & Company is peculiarly a California institution."

To a great extent it was Tevis who transformed Wells Fargo from a New York adjunct of American Express into a sovereign California entity. The torch, or in this case the symbolic stagecoach, had been passed from pioneer expressmen to a new generation of railroad-centered venture capitalists.

During Tevis's twenty-year reign as president the number of offices expanded from 396 to 2,829, stockholders received a steady 8 percent dividend, and the express service was greatly expanded. The predominant brand, used in advertisements and on stationery, changed from a rectangular representation of a steam engine hauling express and passenger cars in the 1870s and early 1880s to a circle enclosing a map of North America crisscrossed by a cobweb of railroad tracks representing "Ocean To Ocean" service in the late 1880s and 1890s.

By 1872 the corporate and operational headquarters had been combined in San Francisco, and five of the nine directors were residents of that city. They were: Collis Huntington (replaced that year by Mark Hopkins); D. O. Mills, a director of the Bank of California who had served on the fleeting Pacific Express board (as had Tevis and Leland Stanford's brother, Josiah); Leland Stanford; Tevis, the newly elected president; and his friend and partner, Haggin, who would soon become vice president. Charles Crocker would join the board in five years. Thus, at one time or another, all of the Big Four served as directors of Wells Fargo. A sick Henry Wells had resigned before the coup d'état. William Fargo remained on the Wells Fargo board while simultaneously serving as president of American Express up until his death in 1881.

California and the West were flourishing, fed by a flood of immigrants transported by the new railroad and a temporarily rejuvenated Comstock Lode. Wells Fargo shared in that prosperity. Shareholders, who had not seen a dividend since 1866, received a total of 6.5 percent in dividends in 1872.

How did Wells Fargo depict itself in terms of a brand at this time? A funnel-shaped stack belching smoke from a steam engine, followed by a coal car, then an express car, and finally passenger cars passing through a bucolic landscape were the predominant Industrial Age symbol.

Crime and Punishment

PROSPERITY, HOWEVER, had its downside; it attracted the criminal element, much as ants swarm to spilled honey. There were trains to rob on the principal routes, and stagecoaches still plied the lesser byways. The latter carried Wells Fargo express shipments and guards but were no longer owned by the company. Both modes of transportation were fair game, as were the tills inside company offices.

Along with Tevis, another man rose to prominence within Wells Fargo at this time and cast his long shadow over the era. While Tevis was concerned with advancing the company's banking and express business within the rarefied confines of boardrooms and private clubs, James B. Hume was mostly outside dealing with the criminal elements who wanted to relieve the company of its assets.

Hume came to the attention of Wells Fargo in 1864 as the under-sheriff of El Dorado County who gave chase to the Confederate stage robbers. Born in upstate New York and raised on an Indiana farm by strict Scotch Presbyterians, young Hume arrived in California in 1850 and settled in the Placerville area.

He prospected and mined without much success for ten years and then took a number of lowly city and county jobs: tax collector, dog catcher, and street sweeper among them. Hume moved up to undersheriff and then sheriff, losing reelection as sheriff after one term. Just before leaving office, he apprehended the robbers who had stolen $1,000 in cash from a Wells Fargo shipment. The company hired him as its first chief special officer; but Hume asked for a one-year leave of absence so that he could attempt to reform the Nevada State Prison—an impossible task, as it turned out.

Hume went to work for Wells Fargo in the spring of 1873 at the age of forty-six, and he would serve as the firm's chief detective for thirty years. Given his duties, abilities, and the wide range of Wells Fargo's interests, along with the notoriety of the criminals he dealt with, Hume became one of the West's most knowledgeable lawmen.

His chief assets were a keen, analytical mind and great persistence. Hume's thin body was topped by a chiseled face with a drooping mustache. He had a piercing stare, somewhat softened by crinkles at the corners of his eyes. "Father was a realist," wrote Hume's son, Sam. "He never read a detective story in his life."

Hume was also what was once known as a company man. Leaving his comfortable office, Hume once spent fifteen hours riding the Sonora stage as messenger with a shotgun and two pistols because of the value of the shipment and the frequency of robberies. He refused an invitation to Thanksgiving dinner in 1878 from his then girlfriend and later wife, Lida Munson. "My time, you know is not my own," he wrote. "I sold it out to Wells Fargo & Co." Sure enough, two weeks later on Thanksgiving day he was thirty miles from Prescott, Arizona, chasing stage robbers with special agent Bob Paul. At a lonely camp in the mountains he ate pork and beans for Thanksgiving dinner while anxiously waiting for Paul to bring in one of the robbers. "Our success before leaving would be very gratifying to me and would be fully appreciated by the Company," Hume wrote to Lida.

Given the times, Hume operated fairly judiciously. There was no American Civil Liberties Union, or its equivalent, in the West; and, in fact, there were very few civil liberties at all for suspected criminals. For instance, most minorities could not testify in court and a suspect was considered guilty until proven innocent. Some suspects never received that chance, for lynching and shooting were not uncommon.

Although only a private detective working for a commercial enterprise, Hume could perform all the duties of a county sheriff except booking a prisoner into jail. Additionally, he could be deputized, perform a citizen's arrest, or dangle substantial amounts of reward money in front of lawmen and citizens, who then became very anxious to do the company's bidding.

Hume could then, as he sometimes did, engage the lawyer who might have effectively defended the prisoner. Wells Fargo paid lawyers to prosecute defendants. The reverse, however, could sometimes be true. Hume had a strict sense of justice and would fight for acquittal, even to the point of engaging a lawyer, if he was convinced a defendant was innocent and being railroaded by local authorities.

The statistics on crime compiled by Wells Fargo and the impressions of its chief enforcement officer are one of the best, if not *the* best, indication of the nature of money-driven illegal activities in the West at the time. Wells Fargo's interests ranged everywhere and crossed the lines of all governmental jurisdictions: whether federal, state, county, city, or remote mining camp. There was no other coordinated assessment of crime—such as FBI statistics—at the time.

Crime cost Wells Fargo a lot of money, but apparently there was an executive decision at Tevis's level that the benefits of attempting to dissuade future robbers outweighed the immediate costs of timely and well-publicized pursuits. From this era, and Hume's activities, the company's slogan, "Wells Fargo never forgets," emerged.

There are two sets of figures that indicate the extent of crime practiced against the private company doing the most business spread over the vastest amount of territory in the trans-Mississippi West.

Hume compiled figures and the company published them in 1885. In the fourteen years between November 1870 and November 1884, there were 378 robberies and burglaries, or attempts at such, and 240 convictions, for a conviction to crime ratio of 63 percent. Interestingly enough, most crime was still being directed at stagecoaches, there being 313 robberies of stages and 4 of trains during this period. Either the stages were easier pickings or robbers also had not adjusted to the new technology.

There was a total of thirty-three killings: four stage drivers were killed, four were seriously wounded; two Wells Fargo guards were killed, six seriously wounded; four passengers were killed, two seriously wounded; and five robbers were killed at the scene, eleven were killed while later resisting arrest, and seven were hanged "by citizens." (The report's terminology has been used.) Additionally, seven horses were killed and thirteen were stolen.

The cost to Wells Fargo for these activities over fourteen years can be broken down into two categories: the amount stolen, $415,000; and the rewards, attorney fees, incidental expenses, and salaries for guards and special officers paid to recover it, which was $513,000. The gross cost was $928,000, or $16 million in current dollars.

There was a second set of figures that takes in a wider span of time. They were not published and can be found amongst Hume's papers in the Bancroft Library at the University of California at Berkeley. A handwritten report titled: "A memorandum of Casualties resulting from attacks upon stages and Railroad Trains carrying Wells Fargo Co's Express from which it will be noted the number of lives lost as a result of robberies and attempted robberies amounts to 147." The report was compiled by "Capt. James B. Hume, Chief special officer, Wells Fargo."

From other papers detailing the crimes that seem to be related to the summary document, it appears that the figures spanned the years from the first robbery of a stagecoach involving Wells Fargo in 1855 to shortly before Hume's death in 1904. This single best snapshot of crime in the nineteenth-century American West indicates that Wells Fargo, and Hume, dealt with more violent crimes than any other single institution, or person. Assisting Hume were three special officers.

Over this wider time span and taking into account the railroad era and the fact that Wells Fargo became a truly national enterprise near the end of the century, there were 482 robberies of stagecoaches and 59 unsuccessful attempts. Beginning with the first robbery of a train in 1870, there were 65 robberies of trains and 25 unsuccessful attempts.

In terms of categories of people killed (the total of which falls seven short of the number on the previous page) and wounded, there were: sixty-five robbers killed outright, twenty-one wounded; sixteen robbers hanged; eighteen officers killed, seventeen wounded; fourteen citizens assisting officers killed, three wounded; six messengers killed, fifteen wounded; six stage drivers killed, seven wounded; six passengers killed, thirteen wounded; seven trainmen (engineers, conductors, brakemen) killed, three wounded; two Wells Fargo agents killed; twelve stage horses killed and fifteen stolen by robbers.

Over the years certain patterns developed. There were few stage robberies in the 1850s; they increased in the 1860s; the climax was in the 1870s and 1880s; they declined in the 1890s. In 1887 Hume said, "Stage robbing is, comparatively speaking, a thing of the past." He attributed the decline to less mining and the new money-order system. Train robberies peaked in the decade of the 1890s, when there were 290 nationally.

Law enforcement officers frequently had to be induced to chase robbers. In the 1870s Wells Fargo rewards varied from $200 to $750, often with an additional one-fourth of the recovered loot going to the lawman who caught the robber. A state or other entity who felt wronged might contribute to the Wells Fargo reward. Expenses, which could be inflated, were paid to salaried officers from public agencies. What went under the table is not known.

Hume was held in great esteem by the press and his employers and was well known to robbers. In a front-page article on the 1885 report in the *San Francisco Call*, the chief special officer was said to be known by "almost everyone on the West Coast" for his detective work. Upon his peaceful death in 1904 at the age of seventy-seven, Hume was lionized by the San Francisco papers, the *Chronicle* calling him in a news story "one of the best and most favorably known figures in Pacific Coast criminal work, if not in the whole police world of the country." An editorial stated: "For more than a generation his name has been a terror to stage and train robbers."

In a letter of introduction to express agents and police chiefs, John J. Valentine, the general superintendent of Wells Fargo, said Hume was "a gentleman worthy of esteem and confidence, both personally and officially." Hume once remarked: "I have reason to believe that I enjoy the entire confidence of the Company, for they require no bonds, and I am yearly entrusted with hundreds of thousands of dollars of their money."

Hume was also known and watched closely, via the newspapers, by those who he pursued. Six weeks and no arrest after a train was robbed near Davis, California, then known as Davisville, Hume received a taunting one-cent postcard from Portland, Oregon. It read:

> Dear Billy. it's awful the way Youse fellows don't KAtch those Awful "Davisville" train robbers. Whatever are you fellows a doin' anyway? I'm tempted 2 think youse Aint doin' ANYthing. What gross dereliction of duty you Are guilty of. You should be bounced. Is it true, As the *Argus* says, that you never catch a train robber? Yea, it would seem so. Why don't you rake the tule Lands? Bestir yourselves. Yours truly, Fly by night.

What remained of the loot was found in the tules near the Sacramento River. The two train robbers who buried the money and the tramp who subsequently discovered it were eventually apprehended.

*   *   *

Wells Fargo had experienced crime before, but not on the scale that it was practiced in the 1870s and early 1880s.

The first teller to commit defalcation, a banking term for embezzlement, stuck his hand in the till in Sacramento in 1855. Others followed in San Francisco, Stockton, Carson City, Virginia City, Gold Hill, and Salt Lake City, where the phrase "Salt-Laking the books" originated and was used by Wells Fargo auditors for years.

Wells Fargo suffered its first robbery in 1855. Rattlesnake Dick robbed a mule train of $80,000 near Mount Shasta. The first attempted stage robbery occurred in 1856, when a fusillade of forty shots was exchanged between the Wells Fargo guard on the Camptonville stage and six bandits from the Tom Bell gang. The gang was driven off. One passenger was killed, two were wounded, and the wounded driver managed to drive the stage to Marysville.

When eventually caught by the law, Dick was shot and Bell was hanged from a tree. Two years later Wells Fargo messengers were armed with heavy-gauge shotguns, whose multiple pellets were more effective than single bullets.

There was a Robin Hood mystique to robbing monopolistic Wells Fargo, although there is no indication that the bandits ever shared the loot with the poor. Hume and the company regarded the crimes with deadly seriousness. Popular accounts that came later tended to treat the criminals rather casually, although deadly bullets had been sprayed over the landscape at the time and innocent people were killed or maimed.

Hume and his special officers sent two unusual robbers, who were both addicted to their craft, to prison. The lives of Black Bart and Bill Miner were later romanticized.

Black Bart's career, punctuated by poetic ditties left at the scene of holdups and signed "Black Bart, the Po8," was spread over eight years. During that time he became Hume's most celebrated case.

Bart's total haul from twenty-eight stages that he robbed with an unloaded, double-barreled shotgun was $18,000. Another oddity was that he did not ride a horse, preferring to walk. A fastidious dresser in San Francisco when not at work in the boondocks of Northern California, the gentleman robber was traced to his apartment by a laundry mark on his handkerchief dropped at the scene of his last robbery.

Bart, whose real name was either Charles E. Bolton or C. E. Boles, was fifty-five when finally arrested in 1883. He was older than most bandits and more mature, which impressed Hume. The gentleman bandit got a special mention—a cross between a description of a suspect and an admiring biography—in Hume's 1885 report and in a wanted poster. The latter read:

> He is a person of great endurance, a thorough mountaineer, and a remarkable walker, and claims that he cannot be excelled in making quick transits over mountains and grades; when reading without glasses, holds paper off at arms length; is comparatively well educated, a general reader, and is well informed on current topics; cool, self-contained, a sententious talker, with waggish tendencies; and since his arrest has, upon several occasions, exhibited genuine wit under most trying circumstances. Has made his head-quarters in San Francisco for past eight years; has made but a few close friends, and those of first-class respectability; is neat and tidy in dress, highly respectable in appearance, and extremely proper and polite in behavior, chaste in language, eschews profanity, and has never been known to gamble, other than buying pools on horse races and speculating in mining stocks.

Hume bridled at the popular concept of Black Bart. This image he described as "a sort of modern 'Robin Hood,' a stage robber of 'heroic mold,' a gallant free lance, who never robbed the passengers or the poor, but confined his attentions entirely to wealthy corporations such as W. F. & Co." The detective said Bart had told him that over the years he had stolen far more from the regular mail carried on the stages than from the express mail.

While Wells Fargo had a policy of reimbursing losses, the U.S. Post Office had no such procedure. Of some two hundred robberies of the regular mail used by less affluent citizens, perhaps one or two had been in-vestigated by federal officers, according to Hume.

Bill Miner, the well-dressed ladies' man portrayed by Richard Farnsworth in the film *The Grey Fox*, began practicing his chosen craft in 1865. Much of the remainder of his life was spent in different jails, from which Miner frequently attempted escape or successfully managed to flee confinement.

In 1880, while the Wells Fargo express shipment on board a stage near Auburn was being robbed, the local congressman just happened to come along in a buggy; and the robber, believed to be Miner by Hume, re-lieved the legislator of his valuable gold watch and $280 in cash. Miner paid a brakeman $5 to stow on board a boxcar at Colfax. He got off in Reno, where he purchased a ticket to Denver, where he pawned the watch for $65.

Miner returned to California the next year and, along with three co-horts, robbed another stage with a Wells Fargo shipment near Angel's Camp in the Mother Lode country. He was caught by a Wells Fargo de-tective near Woodland in the Central Valley and sent to San Quentin Prison. The freedom-loving Miner attempted to escape by placing a dummy in his bed and hiding in the door factory. He was wounded by a guard in a second attempt.

The elderly bandit was released from San Quentin Prison in 1901 and left the state. Near the end of his life Miner specialized in robbing trains in the Northwest rather than stagecoaches in California. His last robbery of a train in 1911 may have been the end of that particular era in the West.

*   *   *

A great deal of blood was spilled over money in the West. Wells Fargo was at the center of the most controversial and notorious shoot-out and the bloodbath that followed.

Two murders and the attempted robbery of a stage carrying a large shipment of currency guarded by a Wells Fargo shotgun messenger set in motion the gunfight at O.K. Corral. (Actually, the gunfight was not in the corral but ninety feet distant in a vacant lot.) Wyatt Earp, who assumed the starring role in the brief battle, was by far the most famous of all Wells Fargo employees.

Many legend-enhancing books, movies, and television shows have celebrated Earp's questionable exploits in Tombstone, Arizona. Tracing the origins of a national gun culture from the country's European heritage to Tombstone in his book *Arming America*, Michael Bellesiles wrote: "Much western violence is mythology." Later in the same paragraph, he added: "Individuals could be just as disappointing."

The history of violent crime in the West and Wells Fargo in particular were intertwined. The possession of money, or valuable minerals that could easily be exchanged for coin, was the common denominator. Wells Fargo guarded it. Others sought it. Wells Fargo then gave chase. Swift retribution or capture and a trial were the usual results.

Wyatt Earp, an opportunist; Wells Fargo, a commercial venture; and Tombstone, a silver mining boomtown had the pursuit of money in common. They were briefly joined. Each became legend. Each benefited from the publicity. Richard Slotkin wrote of the gunfight in *Gunfighter Nation*, a book that documents the creation of frontier myths in the last century: "The national fame of that incident was itself an artifact of Hollywood culture. Neither Earp nor the gunfight had enjoyed any great notoriety outside Arizona until 1920, when the aged Wyatt appeared on a movie lot in Pasadena hoping to cash in on the enthusiasm for 'authentic' western figures."

The life of Earp has been greatly romanticized. To a much lesser extent, it has also been portrayed in a realistic manner or debunked. Like Hamlet, Earp was a complex character who attracted death—a type of person who does not lend himself to easy portrayal. He did not lack for courage; nor did he lack for just plain luck, considering all the bullets aimed his way that never struck their intended target. After the violence had died down in 1888, H. H. Bancroft's San Francisco–based History

Company sent a researcher to interview Earp in Tucson. The admiring scribe wrote: "He is tall, slim, florid complexion, blue eyes, large nose, and quick as a cat. Socially, he could be taken for a minister. He has a heart as big as an ox and feelings as tender as a child."

There are four truths surrounding the events in Tombstone. First, Earp worked for Wells Fargo, a role the company celebrated in 1970 with an ad that promoted Earp, and by extension the bank's customers, as rugged individualists. Second, the attempted robbery of the stage and the murder of the driver and a passenger led to the most celebrated exchange of some thirty shots fired by seven men during a time span of thirty seconds in this country's history. Third, the real Wyatt Earp was not Burt Lancaster, Henry Fonda, Ronald Reagan, James Garner, Joel McCrea, Hugh O'Brian, Walter Huston, Kurt Russell, or Kevin Costner—all of whom, and more, have played the role. And lastly, no single, unequivocal account has emerged to explain these violent events. The truth, if there is a truth, has been lost to time.

*   *   *

If there was a role model to emerge from the cyclonic swirl of history that consumed Tombstone, it was Robert H. Paul. If there was any Wells Fargo employee who distinguished himself it was not Wyatt Earp, the self-proclaimed vigilante who may, or may not, have collaborated with the stage robbers; it was not Jim Hume, who was robbed on a stage near Tombstone while napping; and it was certainly not the local Wells Fargo agent, Marshall Williams, a gambler and drunkard who probably tipped off robbers to the value of shipments and later absconded with company funds.

Paul went from Wells Fargo employment to winning election as sheriff, a position Earp desired but never attained. (In fact, no Earp was ever elected to public office in Arizona. All were appointed by their brothers and others to the various law enforcement positions they held.) Paul outshone the Earp brothers and the local sheriff, who was their nemesis, as a true *peace* officer. The others were prone to violence. After serving as sheriff of Pima County, Paul became a special officer for the Southern Pacific Railroad and then U.S. marshal for the entire territory.

As an honest sheriff, railroad detective, and U.S. marshal Paul pursued his share of criminals, faced them down with a sawed-off shotgun, and brought them back for trial. He didn't go to Hollywood to promote his past, no biographer has sought him out, and he died in 1901 in relative obscurity. Paul was mild mannered, kind, generous, and abhorred killing. He had the wrong stuff to qualify as a western myth.

The fate of big Bob Paul proves how accidental the mantle of hero can be. Even Fred Dodge, like Wyatt Earp a professional gambler, gets far more attention than Paul. Dodge later became a Wells Fargo special officer but claimed at the time of the robberies and killings that he was working undercover in Tombstone for Wells Fargo. That was not the case; and even if it was, Paul was a target for outlaws because he was the company's most visible enforcement presence.

The stage these various characters stepped onto in late 1879 was a dusty mesa elevated slightly above the forlorn landscape of the hot Sonoran Desert. The set was a collection of motley one- and a few two-story structures hastily raised to catch the attention of the newly arrived miners. To Jim Hume, Tombstone was: "Six thousand population. Five thousand are bad—one thousand of them known outlaws." Hume equated the heat of southern Arizona with hell.

A Wells Fargo presence was established in Tombstone in late 1879 or early 1880 by Williams, the agent who worked on a commission basis. Besides conducting Wells Fargo business, Williams sold cigars, stationery, notions, and mining claim and other legal documents in his store.

The deadly robbery, the gunfight, and the resulting vengeance killings were symptoms of a madness that enveloped Tombstone. A satellite mining community was aptly named Contention City. Disharmony was rife. Conflict was bred by a mix of opposites: Republicans and

Democrats, southerners and northerners, townspeople and cowboys (read agricultural settlers versus nomadic herders for an historical equivalent), the Earps and the Clantons, and two badly polarized newspapers that only split the community further with their vitriolic prose. Wells Fargo, being a business, sided with the interests of its customers, whom the Earps—also entrepreneurs—were hired to protect.

Of Bob Paul, Earp later recalled in a backhanded manner: "But of the many daring spirits I have known to imperil their lives in the Wells-Fargo messenger service, I can recall only one who clambered to any eminence out of the hurly-burly of frontier life. And even then it was no very dizzy height that he reached. Bob Paul, as fearless a man and as fast a friend as I ever knew, graduated from a messengership to the Shrievalty [sheriff] of Pima county, Arizona, and from that to the United States Marshalship of the Territory."

Paul and Jim Hume were close. Hume addressed his former employee after he became sheriff as "Dear Friend" in letters seeking and imparting information.

George Parsons, an educated miner regarded as a reliable diarist, wrote of the time of extensive killings: "Paul is here, but will not take a hand. He is a true, brave man himself and will not join the murderous posse here."

Paul had a realistic view of what was happening in Tombstone. Paula Mitchell Marks, an academic, wrote in her book, *And Die in the West: The Story of the O.K. Corral Gunfight:*

> Paul understood the complexities of the situation and held—or had come to—a decidedly dark view of the Earps' activities, classing them with those of the cowboys. He would be asked [in an 1882 newspaper interview] if Doc Holliday was a member of the Earp "gang." He answered: "He was, and in fact was one of the leaders. The so-called Earp gang, or faction if you please, was composed entirely of gamblers who preyed upon the cowboys, and at the same time in order to keep up a show of having a le-

gitimate calling, was organized into a sort of vigilance committee, and some of them, including Holliday, had United States
Marshal's commissions.

The lawman was praised by two Arizona historians. Dan L. Thrapp
described Paul in his *Encyclopedia of Frontier Biography* as "a fearless,
persistent and able detective and lawman of integrity; his adventures
were many." John D. Gilchriese wrote: "Never one to strut in a satin
vest, fancy boots, a sixgun on each hip, Bob Paul perhaps more than any
other single man helped to establish law and order in the two most law-
less frontier regions of the American West—the Mother Lode country of
California and the desert wilderness of Arizona."

A native of Massachusetts, Paul went to sea on a whaler at the age
of twelve. Seven years later he disembarked in San Francisco in the
Gold Rush year of 1849. When problems arose in Arizona, Wells Fargo Superintendent John J. Valentine asked Paul, a former Calaveras County sheriff in California, to visit the territory and look over the situation in 1878.
Valentine suggested that he go in "any guise you may deem necessary."

The six-foot, four-inch Paul, who weighed 240 pounds, went openly
as a Wells Fargo employee whose job descriptions varied as the needs
arose. He was carried on the books as detective, special officer, and messenger over the next three years.

*   *   *

The Earps came to town in December of 1879. Wyatt thought that he
might want to go into the staging business. But that function had already
been preempted by two stage lines. Wells Fargo had a contract with J. D.
Kinnear & Co. to carry their shotgun messenger and the dark green pine
and iron-bound strongboxes. Agent Williams hired Earp, who worked as
a messenger for Wells Fargo for the next eight months at a monthly
salary of $125.

The job of the messenger was to fight, and the job of the driver was to drive, said Earp. He particularly admired the driving abilities of twenty-two-year-old Eli (Bud) Philpot, citing "the accuracy with which he would flick a sandfly off the near leader's flank or plant a mouthful of tobacco juice in the heart of a cactus as we jolted past it."

As the messenger who guarded the box, Earp knew he would draw the gunfire. Not to fear. He and other messengers were armed with a trusty Wells Fargo shotgun, which Earp described as "the homely weapon that makes [the messenger] the peer of many armed men in a quick turmoil of powder and lead." Each barrel was loaded with twenty-one pellets. "That means a shower of forty-two leaden messengers," Earp said, "each fit to take a man's life or break a bone if it should reach the right spot."

Earp explained the advantage of a shortened barrel: "The barrels of the important civilizing agent under consideration are not more than two-thirds the length of an ordinary gun barrel. That makes it easy to carry and easy to throw upon an enemy, with less danger of wasting good lead by reason of the muzzle catching in some vexatious obstruction. As the gun has to be used quickly or not at all, this shortness of barrel is no mean advantage."

The double-barreled, hammer-fired, "cut-off" shotguns, as Wells Fargo called them, were marked with "W. F. & CO. EX." They were, and are, greatly sought after by Earp's contemporaries and modern gun collectors. Up to the mid-1880s, when the company's gun purchases greatly increased, Wells Fargo weapons were obtained from A. J. Plate & Co., Liddle & Kaeding, and Shreve & Wolf of San Francisco.

Earp, in prose crafted by a *San Francisco Examiner* rewrite man, remained absolutely ecstatic about the weapon fifteen years after the gunfight:

The Wells-Fargo shot gun is not a scientific weapon. It is not a sportsmanlike weapon. It is not a weapon wherewith to settle an affair of honor between gentlemen. But, oh! in the hands of a honest man hemmed in by skulking outlaws it is a sweet and a

thrice-blessed thing. The express company made me a present of
the gun with which they armed me when I entered their service,
and I have it still.

When Wyatt was appointed deputy sheriff in the summer of 1880, his
brother Morgan took over as a Wells Fargo shotgun messenger. (All three
brothers were associated with Wells Fargo. Virgil, while never a messenger, was proud of the following inscription on the back of his Tombstone
city marshal badge: "V. W. Earp, with Compliments of Wells, Fargo &
Co." When Virgil showed the five-point star to a reporter in San Francisco, he said he "represented" Wells Fargo.)

Bob Paul ran for sheriff of Pima County in the fall of 1880, but the
election was contested. Paul did not assume office until the Territorial
Supreme Court ruled in his favor on April 12, 1881. Meanwhile, he continued to work for Wells Fargo as a special officer and a messenger.

*   *   *

With Paul the guard and Philpot the driver, the Tombstone to Benson
stage departed at 7 P.M. on March 15, 1881. There was a full load of passengers inside and on top and either $18,000 worth of gold, $26,000 in silver specie, or $26,000 in gold coin in the strongbox. (Accounts varied.) In
any case, the shipment was significant.

Philpot and Paul may, or may not, have switched seats at Contention.
Two miles further north and just before Drew's Station—an adobe ranch,
saloon, and stage stop—the stage crossed an arroyo, or dry gully.

Without warning, shots rang out. A voice shouted: "Halt."

"I halt for nobody," yelled Paul. He emptied both barrels of his shotgun, wounding one robber.

Philpot, killed instantly, fell beneath the wheels of the moving stage,
taking the reins with him.

An outside passenger, Peter Roerig, was mortally wounded. He died
a short time later.

The horses plunged forward, out of control.

Paul tried the brake, to little effect. He talked soothingly to the horses, to no avail.

A fashionably dressed young man shouted up to Paul from the step of the stage: "Put on the brake on the next rise and check them a little while I jump off and head them, if I can."

At the next rise, Paul slowed the stage. The young man jumped, ran, and grabbed the lead horse by the neck, bunching the remaining three horses and bringing the runaway stage to a halt.

Paul retrieved the reins and drove the stage to Benson, where he telegraphed Virgil Earp, the deputy U. S. marshal. The gold and silver remained intact.

An all-star posse was formed. It consisted of Virgil, Wyatt, and Morgan Earp; their friends Doc Holliday and Bat Masterson; and, representing the interests of Wells Fargo, Bob Paul and Marshall Williams.

The posse found Philpot's mangled body and numerous spent shells in the dry wash. The expenditure of ammunition had been considerable. Discarded nearby in some bushes were three disguises, wigs and beards made from twisted strands of rope.

No money had been taken, but two men were dead. Rumors circulated. Philpot and Paul had switched seats shortly before the shooting erupted. Paul was the intended target. A former Tombstone judge, who had run afoul of Earp, wrote the anti-Earp newspaper that Philpot's murder was "the result of a well-concocted scheme, put up by the men who knew all about Wells, Fargo & Company's business, to rob the stage and kill Robert Paul, whose known honesty, energy and bravery was dangerous to the clique that hoped by a monopoly of gambling, stage robbing and dead-fall keeping to control the politics and business of Tombstone."

Tombstone was shaken. The news spread. A one-paragraph story appeared in the next day's *San Francisco Call*. Hume read it. The headline stated: "Shot by Road Agents: A Stage Attacked, the Driver Killed and a Passenger Mortally Wounded."

Events were set in motion. Hume started for Tombstone immediately, arriving three days later. There was no word from Paul and the posse, who were attempting to track the murderers. Wyatt returned to Tombstone. More than three weeks later Paul and Virgil and Morgan Earp, who had kept on the trail, stumbled into town after wandering with little water or food in the desert for four days. In the meantime, Philpot's body had been shipped back to his grieving widow in Calistoga, California, in a casket provided by Wells Fargo.

The wanton murders shocked the West Coast and further embittered the rival groups in Tombstone. The Earps believed that the "cowboys," meaning the ranch-based Clantons and those who accompanied them, were plotting to kill them and had taken a blood oath to that effect. Casey Tefertiller wrote in *Wyatt Earp: The Life Behind the Legend* that there was no proof of such an oath, but "it was not long before blood did flow in the streets of Tombstone."

The reward offered by Wells Fargo, Wyatt Earp's burning ambition, and the differing interpretations of a conversation he held with the leader of the Clantons raised the tension to the level that precipitated the famous gunfight. It worked this way: Wyatt Earp desperately wanted to capture the three murderers in order to enhance his reputation so that he could win election as sheriff. The Clantons might be able to lure the murderers to a place where they could be captured, or preferably killed. The reward money would induce the Clantons to act.

After the gunfight, Earp testified at the preliminary hearing on the murder charges filed against the Earp brothers and Holliday: "I had an ambition to be sheriff of this county at the next election, and I thought it would be a great help with the people and business men if I could capture the men who killed Philpot." The advantage to the Clantons was the $3,600 reward for the three men and getting rid of one of the robbers who was contesting ownership of a ranch they coveted.

For various reasons, not the least of which was the fact that the Clantons would be hunted down and killed if it was known they had fingered the murderers, the reward needed to be valid for dead suspects. Earp had Williams telegraph Wells Fargo's head office in San Francisco. Back came the answer to Williams: "Dead or alive."

The printed posters for semipublic consumption specified that the reward would be given for "arrest and conviction." They were signed "R. H. Paul, Special officer of W., F. & Co." and dated March 23. Virgil confirmed Wyatt's testimony concerning the telegram. Ike Clanton said he was offered $6,000 in reward money; but, understandably, said in court that he turned the deal down. Wells Fargo waffled, stating that rewards were paid if a suspect was killed while resisting arrest and that no telegram had been sent to Earp, agent Williams having been the intended recipient.

The deal was on, said the Earps. But it never came to pass. The three suspected robber-murderers were killed in other disputes. The misunderstandings and fears that mushroomed from this unsavory pact resulted in the gunfight at the O.K. Corral.

*   *   *

When Virgil Earp, the city marshal and deputy U.S. marshal, sought a weapon on that chilly fall day of October 26, 1881, he walked into the Wells Fargo office on Allen Street as if he owned the place and grabbed a shotgun off the rack that had been reserved for his personal use for the last six months.

"No one handed it to me at the time," he said, "I got it myself."

Earp gave the sawed-off shotgun to Doc Holliday, who hid it under his long gray coat.

Then began the celebrated stroll of the four—Virgil, Wyatt, Morgan, and Doc—down Fourth Street, left on Fremont, then left again into the vacant lot between C. S. Fly's Boardinghouse and the Harwood home.

The desert wind kept blowing Holliday's coat open, revealing flashes of dull, gray steel. Those witnesses who saw the metallic object knew what it was; it was an efficient killing machine.

The lot was only fifteen feet wide, an ideal space for the use of such a weapon.

At the other end and ranged along a wall were the Clanton and the McLaury brothers, both from ranching families and armed with six-shooters. A multitude of shots erupted in the small space. Who fired first? In a magazine article that preceded publication of his book, Tefertiller wrote: "Did the Earps gun down unresisting men? Or did the cowboys start the shooting? It depends on whom you believe."

Holliday, the tubercular dentist given to uncontrolled rages, emerged as the most deadly gunman with the most effective weapon. His role in the gunfight is best described by Tefertiller, the most reliable writer among the many scribes who have dramatized the thirty-second gun battle for films, books, and magazines.

Doc Holliday lifted the shotgun from under his gray coat and stalked Tom McLaury behind the house. Holliday closed in, then fired, sending a charge that hit Tom under the right armpit and left him staggering into the street.

There was one remaining shell in the double-barreled shotgun.

Frank McLaury, shot in the stomach, staggered across the street. Morgan Earp and Doc both fired at Frank. Morgan's shot crashed through the right side of McLaury's head. Doc's charge penetrated McLaury's chest.

The McLaury brothers died, as did a Clanton. (Ike Clanton, perhaps the most immediate instigator of the gunfight, fled on foot when the shooting erupted because he had no weapon. So, it was four against three.) Doc was nicked by a bullet. Virgil was shot cleanly through the calf, and Morgan had a shoulder wound. Only Wyatt was unscathed, and thus was born the raw material that would be shaped into myth and legend.

Violence begat more violence. The madness increased in tempo and volume. While the murder charges against the Earps were dismissed, the gunfight could be considered a case of manslaughter—certainly in the literal sense of the word. What followed on both sides, however, was pure murder—execution style.

Through it all Wells Fargo publicly supported their man, Wyatt Earp. Tefertiller wrote: "For Wells, Fargo to come out with such an unqualified statement of support was unusual for the conservative company. It was certainly in response to newspaper editorials throughout the West condemning Wyatt Earp for becoming a law unto himself."

As for what Earp had truly become, Tefertiller had this to say: "Earp became a vigilante, a marshal, and an outlaw all at the same time. He enforced beyond his authority; he punished without due process."

Virgil was wounded and Morgan killed by hidden gunmen. "In response," wrote Tefertiller, "Wyatt led his own posse on a ride through Southern Arizona and into New Mexico that would be called 'The Vendetta.' Before he was through, he killed at least four men he believed were involved in murdering his brother. Wyatt crossed sides of the law."

*　　*　　*

Despite the outcome of the gunfight, Wells Fargo's difficulties in Tombstone continued.

On the night of January 6, 1882, three men stepped onto the Tombstone to Bisbee road and opened fire on the stage, killing a horse. The Wells Fargo messenger, Charley Bartholomew, returned the fire. The stage stopped and the strongbox containing the $6,500 payroll for the miners in Bisbee was handed over, along with the messenger's shotgun.

Thirty-four hours later the Benson to Tombstone stage was rolling along just south of Contention City. Jim Hume, rushing to Tombstone to investigate the latest robbery, was napping inside. At the age of fifty-four, Hume was exhausted by the incessant traveling that his job demanded.

Two masked robbers stopped the stage. From the nine passengers and one driver they extracted a total of $75 and three revolvers, two of which were Hume's fine weapons. Insult was added to injury when Hume recognized the shotgun poked in the passengers' faces as being Wells Fargo property.

Wells Fargo officials in San Francisco were incensed and embarrassed by the two robberies. They threatened to close down their Tombstone office, and they did halt service to Bisbee, a standard practice when robberies got out of hand. As for the losses of the passengers on board Hume's stage, the company offered a reward of $300 and the press had a field day.

Hume and Wyatt Earp conferred.

When Virgil had been seriously wounded ten days previously by shotgun blasts fired by hidden assassins, Wyatt had telegraphed the U.S. marshal for the territory, Crawley Drake, asking that he be deputized with power to appoint deputies. That was done, immediately. So it was with the cover of the law that Earp set out to find the assassins, and only secondarily the robbers of the two stages.

Meanwhile, his new boss, U.S. Marshal Drake, made a trip to San Francisco in January and called upon the executives at Wells Fargo. The government, Drake said, had no funds on hand to pursue the robbers; but if Wells Fargo wanted to advance $3,000 for that purpose, it was all right with him. They would eventually be reimbursed, he said. The firm gave Crawley $3,000. Crawley deposited $2,985 in the bank. Of that amount, Wyatt Earp took $536 and Crawley withdrew the rest, ostensibly to cover expenses incurred while hunting the robbers. Wells Fargo also contributed to a citizens' fund raised by Tombstone businessmen. What happened to all this money was a mystery a special examiner attempted unsuccessfully to unravel.

Company executives must have repeatedly struck their foreheads in despair when they received the next piece of bad news from Tombstone, which, after all, accounted for only a very minor portion of their overall business. Their trusted agent, Marshall Williams, slipped out of town on February 3 with a prostitute—called "a sport" in newspaper accounts—and company funds.

Williams left behind personal debts and rumors that he had tipped off the robbers about shipments. The agent was close to the Earps and Holliday: he hired them as messengers, rode with them on posses, paid their expenses, drank and gambled with them, and was their go-between with the San Francisco office. His reported destination was the Orient.

*   *   *

Agent Williams was not the only Wells Fargo employee who took off westward across the wide Pacific Ocean with stolen company funds. The case of Charles W. Banks illustrates that Wells Fargo may never have forgotten, but it didn't always get its man.

A lot of money surged through San Francisco in the 1880s. It began flowing in the early 1870s—as it had in the early 1850s and as it would again at the end of the last century—from a fleeting source of great wealth, that being the Comstock Lode in Nevada. Wells Fargo president Lloyd Tevis described "the speculation which crazed all classes of society in California" in words that foretold the recent dot-com insanity:

> The spirit of gambling spread through the whole fabric of society. Bankers, merchants, lawyers, doctors, clergymen, manufacturers, farmers, mechanics—even day-laborers and domestic servants, risked means large or small upon the fluctuations of the stock market, and watched its quotations with feverish anxiety. That waste of time and resources, that strain upon energy and morals, which is involved in the grosser forms of gambling took place upon a grand scale, and the dissemination through the community of so much fictitious wealth, which its holders regarded as real, fostered everywhere the greatest extravagance.

Production from the Nevada mines peaked in 1877, the bubble burst, and "that brought the realization of poverty to thousands who had indulged in a fancied possession of wealth," said Tevis. A depression followed. A new state constitution was passed. Business learned to live with it. Good times returned. "That California and the whole Pacific Coast is now passing into an era of the greatest prosperity and most rapid development, there are evidences on every hand," said Tevis.

While production of precious metals declined in Nevada and Utah, it had picked up in Arizona and Colorado. In California, it remained steady, a good sign. "There is no better index of the business of the Pacific Coast than the transactions of Wells, Fargo & Company, and never before have these been larger," Tevis told the bankers assembled in Niagara Falls. Money in the future would flow from agriculture, not mining, Tevis correctly predicted.

As the new decade progressed, San Francisco boomed. Population was up 57 percent. It was the nation's ninth-largest city, the economic capital of the Pacific slope, and almost all money rolled downhill to be deposited in San Francisco banks, which had never been stronger. The city's banks possessed twice the assets of all other California banks combined. The Nevada Bank and the Bank of California were the largest banks. But Wells Fargo had the greatest reach with its express business, which faced virtually no competition in the West. Wells Fargo express had 1,520 offices in 1887; more than 200 were added the next year. Money from the express business flowed into the bank.

At the California and Sansome street bank, there were two officers, four tellers, and a total of approximately thirty employees. The tellers counted gold coins by an expertly developed "grab" method, meaning what they could grab of a particular denomination equaled a certain amount. Large sums of money were scooped up with copper shovels. There were no armed guards. Twice a day a horse-drawn wagon pulled up to the bank, and the gold and silver were tossed in for clearinghouse settlement.

A lot of that Wells Fargo money flowed through the hands of Charles Banks, a trusted employee whose responsibilities had grown in direct relationship to the fortunes of Wells Fargo.

Banks was an Englishman who fought with the New York Volunteers in the Civil War and was wounded in the left leg. He had a slight accent and a noticeable limp. He sharpened his clerk and accounting skills in New York, Washington, D.C., and New Orleans, where he became a naturalized citizen. Banks moved to California in 1871 and went to work for Wells Fargo. Eric Francis, who went to work for Banks at the age of sixteen and remained at Wells Fargo for twenty years, wrote later:

> I have never met a man who was Banks' equal for all around ability. He could add up three columns of figures and could write about five different hands, being a wonderful penman. He could do anything four times as quickly and efficiently as you could. He made me into a lively quick thinking person and kept you on your toes most of the time, too.

Banks rose through the company ranks in the 1870s and early 1880s to become the head cashier for the Express Department. He was married, a neat dresser, member of the right clubs (Union and Bohemian), connoisseur of good wines and food, landowner and vintner in the Napa Valley, liberal tipper, good conversationalist, amateur scientist, Knight Templar, and owner of an impressive library, which included a copy of the unexpurgated edition of Sir Richard Burton's *Arabian Nights*. He kept the book in a locked case in his Wells Fargo office, where fellow members of the Union Club would come to read it from time to time. He was a kind person, noted both Hume and Francis. The young employee worshiped him. The trust the company had in Banks was demonstrated by the fact that he was not bonded.

There are indications that, along with the good life, Banks was in debt. The newspapers would later assert that he "owes his downfall to a woman's wiles." Hume advertised for such a woman, thinking she might lead him to Banks. No such person was ever found. The mystery woman seems to have been an invention of the male-dominated press, as was the subsequently romanticized version of Banks's life in the South Pacific.

Banks planned his getaway to coincide with a two-day holiday. He said he would be at his ranch in the Napa Valley on Monday, November 1, 1886. Tuesday was election day. That meant that his books would not be subject to the regular monthly audit until Wednesday. The auditor alerted bank officials to irregularities on that day. Meanwhile, Banks was on a ship heading westward.

Hume inserted a small notice in the November 8 issue of the San Francisco newspapers titled "Absconded." On the same day he circulated a wanted poster with a photo of Banks and his description. The reward was $1,000 for the arrest and delivery of Banks to any jail in any state or U.S. territory, along with one-fourth of all the monies recovered.

Hume said Banks made off with "at least" $20,000 in the last month; but it was more like $100,000 ($1.8 million in 2000 dollars) or more over a period of five or more years. Ten days later all Wells Fargo employees who handled money were required to post bonds. Young Francis was crushed. He thought his immediate boss and benefactor left because his ambitions had been thwarted at the bank and his wife "was anything but congenial."

By that time the forty-seven-year-old Banks was well on his way to Tahiti on board the barkentine *City of Papeete*. He had shaved his beard and was traveling under the pseudonym of John Scard. From Tahiti he made his way to Rarotonga in the Cook Islands group.

The story, as told in newspapers from San Francisco to New York City, quickly mutated into pure fiction. There is no indication who floated the rumor or whether the newspapers made it up themselves, as was the practice of the times. The fictitious story fit the stereotype of white men lost, killed, or living the South Seas under irregular circumstances.

Banks supposedly had become the consort or favorite courtier of the "dusky sovereign" Queen Makie, his "fair white face and tawny beard" having captured the queen's heart. He was described as the "King of Cook's [sic] Island" or "his kingship" or "King Banks I." The *Express Gazette*, a trade paper, proudly headlined its story, "An Expressman King."

There was absolutely no truth to Banks's reported liaison and idyllic sojourn with the queen, Rarotonga being run by the morally strict Calvinistic strictures of the missionaries who had arrived in the 1820s. The *Gazette* published a retraction in a subsequent issue.

Another version of the Banks saga has him stating that he landed with only $1,700 "as he has got away to save others." The story was repeated by the British resident at an 1897 government hearing on the island. Banks himself sent word back via the captain of the ship on which he had sailed to Tahiti. Returning to San Francisco, the captain showed the letter to a *San Francisco Chronicle* reporter. The following dialogue took place:

CAPTAIN: Here is the letter, and he gives me permission to state this, that Banks says that Wells, Fargo & Co. cannot touch him because three of the Directors of the company stole in partnership with him.

REPORTER: Captain Baruda then showed the letter to the reporter that he might see for himself that this was the very language of his informant.

Wells Fargo denied that others in the company were involved in the fraud. However, at least one former colleague paid Banks a friendly visit and displayed unusual trust, allowing Banks to hold his baby daughter in his arms. Edwin B. Riddell, an auditor, and his wife and daughter arrived on the island in 1892. A photo was taken with Banks holding Riddell's young daughter.

The daughter, Lucile Riddell Andersen, wrote to a Wells Fargo historian in 1966: "My Mother never talked about the trip but did show me the picture of me in Banks's arms—but didn't say who he was—just a Wells Fargo Bandit. I really don't know the real reason my father made the trip except my Mother told me he went to trade goods & met a Bank robber in Rarotonga."

The newspapers could not have been more mistaken about the absconded cashier. Banks led an exemplary life in the Cook Islands, but it was not the life of a rich man. He first went to a smaller island, Atiu, inhabited by only one other white man, and married a native woman, whether before or after his wife divorced him in New York City is not known.

At some point he moved to Rarotonga, where he was employed as a bookkeeper to European traders and bookkeeper and auditor for the native federal government, the latter post at an annual salary of £15. In this dual role he would have had ample opportunity to steal funds. Under first British and then New Zealand rule, Banks's work was considered honest.

The expatriate drank only moderately and was a regular churchgoer. A workaholic, he spent his nonworking hours reading Kipling, playing billiards with his European friends, and bicycling about the island. A Rarotonga historian rated Banks as "too devoid of colour to write about."

Some years later Herbert Shearman, who knew Banks, wrote the deputy resident commissioner of the Cook Islands Administration: "He always wore spotlessly white clothes, with a dark blue or black cummerbund round his waist and a black bow tie. He never went native. He was well liked and trusted by natives and whites. After he went blind he lived for some years in my parents' house and my mother looked after him there until he died." Banks died in 1915 and was buried in the London Missionary Society's graveyard on Rarotonga.

The true significance of Banks's defalcation was not the immediate loss of money and embarrassment, but its contribution to the company's souring on branch banking. The bank shrank to a single San Francisco presence during the first half of the twentieth century. At the same time A. P. Giannini created a banking empire in California based on Bank of America branches.

When Frederick L. Lipman arrived at the bank in 1883, Charles Banks told young Francis: "Do you see that young man? He has a brilliant future and will be heard from." Lipman would work for the bank for

sixty-six years, eventually becoming its president. Like other bank employees, he was shocked by Banks's abrupt departure.

Lipman was forced to spend his honeymooon in Nevada, in order to
audit irregularities at the Virginia and Carson city branch banks in 1891.
Despite new controls imposed by the head office after Banks fled, the
agents in the Virginia City and Carson City offices had made off with a
total of $342,800.

The banks were sold to Isaias W. Hellman, a Los Angeles banker who
would take over the Wells Fargo Bank in 1905. Lipman later came across
similar irregularities at the Salt Lake City bank. The Portland bank lost
money. By 1905 the western branch banks were sold.

Lipman was, in the words of Wells Fargo historian Robert J. Chandler, "forever vaccinated" against branch banking. An interviewer asked
Lipman in 1935 if a correspondent relationship with other banks was
better than branches. "I would say yes," he replied. "Mr. Giannini would
say no."

*   *   *

When Banks absconded, train robberies—mostly in the Southwest—
were occupying the majority of Hume's time. Stage robberies netted bandits only $300 in 1887. "This, of course," said Hume, "leaves a very
narrow margin for the robbers." From 1890 to 1903, however, there were
341 attempted or actual train robberies, resulting in 99 deaths, mostly in
the Southwest.

The train robbers were having a field day in Texas. The *Express
Gazette* trumpeted, "The regularity with which trains are being 'held up'
in Texas is becoming monotonous, and strenuous measures will have to be
invoked to save the fair name of the Lone Star State." Express and railroad
companies huddled with the governor, who said certain key train employees would be deputized as Texas Rangers. Wells Fargo, Southern Pacific,
the state, counties, cities, and the U.S. Post Office all offered rewards.

Wells Fargo had helped finance the Overland Mail Company, which briefly served Texas by stage before the Civil War. The express company did not subsequently enter the state until the Southern Pacific Railroad Company, to whose trains its express cars were attached, reached El Paso in 1881. By 1883 there were forty-four offices in Texas, including one in Houston. Agencies opened in Dallas and Austin in 1886, followed by Fort Worth in 1887. The draw in Texas was agriculture. First Wells Fargo, then the robbers, followed the money trail.

There had been some nasty robberies leading up to the night of October 14, 1887. One train after another fell prey to the bandits that summer and early fall, climaxing in the Flatonia holdup when the robbers tortured the messenger. They pistol-whipped him and slit his ears with penknives in order to force him to reveal where he had hidden the key to the safe.

Two men wearing masks, each holding two revolvers, worked their way over the tender and confronted the engineer on the eastbound Galveston, Harrisburg, and San Antonio Express at 8:30 P.M. on October 14. They told him to halt the train on a curve. Taking the engineer and fireman with them to point out the express car, they made their way back along the train, shooting and cursing along the way. A stick of dynamite blew open the door to the express car. The *Express Gazette* account follows:

> The robbers called the express messenger to come out. The messenger was J. Ernest Smith, and with him was J. R. Beardsley, clerk in the Wells Fargo office at Fort Worth. When they heard the firing they put out the lights and went to the rear of the car. At the command of the robbers they came out, Smith leaving his revolver just inside the door. The robbers ordered Smith and Beardsley to hold up their hands, and then searched them. Smith was then ordered to go back into the car and light the lamp. He climbed back, and the foremost robber started to follow. Smith seized his pistol, placed it almost against the robber's breast and

fired, sending a bullet through his heart. The robber fell back dead, but fired twice at Smith while falling. Smith and the other robber also exchanged shots. The robber then attempted to get his comrade's body on the engine, intending to uncouple it from the train and run on. While he was trying to lift the body upon the engine the messenger got his double-barreled shot-gun, leaned out of the car and shot at him. The robber sank down, then sprang up and ran out of sight. The train returned to this city, the express car was repaired and the train went on, messenger Smith remaining in the city.

The next day a posse found the body of the second robber fifty yards from where the train had been halted. One pellet from the shotgun had severed an artery.

Smith's fellow Wells Fargo employees in the San Antonio office were jubilant, erecting a sign along with his portrait in the flag-draped front windows. It read:

Our Hero, J. E. Smith,
Wells, Fargo & Co.'s Messenger,
Who so bravely resisted train robbers,
Near El Paso, Tex.,
On the night of October 14, 1887.

Smith collected $5,200 in reward money from commercial and government entities and a suit of clothes and a $100 gold medal from the citizens of El Paso.

But the train robberies in Texas and elsewhere continued into the next century. The express and railroad companies sought passage in Congress of a bill that would make train robberies or any felonious assault on a train, or assisting in such acts, punishable by death. Proof of committing or assisting in such an act was not needed for a guilty verdict, just proof that someone had been robbed, injured, or killed. The bills did not pass. Wells Fargo's losses from train robberies ended with World War I, when it left the express business.

Wells Fargo's exposure to crime didn't disappear, however. It merely shifted in more recent years to the most vulnerable links in the money chain.

With holdups of its branches and the introduction of credit cards and the accompanying fraud that they invited, the bank revived the Jim Hume concept of "special agents" in 1967. By 1970 there were six such agents investigating external crime and internal fraud. In 1980, $312,000 was lost in holdups. A single case of internal embezzlement had cost $70,000 a decade earlier, a record that would stand for thirty years.

Most of the losses were in Southern California, the bank robbery capital of the world. When employees and customers were threatened during a $434,000 robbery of the Tarzana branch in 1991, the James B. Hume Reward Program was initiated. Wanted posters were also revived that year, being sent to some 82,000 law enforcement agencies.

Northern California was not immune from crime. Bank robberies were increasing at an alarming rate in the early 1990s. In the San Francisco Bay Area, Wells Fargo hired off-duty police officers as armed part-time tellers in such high-crime areas as Richmond and Oakland. An attorney representing a bystander who had been wounded by an armed teller recalled the days of Wyatt Earp. "It's like Dodge City out there," he said.

Perhaps because of its historical legacy, Wells Fargo was more aggressive than other banks. It offered a $50,000 reward "leading to the identity, arrest, and conviction" of two men who fired a shot at an employee and struck another with his handgun in a 1995 robbery of the Pittsburg, California, branch. The bank's full-page ad in the *Contra Costa Times* stated: "This is terrorism—a wanton disregard of our customers and employees. It cannot and will not be tolerated. Wells Fargo Bank is determined to bring these criminals to justice."

By the end of the century that had begun with concern over train robbers, sixteen computer-equipped "security managers" did the job of three horseback-riding "special officers." The cutting-edge technology was no longer the deadly sawed-off shotgun but rather ATM cameras, digital recording of video images onto computer hard drives, wanted posters on the Internet, tiny tracking transmitters hidden in packets of money, and satellite tracking of mobile ATMs.

A More Ordinary Place

A S OPPOSED to the wilder goings-on in the Southwest and California, Wells Fargo's operations in the Pacific Northwest and western Canada were more prosaic. Along with carrying heavier items, valuable minerals, and providing banking services that were uniquely tailored to the needs of the region, Wells Fargo's mail service bound this more remote part of the country to San Francisco, and from there to the rest of the world.

Eugene Shelby, a messenger in the Portland office, described the arrival of mail on board a coastal steamer from San Francisco in the 1870s. On the trip up the coast, the Wells Fargo messenger sorted the mail in alphabetical order and prepared a list with each recipient's name on it. As the steamer cleared the bar at the mouth of the Columbia River, a signal was flashed to Portland. If it was received during daylight hours, a special flag was hoisted at the downtown Wells Fargo office.

Because of the irregular times of arrival on steamer nights, Shelby and the other employees slept in the office. He recalled, "The agent usually occupied a divan, while the rest of us perched ourselves as comfortably as we could on the counter, on trucks or on chicken coops, the latter being favorites because of their spring."

On being alerted of the imminent arrival of the steamer, everyone sprang to their assigned tasks. "Before the vessel was fastened to the dock at Portland the letter bags were thrown ashore and rushed to the office," Shelby said, "the result being that within thirty minutes after the steamer's arrival we were in position to deliver this mail, the list being conspicuously displayed so that each interested party could find out for himself if there was anything for him." By such tactics, the express company outperformed the U.S. Postal Service.

Shelby documented the total dependence on the mail as the sole form of communication with the outside world and cited the preference for his company's services:

> At that time our letter business was a wonderful factor in mercantile life, and if the steamer reached us anywhere prior to two or three o'clock in the morning nearly every business man of Portland showed up at our office for his mail. The postal service at that time was only slightly patronized, all the merchants and bankers preferring to forward their letters in this Company's franks, which we sold at 5¢ each.

From the Portland hub the mail went south via horseback, stagecoach, and eventually train through the Willamette Valley; north to Washington Territory, Victoria on Vancouver Island, and the Fraser River mining camps in mainland British Columbia; and east via the Columbia River to such remote mining camps in Idaho as Placerville, served on horseback by Charles T. Blake.

The Columbia River tested the mettle of the private express company and the federal Post Office. The river froze in January of 1868. The Post Office declared that such conditions constituted "an act of God" and excused its contractor, as provided for in the contract, from making deliveries. The veteran Wells Fargo messenger T. H. Cann, who had never failed to deliver the mail, set out on the indistinct trail along the river. The *Weekly Oregonian* reported:

In places where no other course was possible, they dug out a trail with axes and picks but in many places, they made no attempt to follow it preferring to cut their way through the underbrush and logs of the bottom lands and swamps of the mountain's base. Thus, for a considerable portion of the way, they literally cut their way through; and considering the distance—one hundred and fourteen miles—the accomplishment of the trip in three and a half days, exhibits a degree of enterprise, activity and endurance seldom found.

Upon Cann's return trip to The Dalles, the local newspaper published an extra edition, and the more distant *Idaho World* declared: "The fact that Wells, Fargo & Co. did run the route proves that it can be traveled, and that the mails can be transported over it." The difference between the performance of the two mail services was not lost upon editors at both ends of the route.

Wells Fargo served the colonists in British Columbia as well. Upon lowering its rates for mail service to the United States, a Canadian newspaper commented: "It is pleasing to observe that this enterprising firm is disposed to give customers the benefit of their enlarged facilities and as rapidity and correctness of delivery are their rules, their liberality will, no doubt, meet with ample reward the public never fails to extend to such a service." Wells Fargo ended its banking service in Victoria in 1873, the mail service ceased in 1895, and its express business was terminated in 1918, the same year it ended in the United States.

One White Male;
Women Employees;
and Minorities

W HAT WAS it like to work for Wells Fargo as a low-ranking employee in the latter half of the nineteenth century? The profitable company ran a tight ship in an era that predated minimum standards for working conditions and pay.

There is no better example of such an employee than Pilsbury "Chips" Hodgkins, who labored longer and harder for Wells Fargo than any other worker in that century. Hodgkins left a diary and daily company journals that Wells Fargo historical consultant William F. Strobridge incorporated into a number of published and unpublished manuscripts.

To sum up, Hodgkins was a company man. Like any loyal, longtime employee he experienced good and bad times.

Hodgkins acquired the nickname Chips while serving as the ship's carpenter on the voyage from Boston to San Francisco in 1849. He headed to the gold fields, where he made a modest living until 1851, when he went to work for an express company. He carried mail and packages on a mule to the miners and returned with gold dust to Sonora. The company was acquired by another in 1853; and in that year of consolidation, the second firm was purchased by Wells Fargo. Hodgkins went to work in the Stockton office loading and unloading stagecoaches and riverboats.

His next job for Wells Fargo was as steamboat messenger on the Stockton to San Francisco run from 1857 to 1870. Hodgkins was entrusted with millions of dollars' worth of valuable minerals and coins without being bonded. During his first year he carried $4,422,000. His single most valuable shipment was $115,400, on July 18, 1859.

The paddlewheelers were unreliable craft and travel on San Francisco, San Pablo, and Suisun bays and the San Joaquin River could be exciting. On his voyages Hodgkins encountered shootings on board, breakdowns, groundings, near collisions, fires, floods so great that the shallow-draft vessels could travel overland on twelve to fifteen feet of water, thick fogs, and one explosion that killed eleven crewmen.

There were tremendously heavy loads to lift, and the messenger repeatedly injured himself in the late 1860s. Hodgkins took time off without pay. His salary was $100 a month, an amount that never varied from 1866 to his retirement in 1891. Meanwhile, Hodgkins's contemporaries were given raises and promotions. Women were hired in the Accounting Department of the main office in the 1880s at $100 a month, and soon their pay was increased.

Work was six days a week, holidays, and many nights without overtime pay. The company gave each employee a turkey and two cans of frozen oysters for Thanksgiving. One week of vacation was granted. In thirty-nine years with Wells Fargo, Hodgkins took twelve weeks of vacation. He was uncomplaining. He married, owned a house in the city, had children, and lived a middle-class existence.

In 1870 Hodgkins went to work as a messenger on the San Francisco, Santa Barbara, Los Angeles, and San Diego coastal run. Wells Fargo had established a presence in Southern California in 1855 with three offices. By 1870 there were fifteen, with the main Los Angeles office located in the Pico House. Hodgkins gained a measure of fame in Southern California. Of his shipboard career, the Los Angeles agent said of Hodgkins: "Never lost a penny. Never lost a package."

The oceangoing shipments of bullion were less than his Mother Lode days but still considerable. The merchandise was varied and reflected the growth of agricultural products and business enterprises in Southern California. There were seeds, orange and magnolia trees, chickens, butter, oysters, fish, ice, machine castings, trunks, valises, and prisoners from Southern California for delivery to San Quentin, the state prison. Between 1871 and 1875 Hodgkins, armed with a pistol, escorted fifty-two prisoners from Los Angeles, San Diego, and Santa Barbara to San Quentin. Four prisoners were returned to Southern California. There were no escapes.

Hodgkins celebrated his twenty-fifth anniversary as an expressman in 1876. A formal photograph shows a strapping, handsome, bearded man with curly hair. Some two hundred guests crowded into his home, including former Wells Fargo director Henry Wells, who was in California to escape the harsh upstate New York winter. A song, "Chips the Messenger," was sung. It ended with the line "Brave Chips, the Faithful Messenger." Wells Fargo employees gave the couple a set of silverware and a miniature silver Wells Fargo treasure box containing $1,000. Hodgkins confided: "They gave me credit of actually handling more money than any other man in the United States."

When Hodgkins arrived in Los Angeles during this period with the latest newspapers from Northern California he generated priceless publicity for Wells Fargo. The Los Angeles *Express* commented on one visit: "We tip our sombrero to Mr. Chips, the genial old stand-by of Wells, Fargo & Co. messenger on the *California*, for late San Francisco papers." Other newspapers printed similar kudos, not only in repayment for the free service but also in appreciation of the company's "popular," "efficient," and "enterprising" messenger.

The messenger became land-based in late 1877, and found that working conditions were more regularized in the San Francisco express headquarters. He arrived in the office at 6:30 A.M. and was usually done by 7:30 P.M., although it could be later. There were light work days and heavy work days. There was sun, rain, and fog.

After working eight years in the Forwarding Department specializing in making steamship connections, Hodgkins was transferred to the Collections Department, where he had to traverse the seamier sections of San Francisco and deal with angry customers. Paper money was still virtually nonexistent in the West, so he lugged heavy bags of coins. He was never robbed on the streets. One of his sons went to work as a Wells Fargo messenger. His wife was active in the California State Floral Society. They went to Admission Day and Maine Day picnics.

After the Banks episode in 1886, Hodgkins had to pay $19.50 annually for a personal bond, despite his many years of honest service. The payment represented one-fifth his monthly salary. It hurt. He was bitter about the bond, which he called "a clear case of robbery of a few poor hard workers that got but bitter wages and the high toned and high salaried officials of Wells Fargo & Co. are the stockholders in the surety company."

The fortieth anniversary of the admission of California as a state was celebrated with a large parade in San Francisco on September 9, 1890. One of the highlights was Hodgkins, billed as "the oldest representative of the express business on this coast," riding down Market Street on a white mule adorned with the saddlebags from his Gold Rush days.

The next year, Hodgkins's last with the company, he took the highly unusual step of complaining about "the privilege of being honest." The Pacific Surety Co. refunded the bond payments of Wells Fargo employees, but Hodgkins refused to collect his money. He insisted that it be sent directly to him, "otherwise they can keep it." Hodgkins became ill in December and never returned to work. He died in 1892. Whether it was bitterness directed at Wells Fargo or nostalgia for the old days, his last words were: "The Express has gone wrong."

The story of Hodgkins is illustrative of a time when employees were loyal to a company under working conditions that would not be tolerated today. What the employees received in return was a sense of belonging. This was true not only of Wells Fargo but held throughout the express industry.

Express company ownership of the bonding companies their employees were forced to use was common practice, as Peter Grossman points out in his book *American Express*. Salaries were low, benefits were nonexistent, hours were long. The express companies were antiunion. An expressman, if he wanted to remain an expressman, could not change jobs. The major companies had a pact that no employee could switch jobs from one company to another without written consent, a policy that prevented competition for labor.

Writing of the last days of the express companies in 1918, Edward Hungerford, a former Wells Fargo executive, said. "The companies had not been too progressive in their personal relationships with the rank and file of their employees. It was not until 1915 that the highly prosperous Wells Fargo came forth with a comprehensive, modern and extensive pension and benefit plan for its workers. The pay in the express as compared with other businesses of a like nature was not high."

*   *   *

At the American Express Company in New York City there was a ban against women employees. A manager wrote President James C. Fargo, a younger brother of William, asking permission to hire a woman stenographer. Fargo replied, "When the day comes that American Express has to hire a female employee, it will close its doors." The objection? Fargo continued: "Every time a woman gets up from her desk three men look up from their work" and "female tears do not correct misspelled letters."

Managers in the field, where there were few men and where women were available at less cost, pleaded with the unyielding, autocratic president. Fargo rejected these requests, stating in a 1884 letter: "We do not believe the time has arrived in this country when it becomes necessary to appoint females as agents of this company, and when a town does not afford a proper male party to represent our business we had better import one for that purpose."

With the president none the wiser, women were employed as substitute freight agents or for their ailing or dead husbands, their gender disguised on the books by using an initial instead of a first name. The first mention of a known woman in official American Express records was an Iowa agent in 1886, the second a clerk in Michigan in 1892.

Hiring practices were different at Wells Fargo in the more democratic West. More than 160 women worked for Wells Fargo during the nineteenth century, not counting those who were identified only by their first initial. Most were in California, some were in the Midwest and Texas, and a few were scattered about Pennsylvania, New Jersey, and New York, the distribution being representative of the geographical spread of offices.

The first woman Wells Fargo employee besides the stagecoach driver Charley Parkhurst may very well have been Mary Taggart, the agent at the Palmyra, Nebraska, office in 1873. She was also the agent for the railroad and the telegrapher. In response to an 1876 article in *The Expressman's Monthly* headlined "Something New under the Sun," Taggart wrote that she was "glad to learn" that she was not the only female agent "in this benighted region." The publication had mistakenly stated that another woman was the first female employee in a prior issue.

Like most male agents, women worked on a commission basis while holding down other jobs. Quite a few were agents for Wells Fargo and the railroad, along with being telegraphers. They were single or widows. A number were also postmasters, one published and edited a newspaper, and some were bookkeepers. Artists, commercial photographers, librarians, schoolteachers, and housewives worked part-time as Wells Fargo agents.

San Francisco newspapers, under such headlines as "Trying Out the Girls" and "Girls to the Front," reported in 1889 what was probably the first group hiring of women at the company's headquarters. Six mature women were hired to replace eight young men who had been making too much noise in the Auditing Department. Their job was "of a purely mechanical nature," but the boisterous males were disturbing the nearby accountants. It was hoped that the experiment would succeed; if it did, other women would be hired in other departments.

To the east of San Francisco in the Mother Lode country, two sisters and a third woman had a lock on the Mariposa agent's job for thirty years. The first woman agent was Lucy S. Miller, recently widowed with a small son. She applied for the job because she did not want to be a financial burden on her father, an attorney. Miller went to work in the Sierra Nevada foothills community on the road to Yosemite Valley in 1885.

Two years later she became the town postmaster after the first applicant, a man, failed to qualify. The post office and Wells Fargo offices were physically combined. (Not all Wells Fargo offices were stand-alones. They could be combined with grocery and dry goods stores or barber shops.) One of Miller's post office duties was to inspect other post offices in Mariposa County. Most were in good order, she reported.

Six days a week Miller got up in the early morning hours and loaded the Mariposa to Merced stage that departed at 5 A.M. Paperwork consumed much of her time, there being more than two dozen forms to use for five basic tasks. She kept a dozen account books and registers, from which she derived her totals.

There were holdups on her routes and losses, which required more reports and energizing local law enforcement officials to chase the robbers. In 1890 the Mariposa *Gazette* ran a headline: "The Mariposa Stage Robbed Three Times within Six Months." The robber was caught and the holdups ended.

Miller reflected on her job: "I have learned much of patience, forbearance and policy, and have acquired some knowledge of human nature, which should be in itself an education."

One of Miller's sisters, Julia L. Jones, a schoolteacher, replaced her as Wells Fargo agent and postmaster in 1892. Jones was thirty-five years old. She is on the far right in a group picture of the Mariposa Chapter of the Native Daughters of the Golden West. Jones's legs are stylishly

crossed, her hair is piled atop her head, and she is holding in her hand
what appears to be a branch with large oak leaves.

Gold mine operations in the region picked up after the financial
panic of 1893, and Jones handled quite a few gold dust and bullion shipments. Gold valued at a total of $251,770 passed through her hands in
1902. Sacks of ore samples weighed sixty-four pounds apiece.

Floods made streams and roads impassable in winter, wreaking
havoc on established schedules. In summer stagecoaches loaded with
tourists on their way to Yosemite Valley taxed the town's overnight ac-
commodations. On top of all her other duties, Jones was elected county
superintendent of schools. She prepared budgets, visited the thirty-
five schools under her jurisdiction, taught, and attended and conducted
meetings.

Besides being active in the schools and club activities, such as the native daughters and the Order of the Eastern Star, Jones was a busi-
nessperson. She owned the Jones Building, which housed a grocery,
jewelry store, and the combined post office and Wells Fargo agency. She
was reelected twice as county school superintendent and only gave up
her Wells Fargo and post office jobs when she was appointed secretary to
the Mariposa County Board of Supervisors.

Miller took over the dual jobs again. Miller's son, now grown, helped
her on occasion. In 1909 she remarried and resigned the positions. Auto-
mobiles had begun showing up on the road to Yosemite, spooking the
stage horses. A railroad reached the edge of the park in 1909. Another
widow, Miriam Isabel Rowland, replaced Miller. Competition cut into
Wells Fargo's business; and the office was closed in 1914, but not before
three women in long skirts had proved they could do the work of three
men in long pants.

*   *   *

In the late 1870s, California whipped itself into a froth of anti-Chinese
fear and hatred. The white population of the Pacific Coast, it was feared,

was about to be inundated by Asian hordes. A report of the Special Committee on Chinese Immigration of the State Senate noted: "Were they sufficiently civilized, well armed, learned, and intelligent, they could spread their rule over the world, and be as dreaded in the nineteenth and twentieth centuries as were the hordes of Atilla, Genghis-Khan, and Tamerlane (all from Chinese territory), from the fifth to the fifteenth [centuries]." In scattered locations throughout the state the Chinese were shot, burned out of their homes, or sealed into ghettos.

Wells Fargo aggressively sought the lucrative business of the Chinese, while taking what might be best termed a middle-of-the-road position on immigration policy. Lloyd Tevis sought to avoid disruption, and he wanted to continue to do business with the better educated, more prosperous Chinese, as he outlined in the 1881 speech to his fellow bankers:

> That the Chinese have been of use in the industrial development of the Pacific Coast is unquestionable, but it is as unquestionable that the antipathies excited by their presence and the fears of their overwhelming influx have been the cause of much social discontent and political agitation. The treaty with China, recently ratified, gives to our Government the power of restricting or prohibiting the immigration of Chinese laborers without interfering with a proper national hospitality towards Chinese students or travelers or merchants, and the enactment of laws in consonance with this treaty, which will doubtless take place at the next session of Congress, will remove a cause of dangerous agitation, and solve a question which though it has attracted comparatively little attention in the Eastern States of the Union, has been to thoughtful men on the Pacific Coast a source of great anxiety.

Such a law, known as the Chinese Exclusion Act, was passed by Congress in 1882. Neither in favor of a liberal immigration policy nor allied with more reactionary businessmen-vigilantes, Tevis sought to maintain ties to the Asian community. Yong Chen, an associate professor of Asian Studies at the University of California at Santa Cruz and the author of *Chinese San Francisco, 1850–1943*, wrote about San Francisco businesses: "At a time of increasing hostility toward the Chinese, these merchants carefully worded their Chinese-language advertisements in an effort to distance themselves from the anti-Chinese forces." Chen named Wells Fargo as one of the merchants.

Wells Fargo pursued the Chinese, the largest minority in California, in an era before the terms *niche market* or *market segment* had been invented. As a result, Wells Fargo was the Chinese bank of choice dating back to the 1850s and forward to the present time. When the writer Amy Tan's heroine tours her mother's flower shop in *The Kitchen God's Wife*, she is told for whom the small table sprays were made: " 'Some for tonight. Some for a retirement dinner,' my mother explains, and perhaps because I don't look sufficiently impressed, she adds, 'For assistant manager at Wells Fargo.' "

After one of San Francisco's frequent fires had swept the city in 1851, a three-floor, granite-faced building was erected on the northwest corner of Montgomery and California streets (across Montgomery from the current headquarters building). The granite was shipped from China. The building's owner, John Parrott, refused to allow the Chinese to perform a ceremony that would exorcise evil spirits. The two largest express and banking companies moved into the new building. They failed in the panic of 1855. Wells Fargo then occupied the Parrott Building. The rest of the story is told in the 1989 Chinese Historical Society's history of San Francisco and Chinatown:

> Before the reopening of the building, Wells Fargo and its Chinese friends had spent much time and made many prayers and offerings to their god of wealth, Choy Pak Sing Kung, to bless the building and look after the welfare of Wells Fargo in its new home.

These efforts must have done the job, because today, more than 130 years later, Wells Fargo is one of the leading banks in the state. And many Chinese are still among its most loyal customers.

Wells Fargo courted the Chinese at a time of intense hatred of the foreigners, called "Celestials" in polite company. It sponsored publication of an English-Chinese phrasebook that included a list of company offices in California, Nevada, and elsewhere. The unusual aspect of such a venture was cited in a history of the Hongkong & Shanghai Banking Corporation: "A phrase book, as such, was rare enough during this era; that it contains a listing of Wells Fargo business offices makes it extraordinary, especially when one considers that it was produced during the height of anti-Chinese sentiment in California."

English phrases for which the equivalent Chinese characters were supplied included the following: "People call him a pedant," "I will leave when my month is up," "The man goes into the sea to attack a crocodile," "I go into the woods to attack a tiger," "I go to the banks for money," "That is the lowest price," "Youth is for learning," "Manhood is for action."

The Chinese characters were indecipherable to Westerners. One Wells Fargo agent, who had difficulty reading a receipt, said they were "barbarous hieroglyphics which resemble so closely crickets & grass hoppers."

Between 1871 and 1882, Wells Fargo published four editions of a "Directory of Chinese Business Houses." Because of the vagaries of census taking, the carefully compiled directories may very well be the best indication of the spread of Chinese population along the West Coast at the time. The last edition contained the following total numbers of Chinese-owned businesses: San Francisco (674); Sacramento (105); San Jose (79); Oakland (69); Portland (65); Stockton (57); Victoria, British Columbia (44); and Marysville and Los Angeles (42).

In 1882, the same year the Exclusion Act passed, Wells Fargo sent a package of materials to all its agents. It included the Chinese directory with a Denver supplement; Chinese business posters, cards, and paper; Chinese shipping stickers; and a poster "relative to [company] identification." The instructions specified that the identification posters printed on cardboard were to be displayed "conspicuously" in the office and those on red paper "hand to your best Chinese patrons." Additional supplies were available "on requisition from offices where Chinese business is of sufficient consequence to make further circulation advantageous."

The Chinese received a wide range of miscellaneous services. When shipments went astray a reward of $70 was offered for the return of a box of opium valued at $150; $10 for a Chinese tea box containing $15 worth of clothes; and $10 for a locked Chinese trunk. A special mail route, called the China Route, served San Francisco's Chinatown. Such special services continued into the early twentieth century, as evidenced by this passage from the company's magazine:

> The remarkable breadth of Wells Fargo service was shown a month or two ago, when our company undertook to carry a Chinaman from Tia Juana, on the Mexican border, to Vancouver, British Columbia. As everyone knows, Chinamen are contraband in the United States, but when the bland Celestial was brought to Tia Juana—which, by the way, can be translated into English as Aunt Jane—Wells Fargo & Company regarded it but as a detail of its business to furnish bond for his safe delivery in Canada.
>
> John Chinaman rode on the express car, properly tagged and waybilled, and a succession of our alert messengers kept their eyes upon him to see that he did not commit *hari kari*, or any other sort of a getaway. Our company, following its custom in moving living animals of all sorts, furnished John with his meals, and he left the United States a brighter and brisker Celestial than he had entered.
>
> There are no limits to Wells Fargo enterprise, and the prob-

lem is yet to be found that is too difficult for this company to undertake.

The language was temperate, considering the overt attitudes and actions of the time against the Chinese: discriminatory legislation, hate-laced literature and speeches, forcible evictions, arson, and outright murders throughout California and the West.

The First Divestment

MEANWHILE, WELLS FARGO continued to perform that function so essential to the smooth functioning of a democracy: delivering the bulk of the mail west of Salt Lake City and Albuquerque. The inevitable confrontation between Wells Fargo and the U. S. Post Office Department in 1880 was a classic example of a private business competing directly and successfully with a government agency.

Faced with minor attempts to capture its business in downtown Manhattan and Brooklyn, the postal service looked westward in order to remove this threatening growth before the cancer spread more widely. It sent special agent B. K. Sharretts to San Francisco. His report was submitted to a committee appointed by the postmaster general.

During the Gold Rush era and shortly afterward, Wells Fargo's private mail system was tolerated because the government recognized that it did not have the same broad reach or the same degree of efficiency. The compromise was double payment in the form of a prepaid government envelope and an additional Wells Fargo stamp. In this way the government got its due and the customer got quicker delivery. By the late 1870s the cost of an express letter was five cents; three cents went to the government and two cents to Wells Fargo, with heavier objects costing more in approximately the same ratio. In a series of directives sent to its agents during the intervening years, Wells Fargo sought to administer the mail service correctly.

What Agent Sharretts found ostensibly shocked the committee. There was "a letter-carrying department of immense magnitude, whose headquarters are in the city of San Francisco, but whose ramifications extend into every one of the Pacific States and Territories, and even into foreign countries." Furthermore, nearly 20 percent of Wells Fargo agents in outlying areas were also postmasters and thus served two bosses.

In San Francisco, the more centrally located green Wells Fargo collection boxes stood next to many of the more widely dispersed red government boxes. The Wells Fargo collection system was "almost as extensive as that of the government," noted the committee's report, and was "more frequent and perhaps more expeditious." Two examples of quicker service in San Francisco were cited by agent Sharretts. Mail on the ferry from Oakland was thrown to a waiting Wells Fargo messenger "while the legitimate mail-carrier is obliged to wait till the boat is made fast." Messengers mounted on horses then dashed to the respective addresses.

In language conveying grave dismay, the committee determined what had been obvious: that Wells Fargo was "carrying on, without any government control or supervision whatever, an extensive postal service of their own, of considerable profit to themselves, which they endeavor by every means in their power to render more efficient than the regular postal service, and which has therefore become a formidable competitor with the government for public patronage." The report added: "The company, no longer catering to any essential public want, should be required to give way, so that the government may exercise its right on the Pacific coast, as everywhere else, to a complete monopoly in the custody and carriage of the mails."

Not so, Lloyd Tevis, president of Wells Fargo, thundered in reply: "We claim that our Letter Service has been a necessity on this coast, is still a convenience, and its continuance desired by the expressed will of the people, and *that the public interest does not require its suspension."*

There were some dry technical issues and legal arguments advanced and countered by both sides that were obscured by the more public and emotional aspects of the controversy. General Superintendent John J. Valentine sent a directive to all agents on April 3, 1880, that cited an Associated Press dispatch from Washington, D.C., stating that it was the intent of the Post Office Department "to break up the postal business of Wells, Fargo & Co."

If the story was correct, Valentine told his 560 agents, "It will require a very general protest from citizens of the Pacific Coast to prevent the Government from abolishing our Letter service." He added, somewhat disingenuously: "We cannot conceive a reason for the hostility exhibited, but it exists, and we must meet it."

An intensive lobbying effort was quickly unleashed. Wells Fargo agents gathered thousands of names on petitions and met with newspaper editors in their regions. Six copies of each story generated by the agents was sent to Valentine. One week later, after being bombarded by petitions bearing "hundreds of thousands of signatures," according to one newspaper account, and the opposition of western senators and congressmen, the Post Office Department relented. Lest the firm be subjected to recriminations, Wells Fargo agents were instructed by Valentine to follow regulations "to the utmost."

Fifteen years later the Post Office had become a model of efficiency; the specter of monopolies, like Wells Fargo, had risen; and the company's letter service had declined. It was time for a delicate retreat. On May 24, 1895, Wells Fargo quietly removed all its collection boxes in San Francisco and on the next day announced that it was ending its letter service.

From a maximum of 15,000 letters daily during the Gold Rush era, the service had fallen off considerably, said general agent Henry W. Titus.

"In the old days," Titus lamented, "we not only competed successfully with the Government, but we beat the postal system at every turn of the road, but now the Federal authorities have adopted all of our plans, and they do the work as well as we do." Wells Fargo's functions had lessened by one; the banking and express businesses remained.

A Midwest Connection

THE BANK fed off the express business and the express depended on the bank. It was a symbiotic relationship. Years later Frederick Lipman, by then president of the bank, explained: "The ownership was with the express company, but the capital was with the bank. Our capital was a funny thing. It was all the capital they [the express] had. . . . The mere fact that we had the express business adjunct helped to keep us [the bank] out of trouble."

In other words, the express company was a cash cow milked by the directors, with the resulting liquid gold flowing directly into the vault of the bank. (The flow could be reversed. Directors received a ten-dollar gold piece, stored in the vault, for attending each board meeting.) Wells Fargo Bank owed its existence to the express company, both as an historical entity and in terms of the economic realities of the late nineteenth century. If not for the huge monthly deposits of the express company and the huge capital reserves they provided, what had become a moderate-sized bank would have been virtually nothing.

For the express business to be profitable, there were two requirements: a close relationship with the railroads and an absolute monopoly on their lines. The result was a triumvirate—express company, bank, railroad—that was not limited to Wells Fargo's operations.

No one was more aware of these realities than William Fargo, who was on the Wells Fargo and American Express company boards in the 1870s. Fargo and some of his close Wells Fargo associates were not adverse to establishing a new transcontinental train route that could harm his namesake company. Making money was the main goal. In the process, Fargo initiated a corporate loop that would eventually arc back to Wells Fargo more than one hundred years after his death.

The Northern Pacific Railroad was chartered by Congress in 1864 and given 47 million acres to build a railroad to the Pacific Ocean. Such a northern railroad, when completed, would flank Wells Fargo's central route, acquired in the 1869 agreement with the Central Pacific Railroad, now renamed the Southern Pacific.

The president of the Vermont Central Railroad, J. Gregory Smith, sought funding for a railroad in 1867 that would begin in Vermont, weave back and forth across the United States–Canadian border, and wind up on the Pacific Coast. Smith searched for important personages in the transportation industry to give his plan public visibility. Four Wells Fargo directors bought four shares at $8,500 apiece. They were Fargo, Benjamin P. Cheney, and the brothers Danforth and Ashbel Barney, both of whom would serve as presidents of Wells Fargo. Fargo was elected to the new railroad's board of directors. Ashbel Barney and Cheney joined the board at a later date.

The financier Jay Cooke signed a contract in 1869 to handle the financing of the railroad. An extensive publicity program sought settlers in the United States, Europe, and Scandinavia. Engineers were sent into the field in 1870. They decided that the railroad, now planned to traverse the northern tier of states and territories, would bridge the Red River at Bogusville, renamed Fargo the next year and known as "Fargo in the Timber" to the troops who were sent to clear the town site of premature settlers in 1872. (Cheney would eventually get a town in eastern Washington state named after him.)

Cooke's firm went bankrupt in the panic of 1873, brought on by the overexpansion of railroads. The railroad was not completed until 1883.

The Northern Pacific Express Co., with Ashbel Barney and Cheney as directors, was formed to operate on the railroad that had been, while under construction, the exclusive province of Wells Fargo. The new express company squeezed Wells Fargo, whose express business was "tremendously damaged" as a result. Wells Fargo filed suit against Northern Pacific. There was a bitter court battle. The Federal District Court in Portland ruled that the Northern Pacific Express Co. had to open its lines to Wells Fargo on an equal basis with other express companies.

Barney and Cheney had potential, if not immediate, conflicts of interest. They were directors of the Northern Pacific railroad, its associated express company, *and* Wells Fargo. Choosing to cast their lot with Northern Pacific, Barney left the Wells Fargo board in 1883 and Cheney departed the next year.

Meanwhile, at the start of construction Northern Pacific Railroad needed a local bank. Northwestern National Bank was established in 1872 for that purpose. The number of initial shares of bank stock was split almost evenly between easterners and midwesterners. Fourteen investors from the East signed up for one-half of the $200,000 stock offering at $100 per share, and thirty-eight Minnesotans took the remainder. Of the easterners, Fargo, Cheney, and Danforth Barney—all directors of the railroad—bought one hundred shares apiece.

The bank was initially the adjunct of the railroad. Of the fourteen out-of-town investors, ten were either officers or directors of the railroad. Of the first board of directors of the bank, one-third were from the railroad. The 1872 city directory published by the *Minneapolis Tribune* noted that the bank "was organized in the interests of the Northern Pacific Rail Road, thus giving that road a convenient banking house for the transaction of its immense business in this section."

The First National Bank of Fargo was established in 1876. The prairie land, just pierced by the railroad, was prime wheat country. Cheney was a part owner of one of the first "bonanza" wheat farms that eventually encompassed 13,440 acres in North Dakota. (For those associated with the railroad as investors, the more immediate return was from land speculation derived from the land grant and the increased value of adjacent lands.)

To fend off corporate raiders from both coasts, the midwestern banks in the region—including those in Fargo and Minneapolis—formed a holding company named Northwest Bancorporation, or Banco, in 1929. The company was dominated by Northwestern National Bank of Minneapolis. From 1930 to 1949 Banco's corporate logo was a covered wagon pulled by two oxen with a pioneer marching alongside, cradling a long rifle in his arms. The prairie schooner was the plains counterpart of the western stagecoach.

A Thanksgiving Day fire in 1982 destroyed the corporate headquarters of Banco, just as Wells Fargo's headquarters in San Francisco were destroyed in the earthquake and fire of 1906. Both banks rebuilt. Northwest then changed its name to Norwest Corporation to reflect a wider range of services than just traditional banking.

In what was called "a merger of equals," Norwest became Wells Fargo in 1998 and moved its headquarters to San Francisco, thus completing the loop. By then both corporations were far removed from their railroad and stagecoach roots, although when merged they retained the horse-drawn coach as the corporate symbol.

Once Again: Growth
and Takeover

THE TRIUMVIRATE of railroad, express company, and bank enabled Wells Fargo to become the first express company that connected one coast, and points in between, to the other coast with goods and services. But the seeds of growth contained the cells of near destruction.

In 1888 Wells Fargo took the giant stride of first reaching Chicago and then New York City with an express service that did not have to seal its doors on sections of the track monopolized by other express companies. It was free to pick up and deliver items all along the way and serve the Orient and Europe with greater ease.

The change was immediately noticeable. The new ocean-to-ocean service accounted for an increase in offices from 1,520 in 1887 to 2,560 in 1889. While Wells Fargo had become a household name in the West, it was now recognized in other sections of the country.

The expansion was surreptitiously fought by American Express; it was achieved at a great monetary cost; and it occurred at a time when the company was raking in record revenues on ten thousand miles of railroad tracks and had a sterling reputation. The trade publication, *Express Gazette*, wrote in 1887: "The general reliability of the company is as widespread as its operations." John Valentine, who played a key role in the expansion, emerged to become a major force in the company just as Tevis was receding from view.

Valentine's code name in sensitive intercompany telegraph messages was Vanilla. He was a straightforward, scrupulously honest taskmaster. Another native of Kentucky, Valentine had joined the company in 1860 as a clerk in the Virginia City office. When a stage became stalled in deep snow, he carried the express items the remainder of the way to Placerville. Valentine was superintendent of the Pioneer Stage Co. when that firm was purchased from Louis McLane. He rose through the ranks, becoming vice president and general manager in 1882 and president ten years later. He served Wells Fargo for forty-one years.

Valentine was a tall, fully bearded, commanding man who wore polished boots instead of shoes in the executive offices. He was the last of the great expressmen when that job description carried with it an aura of a solid, brave individual. No rube, Valentine owned an extensive library, was well read, and was bolstered by his Christian belief system. "Have faith in God and man" was his credo when pessimism was fashionable at the fin de siècle.

Understandably, Valentine was less knowledgeable about the banking functions of Wells Fargo. He also depended on others for information on stocks. Receiving a stock tip from an American Express officer in the days before laws against insider trading, he wrote Hosmer B. Parsons, the head of Wells Fargo's New York bank: "I thought I might make a few dollars on a 'legitimate' stock, and maybe you could also. What do you know about it? Can you get a point from J. C. F. [American Express president James C. Fargo]?"

Meanwhile, American Express was working behind the scenes in 1887 and 1888 to sabotage Wells Fargo's efforts to carry express items on the New York, Lake Erie, and Western Railroad, the last link in establishing a true transcontinental service. Valentine, who had turned down the offer of another railroad to steal an express line from American Express, cited the "comity" between the two companies. He could not understand why American Express objected to Wells Fargo's presence in New York City.

Valentine was ready to deal with American Express on its terms. He sent an unusual "personal and confidential" letter to Parsons in New York that instructed his New York representative to continue secret negotiations. "I duly appreciate the desirability of working harmoniously with the American Express Company," Valentine said, "but I also believe that in order to insure our reasonable independence, it will be very desirable to get the Erie Lines and I trust you will continue to communicate discreetly with Mr. Quintard, as I telegraphed you today before the receipt of your letter."

Just as companies now seek foolproof encryption systems for computers, sensitive telegraph messages between Wells Fargo's San Francisco and New York offices were sent in code. There was a yearly cipher book used to encode and decode correspondence. Messages on each day of the week began with a test word. A message might read: "(Test word) Ambler Alpen Acorn John Doe Boarder Alcohol Front Sketch Beauty Baptist Ardena." That translated to: "Pay John Doe & Co., 45 Front Street, $1,577.50."

One week after instructing Parsons by telegraph code and letter to continue discussions, Valentine told Parsons in early January of 1888: "'Covert' influences [read American Express] have been at work in Chicago with the Northwestern lines, and we have no doubt that it will be exercised in the future if it can be done without fear of consequence and for this reason I continue under the impression that we should establish ourselves on lines to New York."

The Wells Fargo board of directors, ostensibly with the agreement of the American Express representative, authorized a contract with the Erie railroad in March and a contract with the Atchison, Topeka & Santa Fe Railroad in May, the latter providing for service into Chicago. Generally, the two contracts provided the railroads with either 40 or 50 percent of the gross express earnings on the respective lines and a guarantee either in terms of a lump sum or a per mile rate. The contracts with the Southern Pacific in 1869, 1878, and 1893 provided for large amounts of Wells Fargo stock, which would eventually make a difference in who controlled the company. The *sine qua non* of every express company's contract was the exclusive use of the line.

Wells Fargo engaged in what would now be called a marketing rollout or a media blitz. The company bragged in literature that designated 63 Broadway as its main New York office: "It is the only through Express Line between the eastern Seaboard and the Trans-Mississippi States, the Pacific Coast, British Columbia and the Republic of Mexico, and is the only Express upon the Erie, Burlington, Northwestern, Santa Fe and Southern Pacific Railway System."

Valentine issued a revised set of "General Instructions" to all employees in 1888 that contained eighteen items, many aimed at prohibiting activities that could result in defalcations. Item nine was different: "The most polite and gentlemanly treatment of all customers, however insignificant their business, is insisted upon. Proper respect must be shown to all—let them be men, women, children, rich or poor, white or black—it must not be forgotten that the Company is dependent on these same people for its business."

During all this activity, Wells Fargo continued to issue an 8 percent yearly cash dividend to stockholders. Some 6 percent dividend years followed in the 1890s, however. Valentine thought that Tevis, with whom he had differences of opinion, ran a sloppy operation, especially after irregularities were uncovered at the two Nevada banks by Lipman in 1891. Other directors agreed. Tevis lost his positions, first as president in 1892 and then as a director in 1893.

Valentine became president in time to weather yet another financial panic in 1893. He wrote his New York representative and friend a "Dear Parsons" letter at the end of 1894 that contained a private summation of the company's status:

The old year has gone its way, or vanishes tonight, and while I am disappointed officially in my expectations as to net results, it has nevertheless, under all the circumstances, been good to us—in fact, I expect better than to the average interests of the country, because we have earned net over six and one-half percent for our stockholders. We have kept all the time in strong condition financially; have met all the evils and disasters of which there has been a multitude—paid the losses resulting therefrom,—and yet have imposed as little hardship on our employees in the matter of reduction of force or wages as any Company I know of, and less than most of them. In proportion to our Capital Stock our clean net earnings are probably better than nine out of ten of the Railroad Companies—therefore we have reason to be thankful; and I am thankful.

Valentine's message to all employees at the end of the nineteenth century cited the "prosperous conditions throughout the country and in the business of Wells Fargo & Company." There were 5,000 employees in 3,600 express offices and three banks, and the express company was operating on 36,000 miles of railroad tracks. But Valentine would die at the end of 1901, and the next year Wells Fargo would begin to pass, once again, into different hands.

★   ★   ★

The Trans-Mississippi West was unique in terms of transportation. In no other region did a railroad and the express company that attached its cars to fast passenger trains have greater control over moving freight and passengers. Express rates for the extra-fast service were a surcharge above the railroad's rates. Both rate scales were high.

While the octopus image of the Southern Pacific Railroad was exaggerated by the Progressives for political purposes, there is no doubt that the railroad exerted an inordinate amount of power over its shippers. Southern Pacific took the heat from critics and regulators while Wells Fargo hovered in its protective shadow. Then the railroad devoured the express company. In retrospect, there was an element of cannibalism surrounding the act.

The conditions for the next takeover were sown in 1869 when Wells Fargo handed over one-third of its capital to what would become the Southern Pacific in order to gain access to the transcontinental railroad. To renew this contract in 1878, an additional $1,250,000 in stock was given to the railroad. For the same purpose in 1893, the railroad received 16,625 shares valued at $2,161,250. The key provision in the fifteen-year contract that would prohibit the express company from diluting Southern Pacific's control was: "And the Express Company agrees that it will not increase its capital stock during the period of this contract to the injury of the Southern Pacific Company." Wells Fargo now had access to 7,750 miles of Southern Pacific track, but it had been acquired at a great cost.

The express and banking company signed its death warrant for the last time in 1893. Henry E. Huntington, the nephew of Collis P. Huntington, president of the Southern Pacific, was elected to the Wells Fargo board that same year. The younger Huntington was an officer of Southern Pacific.

The unrelenting force that managed the second transformation of Wells Fargo was Edward H. Harriman. Harriman was to railroads what Morgan was to banking, Rockefeller to oil, and Carnegie to iron and steel. The railroads were the sole means of fast transportation, and the express was the speediest means of shipment on the railroads. The expresses then were what overnight coast-to-coast airborne express services are today.

The bespectacled Harriman, who gained a seat on the New York Stock Exchange at the age of twenty-two and came to railroads relatively late in life, stood small, physically. But he operated in the business world in an intense, combative, ruthless manner by means of "volcanic bursts of energy," according to his most recent biographer, Maury Klein.

The relationship between Harriman and Wells Fargo bore a certain similarity to others who had controlled the company. It is ironic that Wells Fargo, which has lasted as an identifiable name for one hundred and fifty years, passed successively through the hands of men more interested in other pursuits. There were Wells and Fargo, involved in the American Express Company, railroads, and other philanthropic and political activities in New York state. Tevis had vast real estate and mine holdings in California and the West, including the legendary Homestake Mine in South Dakota. Harriman sought Wells Fargo for its huge surplus, which he used to rebuild the aging Southern Pacific and Union Pacific systems.

Harriman courted the aging Collis Huntington during the first half of 1900, but to no avail. Then Huntington died in August; and his heirs, including his nephew, Henry Huntington, sold the Southern Pacific to Harriman. It was a time of mergermania and a raging bull market on Wall Street, led by the railroads. "We have bought not only a railroad but an empire," Harriman exulted.

That empire consisted of the largest transportation system in the world: 9,441 miles of railroad tracks and 16,186 miles of steamship routes. And by the way, Wells Fargo was a small part of the deal. Southern Pacific owned 15,300 shares or one-third of Wells Fargo's stock, by far the single largest block. Harriman owned ten shares.

Where before there had been contractual agreements, the merger of the railroad and the express company was a natural. The interests were mutual. The *Atlantic Monthly* surveyed express companies across the country and commented: "Available facts would tend to show that the railways, instead of regarding the express companies as legitimate objects of exploitation, are becoming, through stock ownership and representation on the directorates, personally interested in the management of the express business."

The torch was officially passed in early 1902. John Valentine died in late December of 1901, and Harriman was elected on January 2, 1902 to the old expressman's seat on the board. William F. Herrin, Southern Pacific's political operative and the bête noire of the Progressives, joined the board the next year. Dudley Evans, who had risen through the ranks as an expressman in Oregon, was named acting president on the same date that Harriman joined the board and then became president on September 15. The October meeting of the board of directors was held in Harriman's office at 120 Broadway.

There was no doubt where the power now resided. The geographic focus had also shifted back to New York City. Never president of the company, Harriman was the all-powerful chairman of the board's executive committee. The minutes of the executive committee and the board, never voluminous, now shrank to mere mentions of who was present.

It was Evans who presided over the fiftieth anniversary of Wells Fargo on March 18, 1902. Each employee of the company received a silver medal. Engraved on one side was a stagecoach and horses and a pony express rider shooting at an Indian, who was about to loose an arrow at the mounted man. On the other side were a steam engine, coal car, and railroad express car; factories belching smoke; an oceangoing steamship; and symbols for the express and banking services and "Fidelity," the latter being a clenched fist emitting rays.

Evans, a Kentucky colonel in the Confederate army, was "a gentleman of the old South, handsome, courteous, and courageous," said Hungerford, the former Wells Fargo executive. Harriman, a northerner, was brusque to the point of rudeness. The newly elected president waited to be summoned by Harriman. There was the matter of a contract with the Union Pacific, which Wells Fargo had never been able to secure. Surely the company would now be given the route it had sought since 1869.

The expressman broke down and called on Harriman, who abruptly told him: "We have given the express contract on the Union Pacific to the American Express Company." That was that. Wells Fargo never did conduct business on the Union Pacific line, which extended east from Ogden, Utah.

The venerable express company was experiencing the ebbs and flows in fortune of any longtime business enterprise. It soon received another crippling blow. The express lost its longtime partner, the bank.

*   *   *

The Nevada Bank was founded in 1875 in San Francisco with a huge infusion of money from the Comstock Lode. It was the largest bank in California, and its initial capitalization of $10 million rivaled the largest banking house in New York City. The growing of wheat was the dominant industry in the Central Valley, and the Nevada Bank specialized in risky wheat loans. It handled the huge Southern Pacific Railroad account and the account of Tevis's large landholding company. The Nevada Bank suffered from financial mismanagement, so the directors, including Collis Huntington of the Southern Pacific, looked south to Los Angeles and asked Isaias Hellman if he would run the bank.

Hellman was born in Germany and immigrated to the sleepy pueblo of Los Angeles in 1859. He grew with the city, and the city grew mightily in the late nineteenth century. Starting out working for relatives in a general store, Hellman began to speculate in real estate—a sure winner in Southern California, most of the time. Hellman established a small banking business in a corner of the store, then graduated to a proper building. Like Wells Fargo, Hellman skirted legality in California, since the state constitution prohibited banking—a law that was more honored in the breach.

Hellman's Farmers and Merchants Bank incorporated in California in 1871, while Wells Fargo remained a Colorado corporation. The banker and civic leader, who along with two partners donated the land that became the campus for the University of Southern California, played a key role in bringing the Southern Pacific to Los Angeles, for which Huntington was grateful. When Huntington called about taking over the San

Francisco bank, Hellman considered the move carefully. He headed north to the center of finance on the West Coast, while remaining president of the Los Angeles bank.

With a reputation as a conservative banker who made money, Hellman attracted business when he took over the Nevada Bank in 1891. A biography of the banker stated: "The 1891 reorganization of the Nevada Bank created the spectacle of numerous millionaires—many of them reportedly quite old and feeble—standing in line for hours waiting for a chance to purchase stock. The chance to be associated with a Hellman enterprise was too attractive to miss." Hellman said: "I believe in California enterprises, for I am a Californian. I have no interests in the East. This is my home and I expect to live and die here." And so he did.

Edward Harriman turned to Hellman, who was Southern Pacific's banker, after taking over Wells Fargo. The railroad man was not a banker, and he did not like Wells Fargo's loan portfolio nor the 50 percent surplus over deposits ratio. Harriman was mainly interested in the huge surplus, derived from the express company, which could be used to revitalize the Southern Pacific and Union Pacific lines. He sold the bank to Hellman in 1905.

Commenting on the sale years later as he was nearing the end of his long career with Wells Fargo as president of the bank, Frederick Lipman said: "We were always good. We were good in a sense that we never bragged about it, never thought about it. It was quite a matter of course. We were so good that we couldn't make much money, and that's what finally put us out of business by merging with the Nevada Bank."

On the one hundredth anniversary in 1952, bank president I. W. Hellman III said of the 1905 sale: "The banking adjunct of the Express Company had considerable difficulty in making any showing of earnings because of the large capital allocated to it, capital which was continually being added to by the very prosperous Express Company."

The banking and express functions were now owned by separate entities on both coasts, although there still was a tie that bound the two together. Harriman had received twenty thousand shares of stock in the bank as part of the sale agreement. Harriman and William Herrin were named directors of the new bank while retaining their seats on the Wells Fargo board.

The April 3, 1905, sale agreement allowed both entities to use the trade name of Wells Fargo, the first contractual arrangement that indicated the name had acquired value. It was the Wells Fargo Nevada National Bank in San Francisco, also known as "the Hellman bank," and Wells Fargo & Company in New York City, the Harriman-owned express company. Hellman was president and Lipman was elevated to vice president of the new bank. The Wells Fargo bank in New York was sold in 1911.

The Earthquake
and Fire

A T 5:12 A.M. on Tuesday, April 18, 1906, a moderately strong
earthquake struck northern California. At the Lipman home across
the bay in Berkeley the brick chimney collapsed, as did others in the
neighborhood. But the Lipmans had a gas range, so breakfast was prepared and Lipman left for work at his regular time, carrying his evening
clothes in a suitcase. He and Mrs. Lipman were scheduled to attend the
social event of the year, the fourth performance of the touring Metro-
politan Opera. The company was to perform Wagner's *Lohengrin* that
night.

On the ferry boat Lipman noticed plumes of smoke billowing above
the city, his first indication that there had been extensive damage. When
he landed at the foot of Market Street, horse-drawn fire engines were
frantically dashing about looking for a water main that worked. The cable cars were not running. Lipman, with suitcase in hand, walked up
California Street to the ornate bank building at Pine and Montgomery
Streets.

The Wells Fargo Nevada National Bank opened for business at 9
A.M., manned by virtually all its badly shaken employees. The fires
spread rapidly. The employees were ordered to evacuate by firemen at

10:30 A.M. The bank ledgers were hastily thrown onto the floor of the massive, supposedly fireproof vault on the first floor. Lipman barely had time to take his father's watch that he had inherited from the top drawer of his desk before hastily departing for home.

For three days and nights massive fires consumed three-fourths of San Francisco in what was this country's greatest urban disaster. With the water mains destroyed by the earthquake, firemen and soldiers inexpertly detonated massive amounts of dynamite in futile attempts to create firebreaks. It was probably the dynamite that reduced the bank to rubble and a few stray columns of standing bricks. The relatively new, six-story express building at Second and Mission Streets, where there had been little use of explosives, remained standing, albeit a torched shell, with all the historic company records reduced to ashes.

The two separate entities—the bank and the express company—rose to their greatest challenge.

On Thursday, Lipman sent a telegram from Oakland to banking centers elsewhere: "Wells Fargo Bank Building Destroyed Vault Intact Credit Unaffected." Hellman wrote correspondent banks on Friday that they had not yet opened the vault for fear that "the incoming oxygen will cause the contents to ignite." He reassured bankers elsewhere that the bank was in an "exceedingly strong position," with large cash reserves on hand and considerable balances with correspondent banks.

The bank set up temporary quarters at the undamaged home of Hellman's son-in-law, E. S. Heller, on Jackson Street. It was back doing limited business at the Heller home on Monday. The accumulated mail was sorted on the dining room table. There were no records. Composition books used by children were used to record transactions executed on trust. The losses amounted to less than $200 on thousands of dollars worth of payments.

Years later Lipman was asked by an interviewer in 1946 about a statement in *Time* magazine that Giannini's Bank of Italy was the only bank fully open after the earthquake and fire. He said:

That statement isn't so greatly exaggerated. The fact of the matter was Giannini could have gone to his vault, taken all the contents out. He could do it, but the other banks couldn't do it. We couldn't do it. I think young Giannini, if he had an advantage over the other banks, had a right to use it. I think I would have used it myself.

Giannini had used two wagons to haul the bank's money and records to his home south of San Francisco. The banker hid the cash in the ash pit of his living room fireplace. What would become the gigantic Bank of America literally rose from the $80,000 secreted in those ashes.

As the steel, concrete, and bricks slowly cooled, four guards, in two-man shifts, patrolled the rubble-strewn site of the Wells Fargo bank. A fire was kept going throughout the night to keep the guards warm. In the early morning hours they drank coffee to keep awake.

After two weeks, bank officials approached the vault with great trepidation. They opened it gingerly. The first sight of ashes on the floor was not encouraging. But the $3 million in gold and silver was intact, and there were enough unburned ledgers to reconstruct the bank's balance.

The bank moved eventually into a building at Market and Montgomery streets. Hellman represented the dominant mood of the financial community when he said: "The business men of our community are in buoyant spirits, filled with energy and with the determination, in rebuilding our city, to make it stronger and more beautiful than ever."

The express company and Harriman reacted similarly. At the stables on Folsom Street, three hundred horses and the neatly painted dark blue and gold delivery wagons were loaned to people needing to transport their household effects to a safe place. All the horses and wagons were returned. A circus tent was borrowed and set up on Franklin Street as temporary express headquarters.

Harriman, in his finest hour, rushed westward on a special train, issuing orders at telegraph stations en route that put his railroad and express company at the disposal of the public without charge. He set up headquarters from his railroad car on a siding in Oakland. A list of items from collection points throughout the country that was sent free by order of Harriman to the Episcopal Diocese in San Francisco consisted mostly of clothing for children and adults. Also sent were carpenter tools, books, and a "communion set 'for the sick.'"

Harriman's aid, in the form of free transportation and money, was given impulsively; but it was also a public relations coup. He was often quoted in the newspapers. He departed after two weeks in a rush to get back to New York City, where he faced a crisis with the stockholders of Wells Fargo that would partially dissipate the goodwill he had generated in San Francisco.

The following year, after Congress had appropriated $2.5 million in relief funds, Wells Fargo and other express companies submitted bills for their services that had been understood, at the time, to be free. Andrew Christeson, in charge of West Coast express operations for Wells Fargo, explained: "This company has not charged one cent for regular relief supplies, food, clothing and such things brought into San Francisco by express. We delivered more than 100 carloads of stuff free. . . . We have charged for government shipments. The government is not an object of charity."

The Critics Emerge

A s AN EXPRESS COMPANY and bank, Wells Fargo had courted the newspapers when it had good news to relate or a stage robber to capture. The inner workings and financial details of the company were rarely revealed. There were no state or federal reporting requirements for express companies. All that changed momentarily in the spring and summer of 1906 when the turbulent era of the trustbusters finally caught up with Wells Fargo.

From time to time in the past the powerful express companies had been subjected to fleeting journalistic probes. The *North American Review* pointed out in 1870 that the express companies, unlike the railroads, were "subject to no supervision." Of the four leading express companies with stated amounts of capital totaling $50 million, the magazine said that "probably not $15 million has ever been paid in or is represented by assets." But there was no way to determine the exact amount on which dividends were paid.

In 1905 *The Atlantic Monthly* pointed out that the four largest express firms in the country were Adams, American, United States, and Wells Fargo. The last, at $8 million, was capitalized at the smallest face value. American Express was largest at $18 million. But the western

firm operated over the most extensive and complex transportation system—48,000 miles of railway, steamship, and still a few stage lines.
American Express was right behind Wells Fargo, with freight carried on
45,000 miles of railways.

Referring to the express industry as a whole, the lead article in the
July edition of *The Atlantic* by Frank Haigh Dixon stated:

Of this large transporting agency, whose receipts reach the enormous sum of seventy-five million dollars [now equal to $1.4 bil-
lion] yearly, and which, for certain kinds of service, has become
apparently an indispensable part of our industrial mechanism,
the general public knows almost nothing. The companies neither make reports themselves, nor are reports required of them
by any governmental department. President Ingalls of the Big
Four testified before the Industrial Commission: "They manage
their own business by making agreements. I should be sorry to
have them put on the same [reporting] basis as railroads, so they
could not agree."

Dixon said it was common knowledge that the companies agreed
among themselves on what to charge. Rate wars were practically unknown. "Notices of changes in rates agreed to in conference between express companies appear as news items in the financial journals," the
writer added.

There were some fundamental disparities. That express companies
were common carriers had been determined by judicial review. The express companies derived all the benefits of being common carriers, yet
had none of the obligations of the railroads, who were also common carriers. Express companies and the railroads had merged or had interlocking directorates. Yet express companies, unlike the railroads, did not
come under the jurisdiction of the Interstate Commerce Commission.
Congress had repeatedly refused to pass such legislation.

Their future, Dixon hinted, was uncertain. With development of a

From 1905 to 1920, banker and philanthropist Isaias W. Hellman led Wells Fargo through the turmoil of earthquake and world war.

On April 18, 1906, a massive earthquake rocked San Francisco and destroyed Wells Fargo's bank building. (BEFORE ABOVE; AFTER BELOW) Within days, the bank reopened in temporary quarters in a private home.

Frederick L. Lipman, bank cashier, wired the bank's correspondent institutions: "Building Destroyed. Vault Intact. Credit Unaffected."

THE M.-N.ENG.

By 1904, Wells Fargo's express network reached from ocean to ocean, with 4,143 offices serving customers along 47,000 miles of rail, stage, and steamship lines.

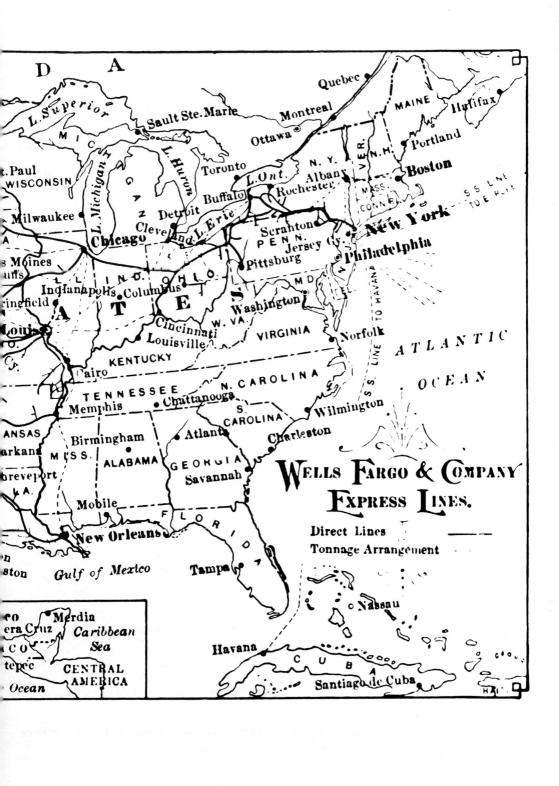

WELLS FARGO & COMPANY
EXPRESS LINES.

Direct Lines ————
Tonnage Arrangement

All across the Midwest and Great Plains, farmers brought their grain to a local elevator, where trains then transported the grain to market. *Courtesy Minnesota Historical Society.*

Wheat was the "gold" that built communities across the Midwest, a region served by Northwest Bancorporation member banks. *Courtesy Minnesota Historical Society.*

From the Farm

The Wells Fargo Food Products Department was organized to assist you in buying fresh produce direct from the country for less than city prices and to enable the farmer or producer to get better prices for what he sells.

We find people in the country who have fresh produce to sell, and arrange to receive weekly quotations from them.

Via Express

Every Monday we issue a bulletin in several cities, showing prices of seasonable fresh country produce.

These bulletins show cost both in the country and delivered to you, and are current during the week.

We send this bulletin to you each week upon request, free of charge.

Address Food Products Department

WELLS FARGO & COMPANY

51 Broadway   New York City

To the Family

Wells Fargo delivered fresh produce from the farm to the family.

Refrigerated railcars rushed fresh fruits and vegetables from growers in Pasadena, Texas, to consumers across the nation.

The original Northwestern National Bank building in Minneapolis, built in 1872, predecessor of the twentieth-century Norwest Corporation. *Courtesy Minnesota Historical Society.*

Bank note signed by Dorilus Morrison, first president of North Western National Bank. *Courtesy Minnesota Historical Society.*

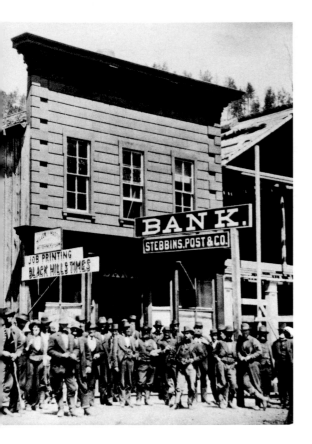

Boomtown bank: First National Bank of the Black Hills in Deadwood, South Dakota, founding member of Northwest Bancorporation. *Courtesy Minnesota Historical Society.*

Fargo, North Dakota, 1873: a town created by the Northern Pacific Railroad and named for William G. Fargo. *Courtesy Minnesota Historical Society.*

Driver Fred DeBenning poses with his wagon in Joplin, Missouri.

Wells Fargo's crew at St. Paul, Minnesota. *Courtesy Minnesota Historical Society.*

BLAZING
a new financial trail

An early ad for Northwest Bancorporation used a Conestoga wagon to advertise its services to the Northwest in the inaugural issue of *Fortune* magazine in 1930.

William Wallop and Frank Tausch at Anaheim, California, circa. 1910. *Courtesy First American Title Insurance Company.*

Driver Harry Kahl (RIGHT) and his motor truck, Detroit, 1917.

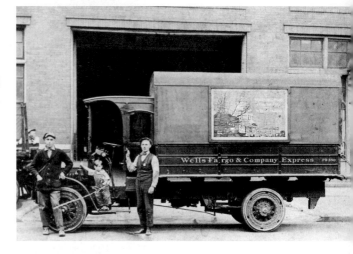

In *The Music Man*, a Wells Fargo wagon brings something special—shiny new band instruments—to the townspeople of River City, Iowa.

Commercial artist Edward Hopper illustrated wartime issues of the company magazine, the *Wells Fargo Messenger*.

The *Wells Fargo Messenger* covered the company's express business from Alaska to New York, Chicago, and the people and places in between.

Women filled the express ranks during World War I. These five held the fort on the home-front in San Diego, California.

Loans to World War I veterans helped boost America out of the Great Depression. Here veterans line up outside Wells Fargo Bank & Union Trust Company in San Francisco.

Two company icons graced this 1923 publication: the stagecoach and the landmark Wells Fargo building in San Francisco.

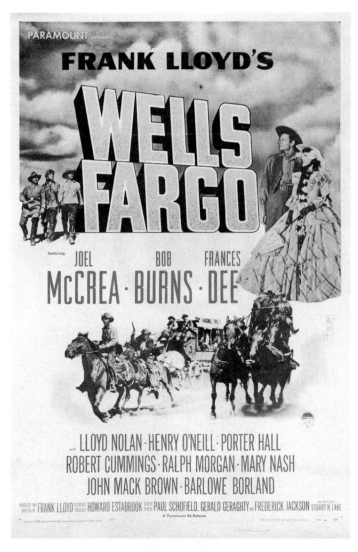

Frank Lloyd's 1937 Paramount feature film *Wells Fargo* starred Joel McCrea and Frances Dee.

Northwestern National Bank adopted a well-known pioneer symbol—the covered wagon. *Courtesy Minnesota Historical Society.*

Northwest Bancorporation banded together community banks like this one in Aberdeen, South Dakota. *Courtesy Minnesota Historical Society.*

Beginning in 1949, a giant weatherball broadcast weather forecasts to Twin Cities residents from the roof of the landmark Northwestern National Bank building in Minneapolis. *Courtesy Minnesota Historical Society.*

Carl E. Reichardt, chief executive officer of Wells Fargo 1982–1994, and Paul Hazen, chief executive officer 1995–1998.

Lloyd Johnson, Norwest chief executive officer 1984–1993.

Richard M. Kovacevich, Norwest and Wells Fargo chief executive officer 1993–present.

parcel post system by the U.S. Post Office not far off and with railways taking over the fast freight business, it might be possible "to do away with the express service altogether." In a dozen years such an unlikely idea would become a reality.

It was the secrecy that mostly bothered Dixon and others like him who had come to distrust monopolies. He said, "Nothing more is known of these great transportation agencies by either national or state government than is known of the operations of a corner grocery in rural New England."

* * *

It was exactly such sentiments being uttered by Wells Fargo express stockholders that Harriman was rushing back to New York to squelch. Harriman, a controversial figure who always courted and attracted press attention, was greeted by a throng of reporters in Grand Central Station who wanted to know about the earthquake *and* the revolt of stockholders that was bringing Wells Fargo unsought and unprecedented publicity.

The express company had been under siege since the beginning of the year to raise its annual dividend. Some stockholders maintained that Wells Fargo had a surplus of $20 million, with an additional $3 million accumulating yearly. Led by Walter C. Stokes of the New York Stock Exchange firm of the same name, the stockholders wanted the dividend doubled from 8 to 16 percent, a more representative board of directors, and an end "to the policy of secrecy."

The Harriman-controlled board of directors said the surplus was needed to purchase express rights on the Union Pacific, which Harriman owned. After Harriman granted those rights to the American Express Company, the directors dropped that particular argument. As the summer of 1906 wore on, what was first described as a mere internal controversy became a full-fledged fight waged openly in the newspapers and unprecedented in the company's history.

Wells Fargo, meaning Harriman, since he was the chairman of the board's executive committee and controlled the most stock through his ownership of the Southern Pacific Railroad, moved to mollify the dissident stockholders. The dividend was raised to 10 percent and a financial report, albeit skeletal, was issued publicly for the first time. The report showed reserves of $20.4 million, including cash, real estate, accounts receivable, and stocks and bonds.

The opposition countered that the stocks and bonds were undervalued, no valuation had been given for equipment, the report lacked specifics, and there was no answer to the question of whether the company had loaned money to its directors, meaning Harriman. The lawyer for the dissident stockholders, Samuel Untermyer, said, "We want to know not only what Mr. Harriman will do but what he has done."

Untermyer and his group filed suit. The New York City judge dismissed it because Wells Fargo was a Colorado corporation. *The New York Times* thought it "a peculiar charter" that allowed Wells Fargo's principal offices to be located outside of Colorado and noted that the charter had been issued when Colorado was a territory with lax laws.

To prepare for the annual meeting, where the fight would be decided, Harriman sent his representatives out into the field to buy stock. They paid $320 a share, when the stock market price was $275. Before the controversy, the stock had sold for $175. Harriman owned ten shares of Wells Fargo stock in his name. *The Times,* giving no specifics, said that the Southern Pacific was "a heavy stockholder."

On July 31, a more detailed financial statement—derived from the court pleadings and thus public knowledge already—was made available to stockholders and the press by Wells Fargo management. It listed the same assets and gave them a total value of $20.7 million. "No loan is made directly or indirectly to any Director," the report stated. The condition of the company was "sound and substantial."

The tumultuous, six-hour annual meeting, orchestrated by the Harriman forces, was held on August 9. The lawyers, Untermyer for the disaffected stockholders and William Nelson Cromwell for Harriman, dueled with both general arguments and specific motions. Votes were taken, but since they had to be counted by hand in another room, the outcomes were not known before the next motion was made and voted upon.

Cromwell made the crucial motion to retain the present dividend with a ringing defense of Harriman that would haunt the railroad magnate. The lawyer said:

> The express business lives by favor. It is entirely dependent upon its railroad connections. There is only one man to be thanked for what the company has gained through the favor of the railroads. It is not on the business acumen of the officers, but on his wonderful executive genius on which the stockholders must rely if the prosperity of the company is to continue. He cannot be replaced, for he moves in *a higher world into which we may not enter* [emphasis added].

The press immediately picked up on the phrase "higher world," and by constant repetition deflated Harriman's elevated status. Harriman won the vote three to one. He died three years later.

LOADING REFRIGERATOR express cars, Angleton, Texas, 1904.
Courtesy Brazoria County Historical Museum.

III

I 9 O 7 – 2 O O O

FEEDING THE NATION

FRANK DIXON, in his remarkably incisive and prescient *Atlantic* article, pointed out that the greatest contribution of the express business was the door-to-door service of perishable food items carried in refrigerator cars. "The individual now has the option between slow shipment by freight at reasonable cost, with an added charge for cartage at destination, and transportation on passenger trains with store-door delivery. For the superior service he pays, on the average, four times as much."

It was worth it for shipment of such foodstuffs as fresh meat, fish, fruit, vegetables, and oysters—the latter previously embedded in ice by Henry Wells in the 1840s for shipment from Albany to Buffalo. The express service had come full circle, except that now whole railroad cars were cooled by ice.

Wells Fargo's fast shipment of foodstuffs, both nonrefrigerated and cooled, from the warm West Coast and the Southwest to the cold Northeast and elsewhere, was its third major national contribution. A healthier diet, for those who could afford the higher-priced food items, was the result. Feeding the nation, although less exciting than operating the Pony Express and chasing outlaws, was far more significant.

The express company was nurtured on mineral wealth in its early years, as was the West. The region would gain a measure of maturity and stability, and California would become the leading producer of agricultural products in the late nineteenth and twentieth centuries.

Lloyd Tevis saw the change coming in 1881 when he addressed the American Bankers Association: "It is already evident, that in the agricultural capabilities of her soil lie the possibilities of California's greatest wealth. California is today not a mining, but an agricultural State." The wheat crop was already three times as valuable as the mineral crop. "But, great as are the possibilities of grain-growing in California," continued Tevis, "it is now becoming apparent that the most valuable of her industries in the future will be that of the vineyard and orchard."

Wells Fargo had been involved in agriculture from the beginning.

From Wayne County, New York, seventeen thousand strawberry plants were shipped by steamer to the Shell Mound Nurseries and Fruit Gardens in the San Francisco Bay Area's Alameda County. Buyers were urged in an ad in *The California Farmer* to contact either the nursery, established by Wells Fargo banker Reuben Washburn in 1852, or the Wells Fargo office in San Francisco.

Washburn and his associates sought free publicity from their marketing efforts. The *Sacramento Union*, commenting on a shipment of strawberries from the nursery, stated in what was clearly a plug for a freebie:

Through Wells, Fargo & Co's Express we were favored recipients on yesterday of a bowl filled to the rim with the handsomest and largest strawberries we have ever seen in this State. A single strawberry picked from the generous pile before us measures three inches and three quarters in circumference. These were all plucked on the 3rd of December, which fact will probably somewhat astound our Baltimore and Cincinnati readers, who are in the same latitude with Alameda.

John Sutter, on whose Sierra Nevada foothills property gold had been discovered in 1848, shipped fruit from his Hock Farm on the Feather River via express in 1856. A native of Switzerland, Sutter wrote a customer: "After having reflected I thought it better to send you the grapes and figs per express so that you receive them without delay because it cannot be much depended on the boats at present and the expenses are not much greater and then the fruit is not exposed to the crew of the boat."

The express company and the wine industry were partners from the start.

Agoston Haraszthy, a Hungarian exile now known as "the father of the modern California wine industry," traveled to Europe in 1861. He toured the wine regions of France, Germany, Italy, Spain, Prussia, and England and shipped back 200,000 cuttings and rooted vines representing 1,400 varieties of grapes that were catalogued under 499 separate names.

What happened next is described in Vincent P. Carosso's *The California Wine Industry: A Study of the Formative Years*: "A gardener cared for the collection en route; at New York they were examined, packed, and shipped by Wells Fargo steamer to California. They arrived in San Francisco 'in the very best condition' in February, 1862." The cost to Haraszthy for shipping via the express company was $1,549. Haraszthy had hoped to recover his travel and shipping costs from the California Legislature, but that never happened. By the next fall 300,000 rooted vines were ready for sale.

Another European émigré played a key role in the Napa Valley. In 1866 Leopold Lazarus, a native of France, was appointed the Wells Fargo agent in St. Helena. In this capacity he served the winemakers in the valley. Lazarus also owned a general store. He purchased sixteen acres near town in 1869 and planted them with some of Haraszthy's vines. The agent-storekeeper-winemaker sold the property in 1881 for $7,500, a tenfold increase over what he had paid for it twelve years earlier, and a harbinger of escalating land values to come.

By 1900 California was producing 80 percent of the nation's wine; but it wasn't very good wine, being mostly *vin ordinaire*. The large dealers in the state had formed the California Wine Association, which graded wines so that quality was consistent and price was tied to quality.

On March 3, 1901 the headline "Hellman Controls the Trade in Wine" appeared over a news story in the San Francisco *Examiner* that began: "Banker Hellman and his financial associates have obtained control of the California Wine Association and with it the control of the viticultural industry of California."

The reporter sought out Isaias Hellman, who owned vineyards in Southern California, the Nevada Bank in San Francisco, and would shortly take over Wells Fargo Bank. He asked if Hellman now controlled the California wine industry. The banker replied:

> We have not formed a combination to raise the price of wine. That must be regulated by supply and demand. The greater part of California wine being made for export, we cannot increase the price very largely, for fear of the competition of the imported wines. We want to assist the wine grower as well as the manufacturer, and propose, as far as we are able, to keep the price of the grape up, so as to encourage the production of good grapes. We deal only in Californian wines, and our ambition is to put the industry on a solid basis, which we believe we have accomplished.

The newspaper story noted that by 1900 all the major wine dealers in the state had joined the association, and added: "Those who sold their stock in the association have been regretting it ever since, for the price of stock has considerably increased."

*   *   *

Wells Fargo's contributions to early agricultural efforts in the state were not limited to the coast. In central California there was a lively farm products trade on the Sacramento Valley Railroad between Folsom and Sacramento. Cheese, butter, eggs, fish, onions, cabbage, grape cuttings, and flowers were dispatched over the line in 1856. Wells Fargo shipped agricultural products to the state fair in Sacramento free of charge.

General superintendent John Valentine encouraged the agricultural trade. In 1879 he issued a "special rate notice" to all agents that lowered the rates for regular dealers and hotel owners. "We hope you will earnestly urge its advantages to shippers," Valentine wrote, "and solicit their business, and thereby promote the company's interest and your own also."

Orchards replaced placer mines in the hilltop town of Newcastle, northeast of Sacramento, and W. J. Wilson and Sons, a Newcastle fruit packer, emerged as the largest shipper of deciduous fruit in the state in 1889. In the record year of 1909 the fruit shipped via one hundred express cars weighed 130,000 tons.

From nearby Auburn, thirteen growers used Wells Fargo's express service to ship a wide variety of fruits, including strawberries, blackberries, raspberries, pears, peaches, apricots, cherries, plums, grapes, nectarines, quinces, apples, and oranges. Close by at Penryn, the Wells Fargo agent pleaded in 1898 with his counterpart in the desert mining town of Eureka, Nevada, to find customers for his fruits and vegetables: "We are shipping more fruit than any other town in the state, getting out from four to eight car-loads a day, so we have plenty of stock to choose from," said the Penryn agent.

California fruit, shipped by Wells Fargo express, was deluging markets from San Diego to Boston. On March 1, 1901, the agent in Haywards, now called Hayward, sent out an advisory. It stated: "I take pleasure in announcing that our vegetable season is now at hand and will be in full blast for the next three months." One Hayward grower, H. W. and W. E. Meeks, also known as the Meeks Estate, shipped asparagus, cherries, currants, gooseberries, and strawberry rhubarb to Fresno, Los Angeles, Riverside, and San Diego in California; Spokane, Washington; Ogden and Salt Lake City, Utah; Butte, Montana; Grand Junction and

Denver, Colorado; Fort Worth, Dallas, and El Paso, Texas; Wichita, Kansas; St. Paul, Minnesota; Boston, Massachusetts; and Mexico City, Mexico.

Wells Fargo agents had a hand in initiating the growing of at least two important crops: cantaloupes and rice. Since they worked at least partially on a commission basis the agents aggressively sought to promote business.

The Indio agent, Duncan Campbell, spotted early maturing cantaloupes in a resident's garden, thus the beginning of the lucrative melon crop in the Coachella Valley, which spread to the nearby Imperial Valley in Southern California. Seventeen freight cars of melons were shipped the first year to Los Angeles and San Francisco in 1901. Seven years later 1,897 carloads were dispatched to all parts of the country.

Sylvester L. Cary, the agent for Wells Fargo and the Southern Pacific in Jennings, Louisiana, was instrumental in starting the rice industry on the Gulf Coast by promoting the settlement of the area. "In the space of ten years the prairies of Louisiana had been transformed from barren land sparsely populated with Cajuns, their cattle, and Providence stands of rice into a booming and highly mechanized rice-growing area," stated a book on the subject.

Wells Fargo employees banded together in Arkansas and purchased 235 acres. They raised strawberries, blackberries, raspberries, and orchard crops on their joint property. *The Express Gazette* congratulated them on their enterprise: "Besides offering a safe method of investment, the fact that expressmen themselves are growers will have a tendency to unite the fruit-growers of that section, and materially help the express business."

Near the end of the nineteenth century the New York–based trade publication, being somewhat protective of East Coast interests, complained about the abundance of California fruit: "Since the vast fruit productions of prolific California, this department of freight, coming as it does over such an immense surface, requires rapid handling to insure delivery in good order; yet the business has assumed tremendous proportions on account of its earlier production, and our markets are literally glutted with California products some weeks in advance of our Eastern fruit harvests."

Wells Fargo was quite active on the East Coast. With its access to the Erie railroad and subsidiary lines, the express company shipped peaches from Northern New Jersey to New York City. There was a bumper crop in 1900. Forty special cars were employed daily to transport between 350,000 and 400,000 baskets of peaches—at twenty-five pounds per basket—from ten stations along the line during the six-week season.

*　　*　　*

Fruits, vegetables, meats, and fish, however, were spoiling on the way to market, thus the invention of refrigerator cars that revolutionized the shipments of highly perishable foods to distant cities. Wells Fargo was the first company to adapt the refrigerator car to the specialized needs of the express trade. It would lead all express companies in shipment of foods via specialized refrigerated cars.

The raising and marketing of such fruits and vegetables was mostly a local affair before the development of refrigerator cars. Now it became national. Specialized crops in certain areas—such as tomatoes in Texas, peaches in Georgia, and oranges in California—were raised, harvested, and transported to where the price and demand were greatest.

Farm towns accordingly grew, thrived, or experienced downturns. Farmers were now at the mercy of distant markets and the monopolies that shipped their products. The carriers, in turn, needed the producers. It was a delicate balance. California fruit growers in 1901 thanked the Southern Pacific for its "improved service" while criticizing the railroad for its "excessive refrigeration rates."

Refrigerator cars achieved for the rural West and Southwest in the early years of the twentieth century what air-conditioning would later accomplish for the urban areas, and that was to greatly hasten development. Perishable fruits and vegetables flowed eastward, and towns grew in the wake of the increased trade.

Looking backward from the vantage point of 1920, a Federal Trade Commission report stated: "If the operation of the refrigerator car was to be profitable, it was necessary not only to solicit the freight for it but also actually to create traffic which would demand such a carrier. The private [nonrailroad] car companies did a great deal in developing specialized productive areas and in thus producing a better and more abundant supply of fresh fruits and vegetables."

The first experiments with refrigerator cars were undertaken in the 1860s. The first patent was issued in 1867. The cars had passed the experimental stage by 1885, but it would be another twenty years before they would be in general use. The meat companies were the first to adopt them. The railroads did not want to invest in something that seemed experimental. Harriman's companies, the Southern Pacific and Union Pacific, leased refrigerator cars from the Armour Company.

The ventilator refrigerator car, as it was technically known, was an insulated freight car with ice bunkers at both ends. The bunkers were filled with ice dropped manually through two hatches. The water from the melted ice flowed onto the tracks through a pipe in the bottom of the bunker. Passenger cars were also cooled by ice at first.

There were two types of bunkers. Both admitted cool air while the train was moving. One bunker was made with overlapping wooden slats that didn't touch; the other was constructed from wire mesh, which allowed more air to circulate through the car. Sometimes small amounts of salt were added to the ice to slow the melting process.

Melting was a problem, particularly in the hot Southwest. Besides the climate, heat emitted from the particular fruit or vegetable was a factor. Ten thousand pounds of ice could be reduced to a negligible amount before the train even left the station.

Huge, expensive precooling facilities were constructed to lower the temperature in the refrigerator cars before they were loaded in Colton, San Bernardino, and Roseville, California. For the first two or three days of the six-day trip to Chicago, or the nine-day trip to New York, the ice melted quickly. Then the rate declined. Re-icing facilities were located along the route. The existing ice was tamped down to make as much room as possible for the new ice.

The cost of shipping rose accordingly, but there were huge benefits. Referring to the history of the California fruit trade, the FTC report said: "The refrigerator car stabilized the citrus-fruit industry and aided in its development until it has now become the most important perishable crop movement in the country."

The refrigerator cars were attached to slow-moving freight trains. To remain competitive, Wells Fargo had to offer a faster alternative. That meant developing a refrigerator car that could be coupled to through passenger trains.

Such a car had to meet special requirements. They included movable trucks, meaning the set of wheels under each end of the car. When operating on different lines, the body of the refrigerator car had to be transferred to those sets of wheels that matched the new line. The refrigerator cars would otherwise have to be repeatedly unloaded and loaded, thus losing precious time and ice. The wheels also needed to be adapted to higher speeds, increased safety requirements, and the height of passenger cars.

Dudley T. Mervine was the Wells Fargo superintendent in Kansas City in 1897. He transformed a small baggage car into a refrigerator car in order to haul butter, eggs, dressed poultry, fruit, and vegetables from stations in agriculturally rich Kansas to the arid mining districts in southern Arizona. The car with built-in ice chests ran once a week and grossed $1,000, of which a tidy $500 went to Wells Fargo.

There was profit in the venture, so ten refrigerator cars compatible with fast passenger trains were built the following year. More were added with the familiar Wells Fargo markings and colors each year, increasing

in total carrying capacity from twenty-five to thirty-seven tons. Pure
ventilator cars, without refrigeration but with increased circulation of
air, were also constructed to carry less perishable items and "dry" express matter, meaning nonfood items.

The minutes of the December 22, 1904 board of directors meeting
noted: "A request from the President was presented, asking for authority
to cause the construction of at least twenty refrigerator cars, found to be
necessary to facilitate the operation of the company and on motion, duly
seconded, he was duly deputed to the effect." By such convoluted language Wells Fargo embarked upon yet another era in its history, which
had begun with the stagecoach and was soon to include the gasoline-
driven truck.

Wells Fargo concentrated on the high-end early-season and late-
season shipments and the crops that spoiled the fastest. Others carried
the bulk of the in-season refrigerated goods in slower moving freight
trains. When the exclusive contract with the Armour Company lapsed in
1906, Harriman organized the Pacific Fruit Express Company as a subsidiary of the Southern Pacific and the Union Pacific. Pacific Fruit became the largest owner of refrigerated cars in the country. But most of its
cars were not compatible with passenger trains. Thus Harriman remained dependent on Wells Fargo for true express shipments. (Pacific
Fruit owned between sixty and eighty refrigerator cars that could be attached to passenger trains. They were referred to as "Wells Fargo cars,"
since they were operated by Wells Fargo.)

By 1912 the 117 cars that Wells Fargo owned were beginning to show
their age. It was necessary to upgrade forty cars to meet the railroads'
standards, and new cars needed to be added to the fleet. At the August
meeting, the board authorized that action. It also decided to begin re-
placing horse-drawn wagons with motor trucks "on a conservative basis" in the outlying areas of large cities "where long hauls were unduly
wearing on horseflesh."

Thirty-five new cars were added to the refrigerator fleet in 1913.
Wells Fargo paid attention to its image. As with the Concord stage-

coaches, appearance was important. "Besides being built for service," the company magazine reported, "the new cars are constructed with an eye for attractive appearance, as they are to be carried only in passenger trains and should be in as good trim as the passenger coaches. In addition, the new cars are finely lettered and bear also the widely familiar Wells Fargo escutcheon."

One hundred and fifty Wells Fargo refrigerator cars traversed 4,540,900 miles of tracks in 1913, "speeding delicate western fruits and vegetables to eastern consuming cities," according to the company's in-house publication, the *Wells Fargo Messenger*. California was the point of origin of most shipments. May was the busiest time of year, with 370 carloads being shipped that month to eastern markets. Chicago received 206 carloads and New York City 247 in 1913.

The beginning of the long journey was documented at Florin, then a small town a dozen miles south of Sacramento, in a 1913 *Messenger* article. The writer was obviously from the home office in New York City.

"About half-past four you'll see them begin to come," says Mr. McKinstry [the Wells Fargo agent], and the words are hardly out of his mouth before they do come, wagon after wagon of them, making a terrific dust down the highway that leads from the county road direct to the little yellow railroad depot. The wagons—there are thirty, forty, fifty of them—sweep around in a circle to a string of our refrigerator cars, "reefers," as the Wells Fargo boys out on the West Coast call them, and the little brown men [Japanese growers] begin transferring the fruit from their wagons into the cars as quickly and as systematically as a three-ring circus come to a small town begins the infinite business of a big day.

To attract more express business, Wells Fargo initiated its "Fargo Fast" service—four days from coast to coast. A huge steam engine was superimposed over the outline of a stagecoach and horses on a 1915 sign advertising the service that read: "Across the Continent the Fargo Way. Once 32 days now 4 days." Hauling seven cars, the express freight train stopped only to change crews and take on fuel and ice.

When the express companies surrendered their businesses to the federal government in 1918, the new Railway Express Agency received seventy-five refrigerator cars from the American Express Company and one hundred seventy-five from Wells Fargo. Years later Dudley Mervine reminisced with fifty-five fellow expressmen at a Los Angeles dinner. "So far as my information extends," Mervine said, "the first express refrigerator car service in equipment specially constructed for passenger train movement was that instituted by Wells Fargo & Company in 1897 while I was superintendent of that company at Kansas City."

The Midwest

With its acquisition of express contracts on regional railroads in 1909 and 1911, some dozen years after initiating its coast-to-coast service, Wells Fargo offices blossomed in such midwestern states as Iowa; and the facilities in the hub cities of St. Louis and Chicago were greatly enlarged.

The Midwest became an important element in the operations of the express company after mining faded in the interior western states and farming expanded elsewhere. The first Wells Fargo agency in Iowa was opened in 1872, then closed shortly thereafter. Ten years later Council Bluffs got its first express office, and the following year three additional offices opened for business in the state.

Stagecoaches fanned out from railroad stops with goods shipped via Wells Fargo for more remote communities. Perishable farm products from Iowa began showing up on tables in New York City. Fresh fish, mail-order goods, and an opera singer's piano were shipped into the state. At least eight Iowa offices had women agents.

The company's office in Mason City was typical of its operations in smaller cities throughout the Midwest. With the acquisition of express privileges on the Chicago, Milwaukee & St. Paul Railroad system in

1909, which connected with the Northern Pacific and the Erie railroads to provide transcontinental service, Wells Fargo entered new territory that included north central Iowa.

The importance of Iowa to Wells Fargo was underscored by the fact that only Wisconsin had more principal agencies in the region in 1909. The region included such populated states as Illinois and less populated ones like North Dakota, where one of the offices was located in Fargo. The territory was the responsibility of Grover B. Simpson, the general superintendent in Chicago. The Iowa Division was ruled by Thomas P. Earl in Des Moines. At the top of the chain of command was Edward Harriman in New York; at the bottom was L. E. Day in Mason City.

The Wells Fargo office was located in the City National Bank building, constructed in 1884 of native limestone in the Italianate style. In 1910 the bank moved across State Street into a new structure that couldn't have been more different in architectural concept. Instead of copying and modifying what was thought to be European, the bank moved into a structure designed in the indigenous Prairie School style by Frank Lloyd Wright.

The new bank building was the talk of the town when Meredith Willson was eight years old. Another major downtown event that occurred while Willson was growing up in Mason City—the River City of his show *The Music Man*—was the fire that destroyed one whole city block in January of 1913. The *Messenger* reported:

> Offices of the telegraph company and the other express companies were completely burned out, but the fire was fairly under control by the time it reached the Wells Fargo office. Our people succeeded in saving everything, including new fixtures, which had been installed during December at a cost of several hundred dollars. The office was pretty well mussed up by the fire, and the exterior was soon encrusted with ice, as can be seen in the photograph carried in these columns.

As a youngster, Willson was acutely aware of sounds, not unusual for someone who would grow up to be a composer, flautist, and conductor. "Sounds stay in your memory longer than anything else, it seems to me," he wrote years later. "The older I get, the clearer I can hear the sounds that were the dimensions of the world during my first seven or eight years in it back in Mason City."

There were the sounds of his mother scraping burnt toast downstairs as he was dressing for school; the screen door slamming in summer; snow shovels scraping in winter; the sound of rugs having the dust beaten out of them during spring cleaning; the click of a peewee being dropped into a box of marbles; roller skates on the sidewalk; the milk wagon; and finally the clip, clop of the horse pulling the Wells Fargo wagon.

The Wells Fargo wagon was an unforgettable sight. They were always kept in neat trim. There were two types, a one-horse and a two-horse version. The lengths of their square beds were either eight or twelve feet. There was a rigid top with mesh curtains that could be raised or lowered. The dark blue wagons had red wheels and were painted light green inside. The lettering in a Roman typeface was gold leaf outlined in red. The driver sat on a raised box. The helper sat in back, ready to jump off and load or unload.

Near the end of Act I of *The Music Man*—book, music, and lyrics written by Meredith Willson—the people are gathered in the center of the town at noon on a Sunday. The stage directions call for "horse music," and Gracie Shinn rushes in exclaiming: "Papa! The Wells Fargo Wagon is just comin' up from the depot."

The crowd replies in hushed anticipation: "The Wells Fargo wagon!"

The scene continues:

(MAYOR) SHINN: "A Likely Story! At this hour of the day? Nonsense! . . . The Wells Fargo Wagon?"
GRACIE: "It could be the band instruments!"
SHINN: "The band instruments!"

> *(The people form, looking up the street listening for the*
> *horse's hooves which are now heard plainly in the music.)*
> THE PEOPLE (sing):
> *"O-ho the Wells Fargo Wagon is a-comin' down the street*
> *"Oh please let it be for me*
> *"O-ho the Wells Fargo Wagon is a-comin' down the street*
> *"I wish, I wish I knew what it could be."*

A recitation of what various voices in the crowd have received via Wells Fargo follows. The items have the ring of authenticity: maple sugar, a gray mackinaw, grapefruit from Florida, a bathtub and crosscut saw from Montgomery Ward, curtains, dishes, a double boiler, salmon from Seattle, a new rocking chair, raisins from Fresno, a cannon for the courthouse square sent by the Daughters of the American Revolution, and, finally and most important, the band instruments.

The curtain rings down on the first act.

Willson, who played in the high school band, based the musical on his memories of Mason City in 1912 when he was ten years old. At the age of sixteen in 1918, Willson left Mason City for New York City to study music. He called the upbeat finale of Act I "theater magic" in his book about the making of the musical.

Also using the services of Wells Fargo in Iowa at this time was Willard W. Beal, who founded the Iowa Securities Company in 1906. The Waterloo company specialized in financing home and commercial construction, rather than the usual farm loans. The Wells Fargo agent in Waterloo—population 12,000—was W. B. Curtis, whose office was at 100 East Fourth Street.

When Northwest Bancorporation acquired Iowa Securities in 1969, the bank's home loan business was substantially increased. Iowa Securities became Banco Mortgage Company and then Norwest Mortgage in 1983. Norwest Mortgage became the nation's leading originator of mortgages and in 2000 changed its name to Wells Fargo Home Mortgage to reflect the merger that had taken place two years previously.

*   *   *

St. Louis and Chicago were urban hubs, meaning that freight generally arrived from greater distances, was unloaded, and then shipped shorter distances to its destination. The reverse could also be true.

The activity in both cities was vastly increased in 1911 when Wells Fargo took over the express business on the Gould System, meaning those railroads bequeathed by the financier Jay Gould to his son, George, who then lost them to Edward Harriman and his bankers, Kuhn, Loeb & Co. The railroads included the Wabash, Iron Mountain, Missouri Pacific, and St. Louis Southwestern. They radiated out from St. Louis in all directions except the southeast.

Inbound freight destined for St. Louis from the north and east passed over one of the marvels of American engineering, the 6,222-foot long Eads Bridge built in 1874 over the Mississippi River, and the newer Merchants Bridge. The *Messenger* described the journey into the heart of the city:

> The passenger and express traffic finds its way through an intricacy of tunnels and of elevated railroad tracks into the broad train-shed of another of the giants of St. Louis—the Union Station. But before it enters the portals of that shadowy train-shed, the express must, perchance, pause at the west side of the tangle of station tracks. Five splendid buildings of brick, devoted to the transportation of small and valuable package freight, stand there. Of these, two are devoted exclusively to the business of Wells Fargo & Company, the one serving as an in-house, and the other—by far the larger, as the out-freight house of our company.

The company's main St. Louis office was located in the Victoria Building at 409 North Eighth Street. The fifty-eight wagons and the horses, which included a prized stallion named "Shamrock," were kept at two separate stables. The wagons served an area that extended beyond the city limits into the county to the west and what was then called University City and Wellston.

Ollie C. Ziegler went to work for Wells Fargo in St. Louis during the transition from horse-drawn wagons to trucks. The seventeen-year-old was a "wagon dog," or helper, on a truck. The federal trucks had solid tires, kerosene lights, and four-cylinder engines. There were no heaters nor any protection from the weather on the cabs' sides. The bed of the trucks resembled the bed of the wagons—solid for a few feet above the flooring and then enclosed in wire mesh with drop curtains suspended from a hard top for bad weather. They could haul three tons, as opposed to the maximum two-ton capacity of horse-drawn vehicles.

The horse-drawn wagons were pulled by matching pairs of Percherons, draft horses originally used in France to haul artillery and heavy coaches. Ziegler described them lovingly:

> When prancing, slow trotting just a bit faster than a walk, their necks bowed, champing at the bits, carrying their tails high, the driver's arms outstretched and holding a tight line, all made a never to be forgotten sight—a beautiful team, gleaming brass and celluloid rings, tassels and a shining well-made wagon. No truck can ever equal this, and I put in a lifetime of driving trucks, many of them new.

The early-morning scene at the express platform at Union Station was a carefully choreographed madhouse. There was the cackling or bawling sounds of livestock, the bang of trucks and wagons against the docks, yelling drivers, the searing blast of locomotive whistles and the woosh of escaping steam. There was the smell of frightened animals, acrid coal, and fresh sawdust sprinkled over everything to absorb the moisture.

Ziegler loaded fruit from Florida and California, large hog carcasses sent from the farm to relatives in the city, barrels of fish, and boxes and packages of every description. The general rule was the first item on was the last to come off. Then he and his driver, Maurice Willey, departed on route #133 in Federal truck #420. Should business not be brisk, they rendezvoused with other drivers at a saloon or restaurant until it was time to return.

During his long career as a trucker, Ziegler drove every type of rig that carried every kind of cargo. His most pleasant memories were of his time with the "old Express Company."

The acquisition of the same railroads that boosted business in Mason City and St. Louis accounted for a brisk increase of trade in the Windy City. Wells Fargo operated on eight railroad lines departing from three stations and the high-speed interurban line in Chicago. Approximately 2,500 employees served the company's local and national operations.

The mail-order catalogue business, centered in Chicago, had exploded; and Wells Fargo was positioned to deal with the heavy traffic that Sears Roebuck and Montgomery Ward generated. Edward Hungerford, the editor of the *Messenger* and in charge of advertising for Wells Fargo, traveled to Chicago in 1913 and was greatly impressed with what he saw: "In Chicago, the mail-order business has reached its very apotheosis. Starting in a variety of humble forms hardly a quarter of a century ago, this business, which must place almost its entire dependence upon national systems of rapid package freight transportation, has grown to proportions that can hardly be within the conception even of the men who gave birth to them."

No longer was each suit, skirt, or shirt home- or tailor-made. Now racks of such clothing were manufactured, advertised in catalogues, ordered by customers, and shipped and delivered by Wells Fargo to such distant communities as Mason City, Iowa, and Nevada City, California.

Hungerford visited what appears to have been the giant Sears plant on the west side, although in deference to the two large Wells Fargo customers in Chicago, he did not specify the plant's owner. The plant was eight stories high, employed nine thousand workers, and sprawled alongside a major railroad line. The editor called it "one of the largest single buildings in the world." Wells Fargo had its own shipping facility inside the plant, as did other express companies. Other Sears facilities, employing even more workers in the aggregate, were scattered throughout Chicago.

Hungerford, who was attuned to the power of advertising, was greatly impressed by Sears's efforts. Twice a year Sears sent out "a massive book of almost 1,500 closely printed pages," clearly the forerunner of today's skinnier, more specialized catalogues and Web pages. He wrote:

> You inquire as to the circulation of this volume.
>
> "Guess," laughs the mail-order man. You guess. Your guess is ridiculously low. You guessed a quarter of a million. The mail-order house last year printed seven million copies of its catalogue [equivalent to 8 percent of the nation's 1910 population]. To print it six acres of spruce forest are bared each day of the year—and it costs twenty-six cents to mail each copy of the book; a little advertising service which the mail-order house performs without cost to its patrons. But it makes up that loss. Advertising does pay. Some sixty or seventy thousand orders come pouring in upon it each working day, and last year it found that it had done a business of something more than eighty million dollars [$1.3 billion today]!

From what had been known as the Polk Street Station, and in 1913 was called the Dearborn Station, the Erie railroad's fastest freight train, the Erie Nine, made the express trip to Jersey City in under twenty-four hours, six days a week. It carried only Wells Fargo cargo. The Erie Thirteen served Wells Fargo's local needs along the same line.

Traditions died hard. The messengers still carried weapons on these counterparts of the stagecoach. Although train robberies had trailed off to nearly zero during the first eighteen years of the twentieth century, arms purchases had increased with the additional traffic. Wells Fargo bought single-action army, new-model army, and, mostly, police positive special revolvers from Colt between 1904 and 1918. Ithaca furnished Wells Fargo with double-barreled ten- and twelve-gauge shotguns with shortened barrels during the same period.

Messengers posed jauntily for photographs with pistols stuck in belts or more properly holstered. At the end of its existence in 1918, the express company employed three thousand shotgun messengers.

End of the Line

WELLS FARGO express became a fixture in New York City after its coast-to-coast service was initiated in 1888. Prior to that year the firm maintained an office in the city for a banking and foreign express business that had a single wagon available for transportation. In 1889 there were four offices scattered about the city and sixty wagons that collected and delivered goods as far north as 59th Street, where a local express company took over. Six wagons served Brooklyn.

The president, Dudley Evans, moved to New York in 1903. The treasurer's and accounting offices followed soon thereafter. All of the nation's large express companies were now located at the tip of Manhattan, at a time when American Express was invading the California market and Wells Fargo was making its presence known in the East. Harriman, through his railroads that gave access to California and ownership of Wells Fargo, made both these ventures possible. He profited mightily from each.

Most of Wells Fargo's headquarters operations were housed in a six-floor building at 51 Broadway, known as "fifty-one" to employees. They worked a six-day week in this city of "strategic importance" to the company's operations, although California still accounted for 35 percent of the business.

The main New York depot was actually located across the Hudson River in Jersey City. The Wells Fargo depot operation was housed in the large Erie railroad complex where the special express trains—like Fargo Fast and the Erie Nine—and the refrigerator cars attached to passenger trains were speedily unloaded and loaded. Ferries transported some four hundred Wells Fargo wagons—at first horse-drawn and then motor-driven—across the river to Manhattan, where they fanned out across the city.

There was a cost to this diaspora. The company suffered a loss of its western essence—its mystique, if you will—with the move back to New York City and the tight control exerted by Harriman. Wells Fargo became just another profitable business driven by one of the most successful capitalists of the day, and then by his bankers, estate, and associated interests after Harriman died on September 9, 1909.

It had been Harriman, through his president and front man, Colonel Evans, who had beaten back the stockholders' revolt in 1906 by successfully making the case against dividends beyond a "scale which may not be maintained and which restricts the growth and resources of the company." In three separate letters to stockholders in July of 1906, Evans had stated the "absolute" need for a large surplus in order to conduct a stable business and provide regular dividends.

Stock from smaller shareholders continued to be acquired after 1906. By mid-1909, the largest shareholders in Wells Fargo were Southern Pacific, Harriman, and various clerks employed in Kuhn, Loeb & Co., the bank that was closely associated with Harriman's Wells Fargo, Southern Pacific, and Union Pacific affairs. After Harriman's death, ownership shifted again.

Two months later the executive committee of Wells Fargo directors formed a special committee to look into "the general question of a dividend increase and a capital adjustment," an increase that would be considerably greater than what the directors had vehemently opposed in 1906.

On December 23, 1909, the board of directors, controlled by Harriman interests and presided over by Evans, approved a onetime $300 per share dividend "out of the accumulated surplus earnings of the company." Sixteen million dollars in new stock was to be offered to existing stockholders, which they could buy in proportions equal to their current holdings. Combined with three payouts of 5 percent dividends in 1910, the total dividend amounted to $26,796,740—the equivalent of 0.5 billion today.

The proportion of the onetime record raid upon the corporate treasury that benefited only a few stockholders was outrageous, even in terms of that laissez-faire era.

There was an explanation for such an unusual action. The Interstate Commerce Commission (ICC) was breathing down the necks of the express companies. In his history of American Express, Peter Z. Grossman mentions a similar raid by the directors of the Adams Express Company, one of the big three: "It looked, correctly, like an attempt to distribute the company's surplus before the ICC forced Adams to reveal just how wealthy it was—a revelation likely to produce stockholder outrage and even lawsuits. Most of all, the surprise dividend suggested that all express companies had much greater wealth than anyone had realized."

It took time for the Progressives to discover the express companies, bigger fish like Southern Pacific having diverted them. "The politicians and the muckrakers attacked the big, visible monopolies," Grossman wrote. "They started with companies like Standard Oil, but inevitably, they soon focused on one of the most secretive and most obvious targets of all, a monopoly business in every town in America, the expresses."

In 1911 Albert W. Atwood, a respected financial journalist, wrote of the huge Wells Fargo dividend of the previous year in *The American Magazine*, which published such crusading writers as Upton Sinclair, Lincoln Steffens, and Clarence Darrow:

Here, then, is a sober recital of Wells, Fargo facts. It is an un-
adorned narrative of how innocent investors were induced to
part with stock which was destined to pay extraordinary dividends, foreknowledge of which did not reach those outside the
"higher realm;" and of how the controlling interests in the company secured nearly all the stock before the dividend was declared. It is not a novel story. There are many counterparts in the
history of our corporations. But the cool effrontery with which
the "insiders" took their 300 percent dividend after having four
years before warned the stockholders against seeking an extra
dividend is without parallel.

With the publication of Atwood's three-part series on "The Great
Express Monopoly" and an investigation launched into express companies by the Interstate Commerce Commission, 1911 was not a banner
year. A synopsis of the company's activities for that year stated: "The
company, together with the other Express Companies, was confronted
with numerous inquiries and investigations by State Commissions and
the Interstate Commerce Commission as to the reasonableness of its
rates, regulations and practices." The dividend retreated to a more modest 10 percent.

From 1909 to 1911 there were four presidents, a period of confusion
ending with Burns D. Caldwell, who would guide the company to its
demise. Caldwell came from outside the expressmen's ranks; he was an
eastern railroad man who had headed various traffic departments. Hungerford, who worked for Caldwell, said: "He was a handsome man with
a great shock of snow-white hair, a million-dollar smile and invariably a
white carnation in the lapel of his coat." Caldwell would need that
smile. One jarring event piled upon the other in the second decade of the
new century.

The chief nemesis of the express companies was Franklin K. Lane,
who was appointed to the Interstate Commerce Commission by President Theodore Roosevelt in 1906 and left the commission in 1913 to be-

come Secretary of the Interior in the administration of President Woodrow Wilson. Lane, who had been the attorney for the City and County of San Francisco and had run unsuccessfully for governor of California, was from the Theodore Roosevelt mold of Progressivism. He was widely praised for his stance against monopolies on the commission but damned by some for approving construction of Hetch Hetchy Reservoir in Yosemite National Park when he became interior secretary.

His fellow cabinet member, Treasury Secretary William G. McAdoo, who would finish off the express companies in 1918, said: "Lane was plump, well fed and well groomed. He had a jolly look and he was charming socially. He loved to go out to dinners; I thought that he impaired his strength and usefulness by too much social life." Others knew Lane as a hard worker and a clear thinker.

With the help and resources of the ICC staff, Lane was able to take a longer, deeper, more incisive look at the express companies than any previous individual or representative of a government agency. He said that he was obsessed with the express case. Lane began an investigation into "the inextricable maze of express company figures" in 1911 at the request of the commission. A fellow commissioner, James Harlan, wrote:

Lane warned a group of high express officials gathered around him that unless they promptly coordinated their service more closely to the public requirements, revised their archaic practices, readjusted and simplified their rate systems so as to eliminate discriminations, the frequent collection of double charges and other evils, and gave the public a cheaper and a better service, the public would soon be demanding a parcel post.

The suggestion was received with incredulous smiles, one of the express officials saying, apparently with the full approval of them all, that a parcel post had been talked of in this country for forty years and had never got beyond the talking point, and never would.

The ICC issued a report, authored by Lane, on express company practices in 1912. It began with the observation that express companies
operating in tandem with the railroads were a unique American institution. Elsewhere the railroads performed the express function by themselves. In the previous year 300 million packages had been shipped over
218,013 miles of railroads, 18,385 miles of steamship and stage lines, and
6,665 miles of electric interurban lines. Up to recently, the companies
had respected each other's "zones of influence," Wells Fargo's zone being
west of the Mississippi River.

The four major firms—the Adams, American, United States, and
Wells Fargo express companies—were so interlocked and so interdepen-
dent—both financially and at the directorate levels—that they "may be
said to be almost a family affair," the report stated.

For instance, the single largest holder of Wells Fargo stock was the
widow of Edward Harriman. Mary Harriman was also the single largest
owner of United States Express Company stock. The second-largest
holder of Wells Fargo stock was the American Express Company. (When
American Express took over the express function on the Harriman-
owned Union Pacific in 1910, part of the purchase agreement called for
American Express to buy the Wells Fargo stock held by the Harriman-
owned Southern Pacific.) Mary Harriman held 27 percent of the total
Wells Fargo shares, American Express had 19 percent, and 53 percent was
divided among 1,991 shareholders. The thirteen Wells Fargo directors
owned a total of 1 percent.

None of the companies would disclose to the ICC the amount of cash
that had actually been invested in their stock, each giving a different ex-
cuse. Wells Fargo cited the 1906 earthquake and fire. "This company,"
said the ICC report, "states that owing to the destruction of old account
books it is unable to state what cash was paid in prior to 1870, and no
cash has been paid in since then excepting such as proceeded from its 300
per cent dividend of 1910."

The complexity and unfairness of the rate system was documented
in the report. "The ordinary express agent was lost in an effort to find a

rate." At the thirty-five thousand express offices in the United States, shippers were being both under- and overcharged, the report stated, and some were discriminated against. The result of the report was that both the ICC and the California Railroad Commission simplified and lowered express rates. Congress authorized the Post Office to undertake a parcel post service that same year, and it went into operation on January 1, 1913.

Wells Fargo responded by going after new business. A Food Products Department, headed by D. G. Mellor, was formed to expand shipment of fresh produce. Agents were encouraged to establish buying clubs within businesses and institutions. Fresh food would be shipped directly to these urban collectives via refrigerator cars. The vast marketing effort was extended to the fields, where agents encouraged cultivation of profitable products and raised the visibility of such crops as California oranges, figs, olives, and raisins that would appeal to new customers.

The company opened a Paris office. Its new traveler's checks were promoted with an advertisement that read: "Even a young girl may travel alone if she carries Wells Fargo Travelers Checks." The New York realist Edward Hopper painted eight covers for the *Messenger* in 1917 and 1918. One cover depicted a frock-coated waiter delivering a small box to an elegant woman in a hotel setting. It was titled: "An Early Morning Surprise—by Wells Fargo." As America became involved in World War I, Hopper's covers became more patriotic. They depicted seeds being delivered for a war garden, the purchase of savings bonds on the home front, and the purchase of Wells Fargo money orders by soldiers in France.

The dividend for 1914 was reduced to 7 percent, but the railroad mileage that Wells Fargo operated on was increased considerably by expansion into the central East Coast states. The Baltimore & Ohio Railroad was the system that brought the express company the most new mileage that year. (Louis McLane's father had been the founder of the Baltimore & Ohio and president from 1834 to 1847.)

By 1916 the number of Wells Fargo offices had reached a record 9,171 and the express agency was operating over 107,529 miles of railroad tracks, more than double the amount in its first coast-to-coast year of 1889. The express business profited greatly from World War I for a time, just as it had during the Civil War. The total dividend for 1916 zoomed up to 39 percent, the third highest in Wells Fargo's history. As the war wound down two years later, the reality of a declining business competing with the Post Office and overseen by government regulators forced the express companies to the bargaining table.

* * *

The March 1918 issue of the *Messenger* was devoted to "Women in the Express." The magazine noted that during the war women "have shown themselves to be competent to do work which, heretofore, has been considered only a man's job." In the future, the company publication pledged, jobs "are no longer to be allotted through sex traditions, but are to go to the persons most fit for them—be they in trousers or in skirts." Alas, the express company that pioneered in the employment of women would not have the chance to put that revolutionary concept into effect.

The railroads had failed to meet the needs of the war effort, so President Woodrow Wilson nationalized them. Treasury Secretary William Gibbs McAdoo was put in charge of the nation's railway system. The government did not honor the complex maze of railroad and express company contracts. The parcel post took business from the express companies. Profits, already shaky, turned to losses.

Representatives from the express companies met with Secretary McAdoo in January of 1918. Charles A. Prouty, a director of the ICC, was put in charge of negotiations for the government. He favored a merger and consolidation of all existing express companies under a single corporate entity that would be controlled by the government. The express companies reluctantly agreed, in principle, and sat down in February for three months of intense and sometime rancorous bargaining on how to divide up the business. Caldwell of Wells Fargo and George C. Taylor, president of American Express, nearly came to blows. Others in the room had to step between the two shouting men.

An agreement was finally reached. Taylor became the president and Caldwell the chairman of the board of the new American Railway Express Company, which would become the Railway Express Agency in 1928. Wells Fargo employees were none too happy that the first word in the new company's name was the same as their rival's, but the name reflected the reality of the merger. The largest financial stake in the new company, some 40 percent, went to American Express.

Wells Fargo directors and stockholders voted to subscribe to approximately one-third of the stock of the new corporation with $10,075,400 in property and cash. Seven shareholders representing 737 shares were present at the stockholders' meeting, and all were satisfied with the arrangement. The vast majority of shares, 173,845, voted in favor by proxy.

At the termination of its express business, Wells Fargo carried goods over 118,000 miles of various types of lines, the longest total distance of the eight express companies involved in the forced merger. (They were: Adams, American, Canadian, Great Northern, Northern, Southern, Wells Fargo, and Western express companies.) Wells Fargo's mileage was broken down in the following manner: railroads 77,400; steamships 35,000; interurban electric lines 4,400; and stage lines 1,200, whether horse-drawn or motorized stage routes was not specified. The most mileage was in Texas; California was second. The New England states, Florida, Georgia, and South Carolina were the only states not served by Wells Fargo in 1918.

The Wells Fargo express company, the lively child born in 1852, was buried sixty-six years later by its sibling. American Express eventually acquired what remained of the gutted company: its traveler's check business, Mexican and Cuban express businesses, certain rights to the name, the Pony Express symbol, and a controlling interest in the remainder of the nonbanking business. A subsidiary of American Express operated the armored car business under the Wells Fargo name and Pony Express logo.

It passed through various hands to become Loomis, Fargo & Company, a subsidiary of Borg-Warner Security Corporation.

But what about the 25,000 employees of the venerable express company? "It was a bitter pill to Wells Fargo men," Hungerford wrote. "That the name of their disliked competitor should be chosen, and that of their own beloved company ruthlessly thrust aside, was bad enough." What was worse, he said, was: "Once the new combination had been made, the Wells Fargo signs and insignia were torn down all the way across the land to be replaced immediately by the signs and insignia of the American Railway Express."

The Bank and the Brand

I N T H E sense of a continuous, traceable line throughout its history, Wells Fargo was now down to a single bank in San Francisco. The line was not straight—for there had been seismic shifts in 1869, 1902, 1905, and 1918—nor would it remain undiluted for the remainder of the twentieth century. But it was, nevertheless, a discernible line for one hundred and fifty years.

The express company had always been the dog that wagged the tail, and now the appendage was on its own. There was only one thing to do if the bank wanted to remain in business, and that was to add gradually to its bulk.

The inheritor of Wells Fargo's western legacy was housed in classically ornate offices remodeled after the 1906 earthquake and fire at the junction of Montgomery, Market, and Post Streets. The bank occupied the basement, first, and second floors of the twelve-story Nevada Bank Building. The liberal use of bronze, Italian marble, mahogany, and Circassian walnut lit by diffused lighting from above combined to project the image of stability, impregnability, and discreet wealth that banks strove to project in that era. The trade publication *Coast Banker* described the bank's unique interior:

The character of the design through the main banking room as well as the ornamental work in the safe deposit department, is worked out in modern Greek, with a feeling leaning towards the Byzantine, but is wholly original and highly decorative, and while the interior will present generally a strictly classical effect, it does not savor of the academic in any sense. The design throughout is very distinctive, and radically different from anything in its class, and carries with it all the dignity and atmosphere desirable for a room of this kind.

Isaias Hellman died in 1920, a much-beloved member of the banking, philanthropic, and Jewish communities in California. At the time he was one of the largest landowners in Southern California and had large real estate holdings in San Francisco. Hellman was succeeded as president of Wells Fargo Nevada National Bank briefly by his son, I. W. Hellman Jr., and then Frederick Lipman. In 1924 another Hellman bank, the Union Trust Company, was merged with Wells Fargo to form Wells Fargo Bank & Union Trust Company. The Union Trust bank building at Grant and Market Streets became a branch of Wells Fargo.

Three years after the merger Ira Cross wrote in his history of California banking: "The Wells Fargo Bank & Union Trust Company is the oldest bank on the Pacific coast from the point of continuous banking service, and is the first bank established in the West which still maintains its original identity in the matter of name." (Kevin Starr, then the San Francisco Librarian and later the California State Librarian, traced the longevity of businesses in the city in 1980. Twenty-three, Wells Fargo among them, had been established by 1852 or earlier. Among others were the Ghirardelli Chocolate Co., Gump's, Levi Strauss & Co., Shreve & Co., and the Tadich Grill.)

By 1928 Wells Fargo was sending and receiving rush shipments of money by airplane, thus making the transition to the next fastest mode of transportation. On March 2 the largest air shipment of money in California's history, $2.5 million, was flown from the state capitol to the San

Francisco bank and was deposited one hour after departing from Sacramento.

During its long history, Wells Fargo had survived eleven major depressions and panics. During the depths of the Depression, it ran an ad in the San Francisco *Examiner* under the headline "80 Years in True Perspective." Only an institution with such longevity, and an institutional memory that was able to recall it, could offer the following perspective—as pertinent now as it was then:

> During 80 years of this bank's existence, business has ebbed and flowed through many cycles . . . from the credit expansion of the '50s, followed by the panic of '57, to the bull-market boom of 1929, followed by the present readjustment period.
>
> The course of business has never followed the horizontal. Ceaselessly it has risen and fallen, risen and fallen. Expansion has been stimulated by the discovery of gold, the building of railroads, the opening of new lands, the supplying of the sinews of war, the development of new industries. And inevitably expansion has gone too far, and then deflationary forces have pulled business back to more solid foundations for growth.

While Wells Fargo could boast of a long history, it was never the dominant bank in San Francisco. First the Bank of California and then the Bank of America controlled most of the business. Then banks in Southern California extended their reach. In the late 1930s, the Bank of America had approximately five hundred branches, California Bank of Los Angeles had fifty-four, Security-First National Bank of Los Angeles had fifty-two, and American Trust Company of San Francisco had twenty-eight.

Lipman, who began his banking career in 1883, would have nothing to do with branch banking because of prior losses, and he had little enthusiasm for the bank's one branch. "We have today one branch—the Union Trust office. That little one-horse bank has $95 million in deposits and still I can't figure out if it pays," he said in 1931. "I know that if we have a $95 million bank with no banking troubles (they are taken care of here at Wells Fargo) it must pay, but it is hard to prove it."

The bank celebrated its one hundredth anniversary in 1952. I. W. Hellman III, the grandson of Isaias, was the president of what was a fairly sleepy financial institution. "In recent years the Country has heard much of branch banking," he said. "In more current times we have added a savings department and all the other ramifications of a modern bank, but we are essentially a commercial bank." Hellman said Wells Fargo operated under less pressure than New York banks.

His operating philosophy was the same as Lipman's:

Rule 1: The bank must be managed so as to be prepared, at all times, and under any conditions, to meet the utmost demands of its depositors. This must come before any other considerations.

Rule 2: Funds arising from the deposits may in part be put to productive use so as to create earnings, but not so as to infringe in any way on Rule 1.

Wells Fargo Bank & Union Trust Company changed its name to the more easily recognizable Wells Fargo Bank in 1954, but six years later the name of another bank was appended when Wells Fargo merged with the American Trust Company, acquiring its 102 branches and adding more in the years to come. The merger created the nation's eleventh-largest banking institution. It was heralded by newspaper ads: "Two oldest banks in the West: now *one* bank."

Wells Fargo Bank & American Trust Company bowed to tradition and became simply Wells Fargo Bank in 1962. History, at least as far as an exact name was concerned, was reclaimed in 1969 when the bank set up a holding company under the historical name of Wells Fargo & Company. Corporate identity was now a major factor in how the bank regarded itself and how it presented its image to the public.

*   *   *

The company's history had begun to be reclaimed around the turn of the century as the frontier faded and nostalgia for the past grew. At the World's Columbian Exposition in Chicago in 1893, Wells Fargo used a Concord stagecoach to advertise its presence.

From 1900 onward, both the express company and the bank made extensive use of the stagecoach and Pony Express as trademarks. When the bank was separated from the express company in 1905, there was no longer any reason to use the locomotive logo. The Wells Fargo name and Pony Express symbol were retained by both the bank and American Express after 1918, leading to later confusion.

In the early years of the century, the express company had three Concord stagecoaches that were displayed at fairs and parades from Astoria, Oregon, to Rochester, New York. The inaugural issue of the *Messenger* displayed a stage on its cover, and two months later the November 1912 issue sported a galloping horse and Pony Express rider. The year after the express business was absorbed by the government, the first issue of the bank's publication, the *Wells Fargo Nevadan*, used a stagecoach and the bank's building as its logo. Hellman's Los Angeles bank also employed the stage as an identifying symbol.

During the 1920s, the bank ran ads with Pony Express themes in all five San Francisco newspapers. One ad cited how the Pony Express "opened up a new era of more rapid communications." California artist Maynard Dixon designed a Pony Express medal for Wells Fargo in 1923, and the bank commissioned his *Lincoln Elected!* painting. The Pony Express icon and accompanying text, without qualifying Wells Fargo's partial role, became the bank's dominant symbol through the first half of the century. The stagecoach was used less frequently.

The bank began being protective of its name in 1922. A corporation calling itself the Wells Fargo Building Company purchased the old express building. The bank's attorneys interceded "in a friendly way," and the new company renamed itself the Express Building Company. As part of the "rather expensive" settlement, said the bank's lawyer, E. S. Heller, Wells Fargo paid the legal fees and the engraving costs of the Express Building Company's bonds.

Two years later the remnant of the express company in New York was about to become a subsidiary of American Express. Attorney Heller, a major bank stockholder and director, wrote Lipman:

> As your Bank is the only going concern in the United States which has the right to the use of the name "Wells Fargo" it has occurred to us that there ought to be no objection to the present Wells Fargo & Company transferring to you prior to its dissolution its trade-name and trade-marks in order that we may in the future protect the name we are proud to bear.
>
> The Express company as you know established the Bank as one of its functions and the bank should have the exclusive right to the name when the Express Company goes out of business.

Lipman adopted a desultory approach to protecting the name. It really had little current value, and he almost gave it away.

The bank president wrote to Davis G. Mellor, a former Wells Fargo express employee and president of the Wells Fargo entity that was about to be taken over by American Express: "Our right to use the name was of course duly confirmed to us in 1905 by Wells Fargo & Company, and the only reason we now have for proposing this resolution on the part of your Board of Directors is to avoid the possibility of some one else using the name in ways that might injure or dilute our prestige." The Wells Fargo that became part of American Express in 1924 kept the name.

Fourteen years later the American Express subsidiary was considering purchasing token interests in small banks throughout the country and licensing the name of Wells Fargo. Lipman appealed elliptically to the president of the company that bore the name of his bank. He first employed the disarming argument that such banks were "a step that seems to an old fogy banker highly perilous." At the time of the merger with the Nevada Bank in 1905, Lipman continued, "The name 'Wells Fargo Bank' was not considered to be of great value." The bank was an "honorable and straightforward" institution, which was all that banks needed to be. The name was retained by Hellman, he said, only to attract the customers of the old bank.

By 1938, with the help of Hollywood, the name had achieved some value. "Nevertheless," Lipman wrote Elmer R. Jones, president of the American Express subsidiary, "the fact remains that today the Bank's standing locally, nationally, and internationally attaches to the name Wells Fargo Bank & Union Trust Co., and it would give us a good deal of pain if a situation should arise that would make us feel compelled to abandon it and take some other name."

And what situation might that be? Lipman did not elaborate.

The mini-bank scheme did not go forward, but not because of any decisive action taken by Lipman to retain the name. For the next twenty years, the bankers in San Francisco showed little interest in gaining back the exclusive use of their brand. American Express retained the name and licensed some Wells Fargo memorabilia. Its right to use the name was broader than the right of the California bank, which could only use it for banking purposes within the state.

The New York company approached Wells Fargo in the 1960s to see if the bank wished to purchase the name of Wells Fargo and the Pony Express symbol for a nominal price. "But the bank's horizons at that time were limited," according to a later memorandum, "and it saw no need to buy anything."

A few years later Wells Fargo Bank, having formed a holding company named Wells Fargo & Company and now seeking to protect that historical name, changed its mind; but the price had gone up. Wells Fargo acquired all the remaining rights from American Express for approximately $2 million in 1969 and hired a San Francisco law firm to aggressively protect its trademark.

Baker Industries, who had purchased the armored car service along with the Wells Fargo name and Pony Express symbol two years earlier from American Express, retained the rights to their use. Wells Fargo Armored Service Corporation, a subsidiary of Baker Industries, displayed the Wells Fargo name and Pony Express icon prominently on the side of their vehicles. The press often confused the armored car company with the bank when a transport was robbed. Borg-Warner acquired Baker Industries in 1977.

*   *   *

Meanwhile, the name had acquired a certain cachet. In the same year that Lipman said the bank might want to assume another name, Hollywood was in the process of boosting the Wells Fargo legend into national prominence. Others would do the same.

Paramount Pictures director Frank Lloyd approached the San Francisco bank and the American Express subsidiary in 1937 for permission to use the words "Wells Fargo" in a movie, first titled *An Empire Is Born* and then retitled *Wells Fargo*. Both entities gave their permission. The movie was made and resulted in priceless publicity for Wells Fargo in 1938.

After viewing the movie, the senior senator from Pennsylvania, James J. Davis, gave a long address over the Mutual Broadcasting System titled "Wells Fargo." Davis attempted to lift the country out of the doldrums of the Depression by citing the history of Wells Fargo, as it had been portrayed by Hollywood. The speech was a long paean to entrepreneurial effort and internationalism on the eve of World War II.

"Wells Fargo rushed forward to meet the future of a growing nation," Davis declared. "Today we must rush forward to meet the urgent demands of a growing world." He added, "Ford, Edison, Burbank, Carver, and Wells Fargo had humble beginnings. Every large business enterprise in this country was once small and unknown." The speech was inserted in the *Congressional Record* by an Oregon senator.

The movie and the subsequent response was a public relations coup of the first magnitude. Two *Stagecoach* movies and one television series,

Tales of Wells Fargo, featured the company's colorful history after the war. Three laudatory histories, the last published in 1968, were written solely about Wells Fargo. There was significant mention of the company in another fifteen books. Dell published *Wells Fargo* comic books. There were numerous monographs in western academic journals and articles in popular magazines and newspapers. Wells Fargo memorabilia—from belt buckles to commemorative carbines—were licensed and sold or auctioned. It is hard to imagine another business in this country that has garnered as much free publicity.

When American Express shipped nearly five tons of historical records and memorabilia to the bank in 1969, a central repository was needed. A bank vice president had been collecting Gold Rush materials since 1920. A small display room had been located off the lobby since 1941. It was moved to its current location at 420 Montgomery Street in 1962. The Wells Fargo History Department was organized and the company archive was established in 1975.

As the brand grew in value, so did the company's history program.

The value of company-sponsored history was demonstrated in the 1960s when a relative of one of the founders of the Pony Express publicly challenged Wells Fargo's role. Waddell F. Smith was a great-grandson of William B. Waddell. Smith would appear at branch bank openings with a sign atop his Cadillac stating: "Wells Fargo Express Never Operated a Stagecoach Line in California," which would have been technically true had he added "under their name." He also claimed Wells Fargo's involvement in the Pony Express was extremely limited.

W. Turrentine Jackson, professor of history at the University of California at Davis, was hired as a consultant. Jackson was a prominent western historian who wrote three books, was a Guggenheim fellow, and served one year as president of the Western Historical Association. He was given a contract to "independently" assess the role of the express. Jackson wrote three major articles, on Wells Fargo and stagecoaching, Wells Fargo and the Pony Express, and Wells Fargo as a symbol of the West. A number of minor articles dealt with the history of Wells Fargo and various states, such as Colorado, Montana, and Idaho.

E. E. Munger, a vice president of marketing who oversaw Jackson's work, sent four articles to his boss in 1973 with the following note: "As you are aware, these meticulously researched and thoroughly documented articles have been of great value to us in repairing the serious damage done to our recognized historical role, credibility, and image by the virulent, anti–Wells Fargo campaign pressed over many years by Waddell F. Smith." Jackson's work for the company, which included being an expert witness in a major trademark case, spanned two decades.

Much of Wells Fargo's history has been produced within the bank since the mid-1970s. Staff members with advanced degrees have written articles for outside professional journals, historical society publications, and educational organizations. The History Department, now known as Historical Services, has produced product, market, and legal histories to support in-house public relations, marketing, and trademark programs.

The valuable Wells Fargo archive is available to researchers. There are six Wells Fargo history museums, five in California and one in Minneapolis. Stagecoaches are available for display or parades. In 2000 there were 623 appearances of Wells Fargo stagecoaches pulled by horses in 23 states, 650,000 persons visited the six museums, and 1,300 school tours were given for 38,000 students (all potential Wells Fargo customers) at the museums.

Few other corporations in this country are as historically conscious—or as dependent on history for its public image—as Wells Fargo. In a 1982 article on corporate history programs, *Newsweek* magazine singled out Wells Fargo for mention:

Delving into corporate history still has some conventional marketing uses. Wells Fargo's history department manages an extensive collection of archives; some are used in the bank's advertising campaigns. But today's corporate historians stress that their research is primarily aimed at giving managers useful information for running their businesses. Sometimes the past proves valuable in simply keeping firms from repeating previous mistakes.

A photograph of Harold Anderson, then in charge of the History Department, accompanied the article. The caption read: "Anderson: a boom in corporate Toynbees." Articles citing Wells Fargo's History Department as an example of corporations paying attention to their past also ran in *The New York Times* and *Industry Week.*

* * *

Since 1956 the stagecoach, in various versions that fit the marketing needs and graphic styles of the moment, has been the dominant company logo. In 1964 the stagecoach appeared on checks, the first use of such illustrated materials. A profile of a stage within an oval was used for a time; it was followed by a profile within a diamond from 1962 to 1986. Carl Reichardt, president and CEO, said in 1982: "We have a name and history, and an ability to market our services that is second to none, and we will continue to build on those strengths, particularly in the West."

In the 1980s the Concord stagecoach, six galloping horses, driver, and shotgun-toting messenger burst forth more energetically in drawings and photographs. The change in design from stasis to movement mirrored the change in banking from government regulation to the free-for-all of deregulation that recalled Wells Fargo's earlier days.

From horses through stagecoaches, trains, trucks, and airplanes Wells Fargo had connected people to goods and money. It was no different with the Internet, the most recent form of communication. Wells Fargo was a pioneer in use of the personal computer for banking and is a recognized leader in the field. The bank teamed up with Prodigy, an interactive personal service, in 1989 to offer on-line banking to its customers. By 1992 the bank had its own disk available for PC and

Macintosh computers. "Call us for a diskette today," it advertised, "and discover the control you get when you boot up your bank."

The first Web site, wellsfargo.com, appeared in December 1994. It featured product information and an historical vignette of agent Charles Blake's welcome arrival in Placerville, Idaho, in 1863. Later versions included wanted posters for current bank robbers. Throughout 2000 the bank ran a full-page advertisement in the Sunday edition of *The New York Times* with a Web format and a Windows type of pull-down menu. The stagecoach was a constant in all these marketing efforts aimed at what was now a computer-literate nation.

By the time Glendale Federal Savings challenged Wells Fargo with a floating banner on San Francisco Bay in 1996, the signature icon was a common target of other banks. Washington Mutual in the Northwest claimed that its new free checking accounts were easier to acquire "than falling off a stagecoach" in an ad with an Old West design motif. Another bank advertised: "Top ten reasons to jump off the stagecoach."

Such imitation indicated the power of the brand. Brand equity, brand standards, brand execution became common words in the 1990s. A Brand Management Division was established. A brand catalogue, which standardized images and lettering, was issued. The bank distributed a poster titled "Building the Wells Fargo Brand" for internal use in late 1998. It stated in boldface type:

> In the 1850s, the reassuring sight of a red and gold stagecoach blazing across the open frontier, or arriving in a township, immediately evoked the name Wells Fargo. It stood for forward-thinking, security and superior service. It still does. The Wells Fargo brand gives us a strong competitive advantage—one that can only be maintained through teamwork and the commitment of everyone at Wells Fargo. Through consistent and repeated use, our brand identity will continue to communicate Wells Fargo's extraordinary heritage and the superior customer-focused financial services for which it stands.

From outside the bank, branding guru David Aaker cited the value of the ubiquitous stagecoach symbol in an industry where similarity was the norm. The accuracy of his assessment, offered at the start of this book, can now be judged in terms of the intervening history. The Old West, horses, and the Gold Rush, he wrote, were linked to "reliability in the face of adversity, adventurousness, independence, and even building a new society out of wilderness."

*   *   *

The brand remained constant, but the players and the assets changed with increasing frequency. With every major merger in the 1980s and 1990s, Wells Fargo doubled in size.

Had anyone been aware that Charles Crocker had staged a successful raid on Wells Fargo in 1869, Wells Fargo's takeover of Crocker Bank in February of 1986 could have been seen as payback. "Look, this isn't a merger of equals; it's an acquisition, so don't expect to be dealt with as though we're partners," a senior Wells Fargo executive told a meeting of Crocker employees.

The blunt-spoken Carl Reichardt, a native Texan, operated like a Gold Rush banker in the early years of deregulation. An entrepreneur, who had replaced the more refined type of banker dominant during the quiet, middle years of the century, Reichardt was gregarious, abrasive, and a shouter who quickly rewarded good work but did not suffer fools gladly. He had joined the bank in 1970 and was aware of its western heritage. Original Frederic Remington drawings adorned his office walls. Reichardt's model for a bank was a fast-food restaurant, such as McDonald's, that had a limited menu, consistent service, and low prices.

The Crocker Bank had a relatively long history by California standards. In 1883 Charles Crocker formed the Crocker-Woolworth Company, and through name changes it became Crocker National Bank and then Crocker Bank. Like Wells Fargo, Crocker had gone through a number of mergers and acquisitions with the name intact. The Crocker name was finally subsumed in 1986 by Wells Fargo—the older, more dominant entity.

Reichardt trimmed staffs, and a leaner, meaner bank emerged in the late 1980s with nearly twice the customer base. More branches were added, particularly in Southern California. Assets, profits, and the stock price zoomed upward. *The New York Times* said, "Wells has clearly become the bank to watch in California." *The Wall Street Journal* noted: "Over the past four years, the bank has cut operating costs like no other large bank in the land. Today, it is the lowest-cost major retail bank in California. And backed by a high-powered sales force unique in banking, it is increasingly one of the most profitable in the U.S."

Clearly, Wells Fargo was beginning to rise once again on the upside of the wave of history. But no wave has a continuously smooth surface.

The bank's profits plunged during the recession of the early 1990s in California. Bad commercial real estate and corporate loans threatened its stability. Confidence, both inside and outside the bank, slipped. A memo was sent to branch managers, reminding them: "Wells Fargo has a long history of succeeding in tough times." The financial panic of 1855, the Civil War years, the disastrous 1906 earthquake and fire, and the Depression years were recalled. The calming message to employees was: "Wells Fargo Bank: Safe and Strong Since 1852."

By 1994, profits were again on the upswing. Reichardt retired at the end of the year. He was succeeded as chairman and chief executive officer of the state's third largest bank by Paul Hazen, a more soft-spoken, analytical presence.

Hazen, the architect of the Crocker deal, made his move ten months later. Where the 1986 merger with Crocker was considered a model of its type, Wells Fargo's hostile takeover of Los Angeles–based First Interstate Bancorp was a near debacle.

On the face of it, the merger looked good. Wells Fargo had a California presence; First Interstate added to that and offered branches in eleven western states once served by Wells Fargo express. *The New York Times* said of the dominant partner: "Wells Fargo is considered one of the best banks in the country, combining low costs with a flair for marketing built around its stagecoach heritage." The *Los Angeles Times*, First Interstate's hometown newspaper, sounded a note of caution: "There would also be a change in climate as Wells, known for its lean, high-tech approach to retail banking, might offer less personal service than some First Interstate customers expect."

There was general approval of the concept. But disaster threatened when the takeover became a reality the next year. First Interstate managers, taking advantage of generous severance packages, resigned throughout the interior West where Wells Fargo had the least presence and lacked knowledge of the different market. Branches were closed; supermarket outlets were opened. There were computer glitches. Deposits were not recorded. Checks bounced. Service was poor. Customers fled or were picked off by such rival banks as Glendale Savings. Hazen said, "The business philosophies we employed are correct, but our merger execution was poor." That would not be the case next time.

Weakened by the First Interstate experience, Hazen turned to the Minneapolis-based Norwest Corporation and its CEO Richard Kovacevich. There had been a tie between Norwest, which ranked number one in mortgage originations nationwide, and Wells Fargo. When the California bank abandoned home mortgages in 1994, it referred its customers to Norwest Mortgage.

This time, on the face of it, there didn't seem to be a match. Geographies and corporate cultures were vastly different. How would a service-oriented midwestern bank with national mortgage and consumer finance businesses get along with a more narrowly focused, leaner-staffed, technology-driven California bank?

Beneath the surface, however, there was another story. Norwest was expanding westward; Wells Fargo was moving eastward. The range of services, the distinct sales-oriented culture, and the Midwestern territory that Norwest brought with it would widen Wells Fargo's narrower base to something comparable to its heyday during the railroad era. In return, Wells Fargo offered Norwest California, which as a state varies between sixth and seventh among the world's economies; boosted Norwest out of the ranks of corporate anonymity with the help of the stagecoach brand (valued at the time of the merger at some $3 billion); and gave it an instant, major Internet presence and new product lines, such as large commercial real estate.

What was called a merger of equals made sense and was carried out with very little pain. Where the First Interstate takeover was rushed, the merger of the two different financial institutions was spread over three years. The technical term applied to the union with Crocker was the same as that affixed to the Norwest–Wells Fargo venture. It was a "value-creating merger." The stock rose. In 2000 analysts called Wells Fargo "one of the best-managed financial institutions in the United States."

Historical serendipity had also intervened. The connection between Wells Fargo directors going back to William Fargo and the Minneapolis bank created by the Northern Pacific Railroad was discovered. Outsiders taking over—like a Tevis or a Harriman—had established precedents. The new Wells Fargo was the product of more than 2,000 mergers and acquisitions. Once again the existing corporate culture had been modified and reinvigorated by the infusion of new styles and procedures.

Kovacevich (pronounced Koe-VAH-suh-vitch), like Reichardt before him, was considered the model banker of his time. The headline on a *Fortune* magazine story read: "Is This Guy the Best Banker in America?" The article implied he might be. *Forbes* called him "the banking industry's king of cross-selling," a reference to Kovacevich's goal to sell more products to the same customers. Raised in Enumclaw, Washington, twenty miles east of Tacoma, the six-foot, three-inch future banker had declined offers from both the New York Yankees and Baltimore Orioles and chose instead to pitch for Stanford University, where he had to give up baseball when he tore the rotator cuff in his throwing arm. Kovacevich obtained his undergraduate and graduate degrees in engineering and business from Stanford, tying for first place in his MBA class.

After graduation, Kovacevich took a sales and marketing job with General Mills. In the mid-1970s, he went to work for Walter Wriston at

Citicorp, where he transformed the New York City branch banking system into a moneymaker and, in the words of *Fortune,* "helped change the face of banking by rolling out Citi's then revolutionary ATMs." Kovacevich went to Minneapolis in 1986 at the invitation of Norwest CEO Lloyd Johnson, a former California banker who was trying to light a fire under a classic midwest bank. Kovacevich was the spark. Three years later he was named president and chief operating officer of Norwest at the age of forty-six.

The collection of Midwest banks and financial services under the corporate umbrella of Norwest had gone through a downturn because of farm loans in a time of low agricultural prices, but the corporation's consumer finance subsidiary had pulled Norwest back to profitability by 1986. Kovacevich wasted no time in making his mark. He restructured the bank's affiliates and doubled their profits in one year. In January of 1993 he became the CEO.

A new sales culture was introduced, one that Kovacevich would take with him to Wells Fargo five years later. Harold Chucker described it in his history of Norwest: " 'To increase profits and then growth, it was necessary to develop a sales and service culture,' Mr. Kovacevich explained. 'Most banks have similar products and services. The difference between them is in the attitudes of employees in selling and serving the customer. The emphasis is put on achieving more business from existing customers.' "

While Reichardt had thought in terms of the limited menu of a Mc-Donald's, Kovacevich used the wider selection available in a Wal-Mart as his example of what he wanted the bank to become. Banking no longer defined Wells Fargo's business. Financial services did. While moving away from its more immediate past, in terms of its core mission, Wells Fargo more nearly matched its distant history in terms of reach.

Kovacevich, a product of the West, had returned home. The integrated Wells Fargo of the first years of the twenty-first century resembled its earlier predecessors. It had, once again, adapted to the natural and human environment of the Trans-Mississippi West.

To deal with the natural disasters that are so common in California, such as earthquakes that had once destroyed San Francisco, there were four data centers spread throughout the region. Booms and busts were recognized phenomena. The bank had avoided loans on high-priced real estate during the technology boom that went bust in the San Francisco Bay Area. "We have a history and are aware of it," said Kovacevich in his office filled with replicas of stagecoaches.

Numbers also told the story of continuity. There were 117,000 employees, called team members, working in 5,400 branches, called stores, in the first year of the new millennium. As with the express company in its last years, the offices were spread nationwide but were concentrated in the West, the majority (1,216) located in California. There were more than 19 million customers spread across fifty states; the District of Columbia; the territories of Puerto Rico, the Virgin Islands, and Guam; and nine foreign countries. The assets had grown from $300,000 in 1852 to $300 billion in 2001.

The Muybridge Mural

THE PAST meets the present in the Wells Fargo Penthouse atop the thirteen-story corporate headquarters at California and Montgomery Streets. An enlargement of Eadweard Muybridge's 1878 photographic panorama of San Francisco is juxtaposed against a view of the city as it exists today.

The seventy-five-foot-long mural that hangs in the teak-paneled penthouse depicts, in a clockwise direction, such landmarks as the Palace Hotel, Union Square, an emerging City Hall, a bare Twin Peaks, the stately Crocker mansion, crowded Russian Hill, the Wells Fargo Bank at the northeast corner of Sansome and California streets, and the express building at Sansome and Halleck streets.

Since 1878 many structures and the various activities they housed have vanished. The city has grown vertically. Bridges now span the bay. Jet airplanes circle above. Cable cars rumble below. The landscape that Louis McLane first saw in 1844 has been greatly altered. Time has passed. It has left new marks and erased old ones.

What's in a name and its accompanying symbol? Are they merely cosmetic or are they rooted in a history that has relevance to the present?

The name Wells Fargo has sheltered a large cast of shifting characters and activities over one hundred and fifty years. Not many commercial enterprises can boast of such longevity, or of being an integral part of their region and of periodic value to the nation for that length of time.

Sources

Three previous histories of Wells Fargo have been published. They are: Edward Hungerford, *Wells Fargo: Advancing the American Frontier*, New York: Random House, 1949; Lucius Beebe and Charles Clegg, *U.S. West: The Saga of Wells Fargo*, New York: Bonanza Books, 1949; Noel M. Loomis, *Wells Fargo*, New York: Clarkson N. Potter Inc., 1968. I used the three books as general guides, but I depended on more original materials to shape my story.

The L. O. Head binder is a typewritten summary of actions taken by the directors of Wells Fargo, with the emphasis on the express business. I referred to the handwritten original minutes for information about times of greater importance. Those minutes are sketchy.

Wells Fargo went through a number of minor name changes during its history. The comma and the abbreviation of the word "company" were the principal alterations.

First it was known as the Wells Fargo History Department, then Wells Fargo Historical Services. The archives are located in the basement vault of the corporate headquarters, and there are extensive files in the second floor offices of the Historical Services department. For convenience, I have referred to all these entities as WFHS.

The sources are arranged in the order they were utilized. The paragraphs correspond to chapters or sections of chapters. I cite the source only when first used.

Preface

Jay Monaghan, ed., *The Private Journal of Louis McLane U.S.N. 1844–1848*, Los Angeles: Dawson's Book Shop, 1971. Over the years, Wells Fargo and the Bank of California have skirmished over the title of oldest bank. Most historians award Wells Fargo the title. "Age Dispute Turns S.F. Banks into Grouchy Old Neighbors," *Banking & Finance Quarterly*, November 25, 1995. "Billboards on the Bay," *San Francisco Examiner*, September 26, 1996. "A Move to Ban Billboards on Bay," *San Francisco Examiner*, March 21, 1997. "Glendale Federal Bank Unveils New Advertising Campaign Aimed at Major Banking Competition" and "Glendale Federal Bank Ad Barge to Float Again on San Francisco Bay," *P.R. Newswire*, Los Angeles, July 25, 1996. David A. Aaker, *Managing Brand Equity: Capitalizing on the Value of a Brand Name*, New York: Free Press, 1991. Henry Wells, "Sketch of the Rise, Progress, and Present Condition of the Express System," a paper read to the American Geographical and Statistical Society, February 4, 1864.

I 1852–1869

Beginnings

Louis McLane to Sophie McLane, Maryland Historical Society, April 2 and April 22, 1850, and September 26, 1851. Wayne E. Fuller, *The American Mail: Enlarger of the Common Life*, Chicago: University of Chicago Press, 1972. A. L. Stimson, *History of the Express Business*, New York: Baker & Godwin, 1881. George L. Priest, "The History of the Postal Monopoly in the United States," *The Journal of Law & Economics*, April 1975. LeRoy R. Hafen, *The Overland Mail, 1849–1869: Promoter of Settlement, Precursor of Railroads*, Cleveland, Oh.: Arthur H. Clark Co., 1926. A strap rail was a bar of iron hastily secured to a "sleeper," or tie. The spikes would loosen with the constant passage of trains, and the rail would curve upward like a poised snakehead and impale the frail bottoms of railroad cars and passengers. Run-offs were derailments. The common road was the carriage path. Henry Wells, "The American Express in Its Relation to the City of Buffalo," a paper prepared for the Buffalo Historical Society, June 1863. Peter Z. Grossman, *American Express: The Unofficial History of the People Who Built the Great Financial Empire*, New York: Crown Publishers, 1987. Ira B. Cross, *Financing an Empire: History of Banking in California*, San Francisco: S. J. Clarke Publishing Co., 1927. Edgar H. Adams, *Private Gold Coinage of California 1849–55*, Brooklyn, N.Y.: Edgar H. Adams, 1913. Dwight L. Clarke, *William Tecumseh Sherman: Gold Rush Banker*, San Francisco: California Historical Society, 1969. Lynne Pierson Doti and Larry Schweikart, *California Bankers 1848–1993*, Needham Heights, Mass.: Ginn Press, 1994. Lynne Pierson Doti and Larry Schweikart, *Banking in the American West: From the Gold Rush to Deregulation*, Norman, Okla.: University of Oklahoma Press, 1991. Robert J. Chandler, "Integrity amid Tumult: Wells, Fargo & Co.'s Gold Rush Banking," *California History*, Fall 1991.

Robert J. Chandler, "William George Fargo," *The Encyclopedia of American Business and Biography*, New York: Facts On File, 1990. Reed Massengill, *Becoming American Express: 150 Years of Reinvention and Customer Service*, New York: American Express Company, 1999. Robert J. Chandler, "Henry Wells," *Encyclopedia of American Business History and Biography*, New York, Facts On File, 1990. Ruth Teiser and Catherine Harroun, "Origin of Wells, Fargo & Company, 1841–1852," *Bulletin of the Business Historical Society*, June 1948. Oscar Osburn Winther, *Express and Stagecoach Days in California: From the Gold Rush to the Civil War*, Stanford, Calif.: Stanford University Press, 1936. Oscar Osburn Winther, *Via Western Express & Stagecoach*, Lincoln, Neb.: University of Nebraska Press, 1969.

Gold Rush California

"Death of William G. Fargo," *The* [Syracuse, N.Y.] *Journal*, August 1, 1881. The actual address of the first office was 114 Montgomery Street, just north of California Street. The addresses were renumbered in the 1860s. Very likely the current corporate headquarters sits on top of the first location. Samuel P. Carter to Edwin B. Morgan, WFHS, June 30, 1852. *Daily Alta California*, August 15, 1852.

Ruth Teiser and Catherine Harroun, "Wells, Fargo & Company: The First Half Year," *Bulletin of the Business Historical Society*, June 1949. Louis McLane to Sophie McLane, Maryland Historical Society, April 30, 1850. Charles T. Blake to his father, WFHS, September 12, 1852. R. W. Washburn to E. B. Morgan, WFHS, September 30, 1852. R. W. Washburn to E. B. Morgan, WFHS, October 15, 1852. Samuel P. Carter to Col. I. McKay (board secretary), WFHS, November 30, 1852. R. W. Washburn to Jas. McKay, WFHS, December 1, 1852. Samuel P. Carter to Col. J. McKay, WFHS, December 31, 1852. R. W. Washburn to E. B. Morgan, WFHS, January 12, 1853. Henry Wells, *Truly Yours, Henry Wells*, Aurora, N.Y.: Wells College Press, 1945.

In the Gold Country

Letters from John Quincy Jackson to various members of his family, WFHS, April 6, 1851; October 14, 1852; October 23, 1852; February 11, 1854; July 30, 1854; September 15, 1854; February 24, 1855; April 14, 1855; June 14, 1855. Various letters from friends and fellow Wells Fargo agents to Jackson, WFHS.

The Post-Gold Rush Years

William T. Sherman, *Recollections of California, 1846–1861*, Oakland, Calif.: Biobooks, 1945. Edward E. Munger to Edward M. Hall, Wells Fargo vice presidents, WFHS, May 19, 1977. Robert S. McBain, Wells Fargo research associate, to Lane P. Brennan, bank vice president, WFHS, August 21, 1980. *San Francisco Bulletin*, April 16, 1866. Alonzo Phelps, ed., Louis McLane, *Contemporary Biography*, San Francisco: A. L. Bancroft Co., 1881. Louis McLane to Sophie McLane, Maryland Historical Society, March 6, 1856. Richard R. John Jr., "Private Mail Delivery in the United States During the Nineteenth Century: A Sketch," a paper presented at the Business History Conference, WFHS, March 13–15, 1986. J. S. Holliday, *The World Rushed In: The California Gold Rush Experience*, New York: Simon & Schuster, 1981. J. S. Holliday, *Rush for Riches: Gold Fever and the Making of California*, Berkeley, Calif.: University of California Press, 1999. William H. Brewer, *Up and Down California in 1860–1864*, Berkeley, Calif.: University of California Press, 1974. Charles T. Blake, "Working for Wells Fargo—1860–1863," *California Historical Society Quarterly*, June 1937. "Report of the Committee Appointed by the Chamber of Commerce of San Francisco," San Francisco, WFHS, September 1864. Carl I. Wheat, ed., "California's Bantam Cock: The Journals of Charles E. De Long, 1854–1863," *California Historical Society Quarterly*, December 1930.

The Pony Express

W. Turrentine Jackson, "A New Look at Wells Fargo, Stagecoaches and the Pony Express, *California Historical Society Quarterly*, December 1966. W. Turrentine Jackson, "Wells Fargo Staging over the Sierra," *California Historical Society Quarterly*, June 1979. W. Turrentine Jackson, "Wells Fargo: Symbol of the Wild West?" *Western Historical Quarterly*, April 1972. W. Turrentine Jackson, "Wells Fargo's Pony Express," *Journal of the West*, July 1972. "Pony Express" and "Wells, Fargo and Company," Howard R. Lamar, ed., *The New Encyclopedia of the American West*, New Haven, Conn.: Yale University Press, 1998.

David Nevin, *The Expressmen*, Alexandria, Va.: Time-Life Books, 1980. John Butterfield, William G. Fargo, Alex Holland, and associates to A. V. Brown, postmaster general, WFHS, June 1, 1857. Frank A. Root, *The Overland Stage to California*, Topeka, Kansas, 1901. Contract No. 12,578 between John Butterfield and six other contractors and four sureties and the postmaster general, WFHS, September 16, 1857. William L. Ormsby, *The Butterfield Overland Mail*, San Marino, Calif.: The Huntington Library, 1988. Samuel Bowles, *Across the Continent: A Summer's Journey to the Rocky Mountains, the Mormons, and the Pacific States with Speaker Colfax*, New York: Hurd & Houghton, 1866. "A Preamble to Pony Express Versus Wells Fargo Express," Waddell F. Smith, *Pony Express History and Art Gallery*, San Rafael, Calif., 1967. Waddell Smith, "Stage Lines and Express Companies in California," *The Far-Westerner*, January 1965. Raymond W. Settle, "The Pony Express: Heroic Effort—Tragic End," *Utah Historical Quarterly*, April 1959.

Mark Twain, *Roughing It*, Berkeley, Calif.: University of California Press, 1993. Prentiss Ingram, ed., *Seventy Years on the Frontier: Alexander Majors' Memoirs of a Lifetime on the Border*, Chicago: Rand, McNally & Co., 1893. William Lightfoot Visscher, *A Thrilling and Truthful History of the Pony Express*, Chicago: Rand, McNally & Co., 1908. Ferol Egan, *Sand in a Whirlwind: The Paiute Indian War of 1860*, Garden City, N.Y.: Doubleday, 1972. Louise Cheney, "The Incredible Story of 'Pony Bob' Haslam: Most Famous of the Old West Mounted Mailmen," *The Texas and Southwestern Horseman*, March 1966. Richard F. Burton, *The City of the Saints and Across the Rocky Mountains to California*, N.Y.: Alfred A. Knopf, 1963.

The Devil in Reality

Carlos Arnaldo Schwantes, *Long Day's Journey: The Steamboat & Stagecoach Era in the Northern West*, Seattle, Wash.: University of Washington Press, 1999. "Hints for Plains Travelers," *Omaha Herald*, October 3, 1877.

Emerson David Fite, *Social and Industrial Conditions in the North During the Civil War*, New York: Frederick Unger Publishing Co., 1968. Demas Barnes, *From the Atlantic to the Pacific, Overland*, New York: D. Van Nostrand, 1866. Horace

Greeley, *An Overland Journey: From New York to San Francisco in the Summer of 1859*, New York: Alfred A. Knopf, 1963. *Omaha Herald*, 1877.

"The Abbot, Downing Company. Manufacturers of Coaches & Wagons," Carriage Association of America, 1984. Harry N. Scheiber, "Abbot-Downing and the Concord Coach," *Historical New Hampshire*, Autumn 1965. Don H. Berkebile, *Carriage Terminology: An Historical Dictionary*, Washington, D.C.: Smithsonian Institution Press and Liberty Cap Books, 1978. Ralph Moody, *Stagecoach West*, New York: Thomas Y. Crowell, 1967.

A. K. McClure, *Three Thousand Miles through the Rocky Mountains*, Philadelphia: J. B. Lippincott and Co., 1869. Albert D. Richardson, *Beyond the Mississippi: From the Great River to the Great Ocean*, Hartford, Conn.: American Publishing Company, 1867. W. Turrentine Jackson, "Salt Lake City: Wells Fargo's Transportation Depot During the Stagecoach Era," *Utah Historical Quarterly*, Winter 1985.

"Instructions to Agents and Employees of Wells, Fargo & Co's Overland Express with Tariff of Rates Etc.," WFHS, New York, January 1868. Archer Butler Hulbert, ed., *Letters of an Overland Mail Agent in Utah*, Worchester, Mass.: American Antiquarian Society, 1929. "Wells Fargo Stage Stations in 1868," pamphlet to accompany an exhibition of Francis L. Horspool paintings, Salt Lake City, 1940. Secretary of War, *War of the Rebellion: A Compilation of the Official Records of the Union and Confederate Armies*, Series I, Vol. L, Part II, Washington, D.C., 1897. Robert D. Livingston, "Wells and Fargo: Western Travelers," *Western Express*, January 1983.

J. Ross Browne, "Washoe Revisited," *Harper's New Monthly Magazine*, May, 1865. "Charley Parkhurst," *San Francisco Call*, January 1, 1880. "The Female Stage-Driver," *San Francisco Call* (copied from the *Providence Journal*), January 25, 1880. "Death Called Charley's Bluff," *San Francisco Chronicle*, November 22, 1967. Edward E. Munger, vice president of marketing and advertising, Wells Fargo, to Basil C. Pearce, vice president history department, WFHS, December 10, 1976. Robert J. Chandler, "Wells Fargo: 'We Never Forget,'" *Quarterly of the National Association and Center for Outlaw and Lawman History*, Winter 1987.

Samuel Bowles, *Across the Continent: A Summer's Journey to the Rocky Mountains, the Mormons, and the Pacific States with Speaker Colfax*, Springfield, Mass.: Samuel Bowles & Co., 1866. Placerville *Mountain Democrat*, July 1, 1865.

Wells Fargo Goes to War

"An American Enterprise," *Harper's New Monthly Magazine*, August 1875. Bray Hammond, *Sovereignty and an Empty Purse: Banks and Politics in the Civil War*, Princeton, N.J.: Princeton University Press, 1970. George Rothwell Brown, ed., *Reminiscences of Senator William M. Stewart*, New York: Neale Publishing Co., 1908. Grant H. Smith, *The History of the Comstock Lode*, 1850–1997, Reno,

Nev.: University of Nevada Press, 1998. Russell R. Elliott, *Servant of Power: A Political Biography of William M. Stewart*, Reno, Nev.: University of Nevada Press, 1983. Russell R. Elliott, *History of Nevada*, Lincoln, Neb.: University of Nebraska Press, 1987. Robert J. Chandler, "Wells Fargo in Sacramento Since 1852," draft manuscript, WFHS, May, 1992. Patrick K. O'Brien, *The Economic Effects of the American Civil War*, London: Macmillan Education Inc., 1988.

Benjamin Franklin Gilbert, "The Confederate Minority in California," *California Historical Society Quarterly*, June 1941. John Boessenecker, "Captain Ingram's Partisan Rangers," Robert J. Chandler, ed., *California and the Civil War 1861–1865*, San Francisco: Book Club of California, 1992. John Boessenecker, *Badge and Buckshot: Lawlessness in Old California*, Norman, Okla.: University of Oklahoma Press, 1988. Richard Dillon, *Wells, Fargo Detective: A Biography of James B. Hume*, Reno, Nev.: University of Nevada Press, 1986. "Daring Stage Robbery," *Sacramento Daily Union*, July 4, 1864. "The Late Stage Robbery," *Sacramento Daily Union*, July 6, 1864. "The Late Robbery on the Placerville Route," *Sacramento Daily Union*, July 7, 1864. "The Placerville Highwaymen," *Sacramento Daily Union*, September 9 and 10, 1864.

End of an Era

W. Turrentine Jackson, "Wells Fargo in Colorado Territory," *Colorado Historical Society Monograph Series*, Number 1, 1982. Leonard J. Arrington, "Banking Enterprises in Utah, 1847–1880, *The Business History Review*, December 1955. W. Turrentine Jackson, "Wells Fargo Stagecoaching in Montana Territory," *Montana Historical Society Press*, 1979. John and Lillian Theobald, *Wells Fargo in Arizona Territory*, Arizona Historical Foundation, 1978. "Important Consolidation of Express and Stage Lines," New York *Tribune*, November 6, 1866. *San Francisco Bulletin*, April 16, 1866.

Robert J. Chandler to Andy Anderson, WFHS, May 8, 1980. Robert J. Chandler to Cary Edwards, WFHS, November 9, 1984.

I. W. Hellman, "Wells Fargo Bank & Union Trust Co.," the Newcomen Society in North America, 1952. *Concord Daily Monitor*, April 18, 1868. *New Hampshire Statesman*, April 17, 1868. Board of Director minutes, WFHS, May–October, 1868. Louis McLane to Sophie McLane, Maryland Historical Society, August 3, 1868. J. Turrentine Jackson, "Newspaper Research Project for Wells Fargo Bank," Report No. 1, WFHS, undated. Charles Crocker, "Reminiscences," manuscript dictated for H. H. Bancroft's *Chronicles of the Builders of the Commonwealth, 1865–1890.* John Hoyt Williams, *A Great and Shining Road: The Epic Story of the Transcontinental Railroad*, New York: Times Books, 1988. Angus D. McDonald, "A Message From the Southern Pacific," *Wells Fargo Messenger*, May, 1940. David Howard Bain, *Empire Express: Building the First Transcontinental Railroad*, New York: Viking, 1999. Stephen E. Ambrose, *Nothing Like It in the World: The Men Who Built the Transcontinental Railroad*, New York: Simon & Schuster, 2000. Committee on Rail Roads of the First Nevada Legislature, *Evidence Concerning Projected Railway Across the Sierra Nevada Mountains From Pacific Tide Waters in California and the Resources, Promises and Action of Companies Organized to Construct the Same; Together With Statements Concerning Present and Prospective Railroad Enterprises in the State of Nevada*, Carson City, Nevada, 1865. Carl I. Wheat, "A Sketch of the Life of Theodore D. Judah," *California Historical Society Quarterly*, September 1925. David Lavender, *The Great Persuader*, Garden City, N.Y.: Doubleday & Company, 1969. Robert D. Livingston, "Pacific Expresses: Many with Short Lives," *Western Express*, October 1986. Testimony of Lloyd Tevis before the United States Pacific Railway Commission, *Investigation of the Books, Accounts, and Methods of Railroads Which Have Received Aid From the United States, and For Other Purposes*, Vol. VI, Washington, D.C., 1887. W. Turrentine Jackson, "Racing From Reno to Virginia City by Wells Fargo and Pacific Union Express," *Nevada Historical Society Quarterly*, summer 1977. Pacific Express Company, Articles of Incorporation, San Francisco, filed July 5, 1869. "Dear Sir" letter to stockholders, Wells Fargo Board of Directors minutes, June 15, 1870.

II   1870–1906

The New Regime

Lloyd Tevis entry in Alonzo Phelps, *Contemporary Biography of California's Representative Men*, San Francisco: A. L. Bancroft and Company, 1881. "Lloyd Tevis Passes Away after a Brief Illness," *San Francisco Chronicle*, July 25, 1899. Oscar T. Shuck, *Bench and Bar in California: History, Anecdotes, Reminiscences*, San Francisco: Occidental Printing House, 1889. Eric Francis, "Reminiscences," Vol. II, WFHS, undated. Lloyd Tevis, address to the American Banker's Association, Niagara Falls, New York, August 10, 1881. Andy Anderson and Gus Brandenburg, "Wells Fargo Dividend History," WFHS, February 29, 1988. Various advertisements, including two in the Portland Directory of 1871 and 1872 for "Wells, Fargo & Co., Express & Exchange Company, and Overland Stage Company."

Crime & Punishment

James B. Hume Papers, undated typewritten note, Bancroft Library, University of California at Berkeley. Undated photo by J. H. Hogan Photo, Oroville, Calif., Hume papers. James B. Hume to Lida Munson, November 7, 1878. Hume to Munson, Thanksgiving Day, 1878. Hume to Munson, December 14, 1878. Robert Pacini, WFHS, to the *International Police Association Journal*, Auckland, New Zealand, January 27, 1978. "Report of Jas. B. Hume and Jno. N. Thacker, Special Officers, Wells, Fargo & Co's Express, Covering a Period of Fourteen Years, Giving Losses by Train Robbers, Stage Robbers and Burglaries, And a Full Description and

Record of All Noted Criminals Convicted of Offenses Against Wells, Fargo & Company Since November 5th, 1870," San Francisco, 1885. "Stage Robbing," *San Francisco Examiner*, April 3, 1887. "Stand and Deliver," *The* [San Francisco] *Call*, February 5, 1885. "Death Closes a Notable Career," *San Francisco Chronicle*, May 19, 1904. "Passing of a Great Detective," *San Francisco Chronicle*, May 20, 1904. "James Bunyan Hume Dies at His Home in Berkeley Hills," *The Call*, May 19, 1904. To Express Agents and Police Chiefs from John J. Valentine, March 20, 1878.

"Wells Fargo Security," Robert J. Chandler, unpublished manuscript, WFHS, 1998. "Report of the Finance Committee to the President and Board of Directors of Wells Fargo & Company," San Francisco, December 15, 1891. Black Bart Description, Wells, Fargo & Co's Express wanted poster, signed by "J. B. Hume, Special Officer's Department, San Francisco, November 30, 1888," WFHS. *The Call*, February 5, 1885. "Stage Robbing," *San Francisco Examiner*, April 3, 1887. Hume thought it was Miner who robbed the stage and the congressman, but he may have been mistaken.

Casey Tefertiller, *Wyatt Earp: The Life Behind the Legend*, New York: John Wiley & Sons, 1997. Paula Mitchell Marks, *And Die in the West: The Story of the O.K. Corral Gunfight*, New York: William Morrow, 1989. "Gunfight at O.K. Corral Still Echoes," *Los Angeles Times*, October 24, 2000. Casey Tefertiller, "Wyatt Earp's Last Stand," *Image* (*San Francisco Examiner* Sunday supplement), October 17, 1993. John and Lillian Theobald, *Wells Fargo in Arizona Territory*, Tempe, Ariz.: Arizona Historical Foundation. Michael A. Bellesiles, *Arming America: The Origins of a National Gun Culture*, New York: Alfred A. Knopf, 2000. Richard Slotkin, *Gunfighter Nation: The Myth of the Frontier in Twentieth Century America*, New York: HarperPerennial, 1993. Leo W. Banks, "Wyatt Earp: In Myth and Legend," *Arizona Highways*, July 1994. "Dictation of Wyatt Earp," the History Company Publishers, Bancroft Library, 1888. Richard A. Pope, account executive for McCann-Erickson, Inc., to John D. Gilchriese, field historian, University of Arizona, September 18, 1970.

Stuart Lake, *Wyatt Earp: Frontier Marshall*, Boston: Houghton, Mifflin, 1931. Carolyn Lake, *Undercover for Wells Fargo: The Unvarnished Recollections of Fred Dodge*, Boston: Houghton, Mifflin, 1969. Robert J. Chandler, "Undercover for Wells Fargo: A Review Essay," *The Journal of Arizona History*, spring 2000. After plowing through the Wells Fargo archives, I concluded that Dodge, at the very most, was an informal conduit of information on an intermittent basis. Don Chaput, "Fred Dodge: Undercover Agent, or Con Man?" *Quarterly of the National Association for Outlaw and Lawman History, Inc.*, January–March 2000. James B. Hume to Lida Munson, WFHS, March 19, 1881. John Richard Stephens, ed., *Wyatt Earp Speaks! My Side of the O.K. Corral Shootout, Plus Interviews With Doc Holliday*, Cambria, Calif.: Fern Canyon Press, 1998. Donald Chaput, *Virgil Earp: Western Peace Officer*, Encampment, Wyo.: Affiliated Writers of America, 1994. Alford E. Turner, *The Earps Talk*, College Station, Tex.: Creative Publishing Co.,

1980. "Wyatt Earp Tells Tales of the Shotgun-Messenger Service," *San Francisco Examiner Sunday Magazine*, August 9, 1896. James B. Hume to R. H. Paul, Hume papers, December 11, 1883. Dan L. Thrapp, *Encyclopedia of Frontier Biography*, Spokane, Wash.: The Arthur H. Clark Co., 1990. John D. Gilchriese, "The Life of Robert Paul," *Arizona Currents*, February 1966. James Long, "Bob Paul, Shotgun Marshal," *Real West*, May 1965.

Philpot's last name has been variously spelled with one *t* and two. I have opted for the spelling in the earliest accounts. Robert J. Chandler, "Wells Fargo: We Never Forget," *Quarterly of the National Association and Center for Outlaw and Lawmen History*, Winter 1987. Robert J. Chandler to Colonel Charles W. Pate, WFHS, December 14, 1979. John G. Hamilton, "Wells Fargo & Co. History-Firearms-Accouterments," *Gun Report*, July, 1990. "Virgil Earp: He Comes to San Francisco for a Surgical Treatment," *San Francisco Examiner*, May 27, 1882. Richard E. Erwin, *The Truth About Wyatt Earp*, Carpinteria, Calif.: The O.K. Press, 1992. General cash books, Wells, Fargo & Co., WFHS, for 1880 and 1881.

Marks and Tefertiller divide on the seat-switching issue, as do others. If they did switch because Philpot was ill, the significance is that it could have been an assassination attempt aimed at Paul, the Wells Fargo special agent in Tombstone and the sheriff of Pima County in waiting. Hume, who investigated the incident, said unequivocally: "They opened the attack by firing a volley at the stage *before ordering a halt*" (emphasis added). Hume papers, 1881 entry, unpublished manuscript. *Denver Republican*, May, 20, 1882. *San Francisco Chronicle*, December 11, 1896. "Shot by Road Agents," *The Call*, March 16, 1881. "The Cowboys: What Wells-Fargo Detectives Know About Them," *San Francisco Examiner*, March 23, 1882.

"Determined Attack On a Stage by Arizona Brigands," *San Francisco Call*, January 8, 1882. "A Daring Deed by Two Masked Highwaymen in Arizona," *The Call*, January 9, 1882.

To add insult to injury, Banks's middle initial W. stood for Wells. William Issel and Robert W. Cherny, *San Francisco, 1865–1932*, Berkeley, Calif.: University of California Press, 1986. Wells, Fargo & Co.'s Express, "List of Offices, Agents," January 1, 1887 and 1888. J. B. Hume, "Description of Charles W. Banks," November 8, 1886. "Defaulter Banks," *San Francisco Daily Examiner*, November 11, 1887. "The Absconding Cashier," *San Francisco Chronicle*, November 18, 1887. "Defaulter Banks," *San Francisco Chronicle*, January 15, 1887. "A Defaulter's Flight," *Express Gazette*, March, 1887. Wells Fargo Finance Committee, December 15, 1891. "Charles W. Banks," auditor's report, WFHS, November 12, 1887. *The Daily Appeal*, November 18, 1886. "Queen Makie's Guest," *San Francisco Daily Examiner*, March 20, 1887. "The Illustrious Banks," *The Call*, March 20, 1887. "An Expressman King," *Express Gazette*, August 1887. "Charles W. Banks: Wells, Fargo & Co. Do Not Believe the Fishy Story," *San Francisco Chronicle*, April 19, 1887. Richard H. Dillon, "Wells, Fargo's Jekyll and Hyde," *The America West*, March 1971. Three letters from Lucile Riddel Andersen, the daughter, to WFHS, one undated and the others February 25, 1965 and March 28, 1966. Wells Fargo Finance Committee, December 15, 1891. "Inquiry Before Sir James Prendergast, at Rarotonga, Friday, 24th December, 1897," *Appendix to the Journal of the House of Representatives of New Zealand*, Vol. I, 1893. W. H. Percival to R. A. Langdon, Pacific Manuscripts Bureau, Australian National University, Canberra, Australia, November 27, 1968. Deputy Resident Commissioner, Cook Islands Administration, to Ruth Teiser, November 21, 1946. Lynnden Pogson, archivist, New Zealand National Archives, Wellington, New Zealand, to Richard H. Dillon, February 4, 1969. W. G. Coppell, "Was Banks Covering Up for Others?", *Pacific Islands Monthly*, February 1971. "Cashier Banks, the Honest Absconder," unpublished manuscript, WFHS, Ruth Teiser, undated. "C. W. Banks Heard From," *San Francisco Chronicle*, April 17, 1887. Frederick L. Lipman interview, WFHS, November 25, 1931.

John Bessenecker, "Bandit Hunting Was in His Blood," *True West*, July 1955. *San Francisco Examiner*, April 3, 1887. "Express Services," *Express Gazette*, July, August, and October 1887. "Wells Fargo in Texas," WFHS information sheet, undated. "A Brave Messenger: Kills Two Train Robbers Single-Handed," *Express Gazette*, November 1887. "The Duty of Congress," *Express Gazette*, January 15, 1901. "Bank Revives the 'Wanted' Poster to Fight Crime," *Wells Fargo News*, January 1992. "Banks Revive Wanted Posters—with 90s Flair," *Orange County Register*, October 7, 1992. "These Tellers Tote Cash, Guns," *Contra Costa Times*, September 23, 1992. "$50,000 Reward!" *Contra Costa Times*, May 9, 1995.

A More Ordinary Place

Eugene Shelby, "Reminiscences," WFHS, undated. W. Turrentine Jackson, "Portland: Wells Fargo's Hub for the Pacific Northwest," *Oregon Historical Quarterly*, Fall 1985. W. Turrentine Jackson, "Banking, Mail, and Express Service in British North America," *Pacific Northwest Quarterly*, October 1985.

One White Male; Women Employees; and Minorities

William F. Strobridge, "Pilsbury (Chips) Hodgkins: Gold Miner to Gold Messenger," *CHISPA* (Quarterly of the Tuolumne County Historical Society), July–September 1994. William F. Strobridge, "Chips Hodgkins: Wells Fargo's Messenger on the San Joaquin River," *San Joaquin Historian* (Quarterly Journal of the San Joaquin County Historical Society), Spring 1994. "Women," Robert Chandler, WFHS, 1993. William F. Strobridge, "Pilsbury 'Chips' Hodgkins: Wells Fargo's Southern California Messenger," *Historical Society of Southern California Quarterly*, Winter 1995. William F. Strobridge, "'Chips' the Wells Fargo Messenger," unpublished manuscript, WFHS, February 2, 1993. William F. Strobridge, "Chapter Four: Downtown Messenger," unpublished manuscript, WFHS, undated. W. Turrentine Jackson, "Stages, Mails and Express in Southern California: The

Role of Wells, Fargo & Co. in the Pre-Railroad Period," *Historical Society of Southern California Quarterly*, Fall 1974. Elizabeth C. MacPhail, "Wells Fargo in San Diego," *The Journal of San Diego History*, Fall 1982.

William F. Strobridge, "Wells Fargo Mariposa Office, 1885–1914," unpublished manuscript, WFHS, February 22, 1998. "The Old Adage Verified—Nothing New under the Sun," *The Expressman's Monthly*, October 1879. William Strobridge, "A Turn-of-the Century Sister's Act: Mariposa's Wells Fargo Ladies," *The Californians*, Volume 11, no. 3. Marshall Cushing, *The Story of Our Post Office: The Greatest Government Department in All Its Phases*, Boston, Mass.: A. M. Thayer & Co., 1893.

California State Senate, Special Committee on Chinese Immigration, *Chinese Immigration; Its Social, Moral, and Political Effect*, Sacramento, 1878. Philip L. Fradkin, *The Seven States of California: A Natural and Human History*, Berkeley, Calif.: University of California Press, 1997. Yong Chen, *Chinese San Francisco, 1850–1943*, Stanford, Calif.: Stanford University Press, 2000. Ronald Takaki, *Strangers from a Different Shore: A History of Asian Americans*, New York: Penguin Books, 1990. Amy Tan, *The Kitchen God's Wife*, New York: G. P. Putnam's Sons, 1991. Thomas W. Chinn, *Bridging the Pacific: San Francisco Chinatown and Its People*, San Francisco: Chinese Historical Society of America, 1989. Harold P. Anderson, "Wells Fargo and Chinese Customers in Nineteenth Century California," Frank H. H. King, ed., in *Essays in the History of the HongKong and Shanghai Banking Corporation*, London, England: Athlone Press, 1983. Wong Sam, "An English-Chinese Phrase Book," San Francisco: Ubery & Co., 1875. "Nineteenth Century Cultural Diversity and Participation at Wells Fargo & Company," Robert J. Chandler, WFHS, October 15, 1992. "Directory of Chinese Business Houses," *Wells Fargo & Co's Express*, 1871, 1873, 1878, 1882. "To agent," *Wells Fargo & Co's Express*, September 12, 1882. Ian Paton, "12: 1880s Wells, Fargo China Route," *London Philatelist*, March 1994. "December, 1912," *Wells Fargo Messenger*, December 1912.

The First Divestment

Numerous directives "to our agents" from the San Francisco office of Wells, Fargo and Co., WFHS, 1858–1877. U.S. Post Office Department, *Report of a Committee Appointed By the Postmaster-General January 5, 1880, To Take Into Consideration the Matter of the Letter-Express Business of Wells, Fargo & Co., As Shown by Letter of Special Agent B. K. Sharretts, Dated December 31, 1879*, Washington, D.C., March 9, 1880. Lloyd Tevis to Postmaster General D. M. Key, April 20, 1880. John J. Valentine to agents, WFHS, April 3, 1880. "Wells, Fargo & Company," San Jose *Pioneer*, April 10, 1880. John J. Valentine to agents, WFHS, June 1, 1880. John J. Valentine to agents, WFHS, March 31, 1883. "No More Express Letters," *San Francisco Examiner*, May 25, 1895. "Wells-Fargo," Sacramento *Record Union*, April 20, 1895.

A Midwest Connection

John L. Harnsberger, *Jay Cooke and Minnesota: The Formative Years of the Northern Pacific Railroad 1868–1873*, New York: Arno, 1981. Louis Ruck Renz, *The Northern Pacific Railroad*, Fairfield, Wash.: Ye Gallon Press, 1980. Sig Mickelson, *The Northern Pacific Railroad and the Settling of the West: A Nineteenth Century Public Relations Venture*, Sioux Falls, S.D.: Center for Western Studies, 1993. "Norwest at Sixty: A History of Norwest Corporation 1929–1989," Harold Chucker, Norwest Corporation, Minneapolis, Minn., 1989. Doniver A. Lund, untitled manuscript prepared for the 1976 Bicentennial, WFHS, 1976. Miscellaneous Norwest items in the WFHS files, such as "1872: Original Subscribers for Stock of Northwestern Nat'l Bank."

Once Again: Growth and Takeover

John J. Valentine to H. B. Parsons, Parsons collection at the Huntington Library, January 3, 1888. John J. Valentine to H. B. Parsons, December 31, 1887. John J. Valentine to H. B. Parsons, September 6, 1880. "Social Evolution," John J. Valentine, commencement address, Nevada State University, Reno, May 30, 1897. "No. 339 Cipher," Wells Fargo & Co.'s Bank, 1894. John J. Valentine to H. B. Parsons, January 6, 1888. "From Ocean To Ocean," WFHS, undated advertisement. "General Instructions," John J. Valentine, vice president and general manager, WFHS, San Francisco, July, 1888. Lloyd Tevis to H. B. Parsons, December 30, 1888. John J. Valentine to H. B. Parsons, December 31, 1894. F. L. Lipman interview, WFHS, November 13, 1931. "To the Employees of Wells Fargo & Company," San Francisco, December 20, 1900, John J. Valentine, WFHS.

James J. Rawls and Walton Bean, *California: An Interpretive History*, Boston: McGraw-Hill, 1998. William Deverell and Tom Sitton, *California Progressivism Revisited*, Berkeley, Calif.: University of California Press, 1994. William Deverell, *Railroad Crossing: Californians and the Railroad 1850–1910*, Berkeley, Calif.: University of California Press, 1994. "Contract Between the Southern Pacific Co. and Wells Fargo Company: Term, 21 years from January 1, 1894 to January 1, 1915," WFHS, October 9, 1893. Maury Klein, *The Life and Legend of E. H. Harriman*, Chapel Hill, N.C.: University of North Carolina Press, 2000. "Wells, Fargo & Co.'s Semi-Centennial," *The Express Gazette*, March 15, 1902. James Thorpe, *Henry Edwards Huntington: A Biography*, Berkeley, Calif.: University of California Press, 1943. Various minutes of the board of directors and the executive committee of Wells, Fargo & Co., WFHS, 1901-1905.

Larry Schweikart, ed., *Encyclopedia of American Business History and Biography: Banking and Finance to 1913*, New York: Facts On File, 1990. Agreement between the Nevada National Bank of San Francisco and Wells Fargo and Company, WFHS, April 3, 1905.

The Earthquake and Fire

Gordon Thomas and Max Morgan Witts, *The San Francisco Earthquake*, New York: Stein and Day, 1971. Robert J. Chandler, "How Three Banks Survived a Disastrous Earthquake," *Wells Fargo News*, April 6, 1987. Isaias W. Hellman to "Our Correspondents," WFHS, April 21, 1906. Edwin McAfee, "Guarding the Vault," *The Wells Fargo Nevadan*, December 1919. "Recalling Our Past," *Retail Bank Newsletter*, April 9, 1979. "Wells Fargo & the San Francisco Earthquake, 1906," William F. Strobridge, WFHS, July 18, 1994. "Banks Change Locations," *San Francisco Chronicle*, February 16, 1907. Philip L. Fradkin, *Magnitude 8: Earthquakes and Life along the San Andreas Fault*, Berkeley, Calif.: University of California Press, 1999. "Reminiscence of Mr. F. L. Lipman on the Period of the 1906 Earthquake and Fire," WFHS, attached to an 1943–1944 interview by Catherine Harroun. *San Francisco Chronicle*, January 10, 1907.

The Critics Emerge

"An Express War," *Express Gazette*, WFHS, (undated) 1877. Charles F. Adams Jr., "Railway Problems in 1869, *North American Review*, January 1870. Frank Haigh Dixon, "Publicity for Express Companies," *Atlantic Monthly*, July 1905. "Harriman Buys Fargo Stock," *The New York Times*, June 27, 1906. "Harriman's 'Blind Pool' in Wells, Fargo & Co.," *The New York Times*, July 17, 1906. "Want Harriman to Tell about Past Surpluses," *The New York Times*, July 20, 1906. "Court with Harriman in Wells-Fargo Fight," *The New York Times*, July 28, 1906. "Wells, Fargo & Co. Deny Profits Are Concealed," *The New York Times*, July 31, 1906. "Harriman Smothers Wells-Fargo Minority," *The New York Times*, August 10, 1906.

III 1907–2000

Feeding the Nation

"Horticultural, &c.," *The California Farmer*, March 15, 1855. Signed, holograph letter of John Sutter, Sr., catalogue for the sale of the library of Dr. Roger K. Larson, Pacific Book Auction Galleries, September 28, 1995. Vincent P. Carosso, *The California Wine Industry: A Study of the Formative Years*, Berkeley, Calif.: University of California Press, 1951. "Hellman Controls the Trade in Wine," *San Francisco Examiner*, March 3, 1901.

Penryn agent to C. C. Whitmore, Eureka, Nevada, WFHS, June 15, 1898. "Special Rate Notice," John J. Valentine to agents, WFHS, June 5, 1879. "Wells Fargo and the Western Harvest," *Wells Fargo News*, June 20, 2000. "Vegetable History,"

Western Grower & Shipper, May 1979. Pete Daniel, *Breaking the Land: The Transformation of Cotton, Tobacco, and Rice Cultures since 1880*, Urbana, Ill.: University of Illinois Press, 1985. Henry C. Dethloff, *A History of the American Rice Industry, 1685–1985*, College Station, Tex.: Texas A & M University Press, 1988. "Expressmen as Fruit-Growers," *The Express Gazette*, September 15, 1897. Claude B. Hutchinson, ed., *California Agriculture*, Berkeley, Calif.: University of California Press, 1946. "The Fruit Business," *The Express Gazette*, October 5, 1897.

Federal Trade Commission, *Report of the Federal Trade Commission on Private Car Lines*, Washington, D.C., 1920. D. T. Mervine, "Express Refrigerator Car Service," *The Express Messenger*, March 1929. John J. Valentine, vice president and general manager, Wells, Fargo & Company, to C. W. Smith, vice president, Atchison, Topeka & Santa Fe Railroad, WFHS, August 6, 1887. "Correcting Economic Waste," *Coast Banker*, December 1912. "A National Problem," *The Northern Crown*, October 1913. State Board of Horticulture, "Transportation, Refrigeration, Time-Scheduling," Fruit Growers of California, report of the Committee on Transportation, San Francisco, 1901. Anthony W. Thompson et al., *Pacific Fruit Express*, Wilton, Calif.: Central Valley Railroad Publications, 1992. E. E. Munger to Pat Pope, Wells Fargo vice president, advertising, WFHS, March 23, 1977. Minutes, Wells Fargo Company Executive Committee, WFHS, December 24, 1904. "Our Refrigerator Fleet," *Wells Fargo Messenger*, September 1912. "Our Ventilator Cars," *Wells Fargo Messenger*, April 1913. "Work of Our Refrigerator Fleet," *Wells Fargo Messenger*, May 1914. "How Wells Fargo Handles Fruit in California," *Wells Fargo Messenger*, August 1913. "A New Transcontinental Express Train," *Express Gazette*, January 1912. Various copies of 1915 advertisements for the "Fargo Fast," WFHS. Minutes of the board of directors, August 29, 1912, WFHS. Commission on Railway and Steamship Refrigeration of the American Association of Refrigeration, Bulletin No. 1, Chicago, 1913.

The Midwest

"Wells Fargo in Iowa," WFHS, undated. "Some Prospective Changes in the Express Map," *Express Gazette*, February 15, 1909. "Wells, Fargo & Co.'s New Territory," *Express Gazette*, May 15, 1909. "Wells Fargo & Company Express, Principal Agencies in Illinois, Iowa, Michigan, Minnesota, Missouri, Montana, Nebraska, North Dakota, South Dakota and Wisconsin," WFHS, supplement to official directory, January 1, 1909. "Dakota Division," *Wells Fargo Messenger*, March 1913. "Mason City, Iowa, an Architectural Heritage," Department of Community Development, 1977. "Joyously High-Stepping 'Music Man,'" *San Francisco Examiner*, April 2000. Peter Gammond, *The Oxford Companion to Popular Music*, Oxford, England: Oxford University Press, 1991. Meredith Willson, *And There I Stood with My Piccolo*, Garden City, N.Y.: Doubleday & Company, 1948. Meredith Willson, *The Music Man*, New York: G. P. Putnam's Sons, 1958. Meredith Willson, *But He Doesn't Know the Territory*, New York: G. P. Putnam's Sons,

1959. "Wells Fargo and Music," Robert J. Chandler, WFHS, July 29, 1997. "History of Banco Mortgage Company," Robert Beal, Minnesota Historical Society, January 10, 1977.

Ollie C. Ziegler, *Memoirs of Ollie C. Ziegler, St. Louis Wagonmaster*, Columbia, Mo.: University of Missouri Cultural Heritage Center, 1993. "Saint Louis," *Wells Fargo Messenger*, January 1913. W. P. French, "Our Company at Saint Louis," *Wells Fargo Messenger*, January 1913. "Chicago—Wells Fargo Hub," *Wells Fargo Messenger*, March 1913. "Wells Fargo Growth at Chicago," *Wells Fargo Messenger*, March 1913. James Lynn Bartz, *Company Property of Wells, Fargo & Co's Express 1852–1918*, Lake Forest, Calif.: The Westbound Stage, 1993. Michael McIntosh, *The Best Shotguns Ever Made in America: Seven Vintage Doubles to Shoot and to Treasure*, New York: Charles Scribner's Sons, 1981. Robert J. Chandler to Charles W. Pate, WFHS, December 14, 1979

End of the Line

"When Wells Fargo Came to New York," *Wells Fargo Messenger*, April 1914. "New York—Our Eastern Gateway," *Wells Fargo Messenger*, April 1914. Letters to stockholders, H. B. Parsons, vice president and secretary, and Dudley Evans, president, July 3, July 18, July 30, 1906, WFHS. Minutes of the executive committee, November 15, 1909; board of directors meeting, November 18, 1909; stockholders' special meeting, December 22, 1909; board of directors meeting, December 23, 1909, WFHS. Atwood wrote a three-part series in the February, March, and April 1911 editions of *The American Magazine* on "The Great Express Monopoly." Edward Hungerford, who joined Wells Fargo as editor of its in-house publication and advertising manager the next year, stated in his history of the company: "Atwood was accurate in his facts and figures. . . . I saw, myself, a dividend check of over $2,400,000 made out to a single member of the Harriman family. This was a big melon cutting." Albert W. Atwood, "The Story of the United States Express Company and of Its Government Contract," *The American Magazine*, April 1911. William G. McAdoo, *Crowded Years: The Reminiscences of William G. McAdoo*, New York: Houghton Mifflin, 1931. Anne Wintermute Lane et al., eds., *The Letters of Franklin K. Lane: Personal and Political*, New York: Houghton Mifflin, 1922. Keith W. Olson, *Biography of a Progressive: Franklin K. Lane 1864–1921*, Westport, Conn.: Greenwood Press, 1979. "A Railway Regulator," *The Outlook*, January 25, 1913. Interstate Commerce Commission, *In the Matter of Express Rates, Practices, Accounts, and Revenues*, Opinion No. 1967, Washington, D.C., 1912. Franklin K. Lane, "The Federal Hand on Express Business," *The Independent*, January 9, 1912. Edward Hopper entry, Peggy and Harold Samuels, *The Illustrated Biographical Encyclopedia of Artists of the American West*, Garden City, N.Y.: Doubleday, 1976. *Wells Fargo Messenger*, July 1914. D. G. Mellor, "Twentieth Century Marketing," *Wells Fargo Messenger*, July 1914. "A National Problem," *Wells Fargo Messenger*, August 1913. "Mellor in the Imperial Valley," *Wells Fargo Messenger*, November 1915.

Minutes of Wells Fargo board of directors meeting of June 4, 1918 and the shareholders' meeting of July 18, 1918, WFHS. Interstate Commerce Commission, *Ninth Annual Report on the Statistics of Express Companies In the United States For the Year Ended December 31, 1918*, Washington, D.C., 1920. "Robbery Prompts Confusion: No Connection Between Bank, Armored Cars," *Wells Fargo News*, May 20, 1985.

The Bank and the Brand

"Wells Fargo Nevada National Bank," *Coast Banker*, August 1911. "Business Pioneers Who Built a Far West Metropolis," *San Francisco Sunday Examiner & Chronicle*, October 19, 1980. "The Nation Greets Air Express," *The Express Messenger*, October, 1927. "$2,500,000 Sent by Plane from Capital to S. F.," *Sacramento Union*, March 3, 1928. "80 Years in True Perspective," *San Francisco Examiner*, May 19, 1932. "These Last Thirty Years," *Coast Banker*, December 1938.

Robert J. Chandler to Andy Anderson, WFHS, May 8, 1980. Numerous copies of advertisements, WFHS. *Wells Fargo Nevadan*, vol. I, no. 1, August 1919. "Merchants National Trust and Savings Bank of Los Angeles: A Consolidation of Hellman Commercial Trust and Savings Bank and the Merchants National Bank of Los Angeles," *Coast Banker*, November 1926. E. S. Heller to F. L. Lipman, WFHS, September 10, 1924. F. L. Lipman to D. G. Mellor, WFHS, September 12, 1924. F. L. Lipman to E. R. Jones, WFHS, May 10, 1938. I. W. Hellman to H. E. Turpin, WFHS, March 31, 1960. "Protecting the Wells Fargo Name," *Wells Fargo Banker*, January 1971. "Some Key Dates In Establishing Our Rights in the 'Wells Fargo' Name and the Stagecoach," WFHS, undated. "Wells Fargo: A Brief History," WFHS, August 1979. George Caulfield to Dick Jackson, WFHS, August 18, 1978. "Wells Fargo Armored Service Corporation Robbery," Bill Zuendt, WFHS, May 1, 1985.

G. W. Wickland of Wells Fargo to Frank Lloyd of Paramount Pictures, WFHS, July 13, 1937. Frank Lloyd to Elmer R. Jones, president of Wells Fargo, July 20, 1937. U.S. Senate, *Congressional Record*, "Radio Address by Hon. James J. Davis of Pennsylvania," Washington, D.C., February 8, 1938. Thomas T. Townsend, "Wells Fargo Bank History Room: A Public Relations Program," thesis for the School of Financial Public Relations, Northwestern University, May 1955. Robert J. Chandler to R. L. Wilson, Wells Fargo Financial Services, January 12, 1981. Some of Jackson's published journal articles identified him as a Wells Fargo consultant; others only cited his academic background. E. E. Munger to A. Kent Tichenor, WFHS, October 30, 1973. Margaret Price, "Corporate Historians: A Rare but Growing Breed," *Industry Week*, March 23, 1981. "Historians Find They're Sought by U. S. Businesses," *The New York Times*, April 23, 1982. "Profiting From the Past," *Newsweek*, May 10, 1982. Harold P. Anderson, "Banking on the Past: Wells Fargo & Company," *Business History Bulletin*, vol. 1, no. 1.

Wells Fargo Banker, January, 1982. *The Los Angeles Times* credited Wells Fargo with being the first large bank to open a site on the Internet. "Wells Fargo Makes $10.9-Billion Bid for First Interstate," *The Los Angeles Times*, October 19, 1995. "Wells OKs Banking by Modem," *San Francisco Examiner*, October 5, 1989. Advertisement, *San Francisco Chronicle*, October 31, 1989. Advertisement, *Bay Area Computer Currents*, August 24, 1992. "Wells Fargo Home Page," December 12, 1994. "Wells's Milestone Gives It More than 10 Percent of Internet Bank Accounts Nationwide," *Minneapolis Star Tribune*, August 12, 1999. Advertisement, *The New York Times*, August 6, 2000. "Building the Wells Fargo Brand," WFHS, December, 1998. "At Banks, Logo Revamps Go with the Territory," *American Banker*, June 28, 2000.

"Carl Reichardt's California Playpen," *The New York Times*, February 16, 1986. "Bold Banker: Wells Fargo Takeover of Crocker Is Yielding Profit but Some Pain," *The Wall Street Journal*, August 5, 1986. "Driving That Stagecoach," *The Los Angeles Times*, April 6, 1994. "Crocker Bank Overview," Robert J. Chandler, WFHS, April 1, 1986. "A Turn in the Spotlight for Wells' Hazen," *The Los Angeles Times*, June 25, 1994. "Wells Fargo Bank: Safe and Strong Since 1852," Bill Zuendt to retail managers, WFHS, January 4, 1991. Sam Zuckerman, "Brilliant Mind, but Is He a Leader?" *USBanker*, February 1995. "$10 Billion Hostile Bid By Wells Fargo For First Interstate," *The New York Times*, October 19, 1995. "Wells Grabs For First Interstate," *San Francisco Chronicle*, October 19, 1995. "Wells Fargo Makes $10.9-Billion Bid For First Interstate," *The Los Angeles Times*, October 19, 1995. "After Devouring First Intersate, Wells Experiences Some Indigestion," *The Los Angeles Times*, April 16, 1997. Kenneth Cline, "The Devil in the Details," *Banking Strategies*, November/December 1997. "Seeking the Next Gold Rush," *The New York Times*, November 22, 1995. Erika Rasmusson, "An Emerging Success," *Sales & Marketing Management*, October 7, 1999. "Wells Fargo & Company," ING Barings, November 21, 2000. Wells Fargo Annual Report, 1999. Bethany McLean, "Is This Guy the Best Banker in America?" *Fortune*, July 6, 1998. Phil Roosevelt, "King of the Cross-Sell," *Forbes*, October 11, 1999. "Stage Set for Wells' Minn. Conversion," *American Banker*, June 28, 2000. "Wells Fargo Annual Report," 2000. Richard Kovacevich, San Francisco, April 12, 2001.

The Muybridge Mural

"San Francisco 1878: Eadweard Muybridge's Portrait of the City," WFHS, 1978. Wells Fargo annual meeting, April 24, 2001.

INDEX